# Puppets, Gods, and Brands

Asia Pop!

**ALLISON ALEXY**

*Series Editor*

# Puppets, Gods, and Brands

Theorizing the Age of Animation from Taiwan

Teri Silvio

University of Hawai'i Press
Honolulu

24  23  22  21  20  19       6  5  4  3  2  1

**Library of Congress Cataloging-in-Publication Data**

Names: Silvio, Teri, author.
Title: Puppets, gods, and brands : theorizing the age of animation from
  Taiwan / Teri Silvio.
Description: Honolulu : University of Hawai'i Press, 2019. | Includes
  bibliographical references and index.
Identifiers: LCCN 2019021387 | ISBN 9780824881160 (paperback) | ISBN
  9780824876623 (cloth)
Subjects: LCSH: Characters and characteristics in mass media. | Cartoon
  characters—Social aspects—Taiwan. | Computer animation—Social
  aspects—Taiwan. | Figurines—Social aspects—Taiwan. | Puppet
  theater—Social aspects—Taiwan. | Video game characters—Social
  aspects—Taiwan.
Classification: LCC P96.C432 T3 2019 | DDC 306.4/8—dc23
LC record available at https://lccn.loc.gov/2019021387

Cover art: Characters from the Pili puppetry video series, *(front)* Dirulai and *(back)* Hudie
Jun. Reprinted with permission of the Pili International Multimedia Company, Ltd.

For my mentors, my *mishpocheh*, and my *tongzhimen*

# Contents

# Series Editor's Preface

From its opening pages, *Puppets, Gods, and Brands* engages experiences that nearly all of us has had. Even if we are not eagerly awaiting the new *Toy Story* film or the next role-playing video game in the Final Fantasy franchise, we are living in what Teri Silvio calls an "Age of Animation." Moving through a normal day, we encounter animation in unmarked and unremarkable ways, from Disney characters on car windshields and popular anime heroes on phone cases to *Lego Movie* airline safety videos. As cosplay continues to gain popularity, more people find real pleasure in dressing up as their favorite characters, literally embodying otherwise two-dimensional personifications. Silvio analyzes the ubiquity of animation as more than simply escapism, globalization, or mimesis: She brilliantly uses her rich ethnographic evidence to retheorize the centrality of performance in cultural logics, suggesting that theories of animation might more fully capture contemporary life-worlds.

In its myriad contributions, *Puppets, Gods, and Brands* connects Taiwanese cultural particulars with globalized trends, builds ethnographic data into provocative social theory, and demonstrates the benefits of taking popular culture seriously. Fundamentally interdisciplinary and transcultural, the book contains compelling examples that practically dance off the page. I fully expect that many readers will recognize parts of themselves—as creators, as fans, as digital citizens—in Silvio's analysis and will connect with this cutting-edge work by reflecting on their own experiences. I am excited to see how *Puppets, Gods, and Brands* will enter the world, be taken up by readers, and acquire a life of its own. I welcome this powerful contribution to the Asia Pop! series and the vital conversations it will provoke.

# Preface

This book has been about fifteen years in the making. In it, I argue for a paradigm shift that I have seen developing throughout the twenty-first century, a shift from seeing what we do, as human beings and as members of societies, as performing identities, toward seeing our actions in terms of animating worlds. In particular, I look at how this view of human action has been developing in the intersections of globalized popular culture, local creative industries, and Chinese folk religion in Taiwan.

The world is changing fast, and I cannot guess now whether, by the time you read this book, it will still be a work of contemporary anthropology or it will be a historical record. So this preface is a sort of postcard from July 2018, which may seem to you like yesterday or like a thousand years ago.

The majority of research for this book was conducted between 2003 and 2015. This was a period during which, in the parts of the world where I expect most readers of a book about Taiwan written in English will be located (North America, Europe, the Antipodes, and East Asia), the ideologies and policies of neoliberalism, in different forms, were dominant.

Since then, much of the Western world has been changing so fast that many of us are feeling whiplash. In the past few years, we've seen the election of Donald Trump as president of the United States, the vote for the UK to leave the European Union, the largest refugee crisis since World War II, and the rise of far right parties determined to keep refugees out of their countries in North America, Europe, and Australia. We have also seen the rise, in response, of new progressive activist coalitions and mass demonstrations larger than any since the 1960s. Many people see these developments as the result of decades of neoliberal policy. The globalization of supply chains and markets, with manufacturing industries moving from the global North to the global South; deregulation that weakened protections for workers and for the environment; the privatization of government functions such as infrastructure and education; and the shrinking of social welfare programs—all widened the gap between rich and poor, creating conditions for resentment and backlash, while the increasing influence of corporate money and interests in democratic politics made it easier for newly elected governments to become more authoritarian very quickly.

But while the West seems to be rapidly moving from neoliberalism into some kind of post-neoliberalism, change has been much less dramatic in East Asia. Taiwan—along with China, Japan, and South Korea—has been relatively insulated from the wars and political upheavals taking place in much of the rest of the world. Local versions of neoliberalism, which combine corporation-friendly policies with an ideology that stresses social harmony and the maintenance of basic social services, continue to develop. While ethno-nationalism is on the rise throughout the region, especially in Southeast Asia, in the Chinese-speaking world it is technocratic ideology that continues to guide most government policies. China's international influence is rising, largely because of its Belt and Road development programs, and most people here in Taiwan are more concerned with "the China factor" than with other international developments.

However the world has changed by the time you read this book, I hope it will prove relevant and useful to you. The ethnographic record has its own value. If you are reading this because you are interested in Taiwan or in East Asian popular culture and animation, then you should find some interesting information here that you won't find elsewhere, and I hope that the idea of the *ang-a* mode of animation as a cultural logic will be intriguing to you. If you are reading primarily for the anthropological concept of animation I elaborate, I hope it won't seem that the Age of Animation is already slipping away with its possibilities for the future, that the critiques I make here of identity and disenchantment won't be just ethereal thought exercises. I suspect, given the deep connection between digital technology and the emergence of animation as a concept, that these ideas will still prove useful, and I hope that you will find something in this book that is good to think with, and maybe act on, wherever you are. At any rate, like any other thing that human beings have put part of their soul into, this book will have its own, unpredictable, life.

# Acknowledgments

$A$ huge number of people have contributed to creating this book, way more than I could thank in this short space. I'm going to do my best, but inevitably many people without whom this book would have been poorer will be left out. I hope you know who you are, and that I appreciate all your help.

First and foremost, I need to thank all the people who allowed me to interview them, hang out with them, and watch them go about their work. I am especially grateful to Chris Huang (Huang Qianghua) and Vincent Huang (Huang Wenze), the CEO/script supervisor and managing director/voice artist of the Pili International Multimedia Company, as well as Jill Huang, who helped me arrange so many interviews, and all of the script-writers, puppeteers, directors, and other workers at the Pili Company that I met. They were incredibly welcoming, not only accepting interviews but allowing me to observe the entire production process for their puppetry series, including sitting in on script meetings and in the editor's booth, and inviting me to events. I must also thank all of the Pili fans who patiently answered my questions, explained complex plots, invited me to events large and small, and showed me their fan fiction, their cosplay, and their collections. Lin Chin Mei and the other members of the Limitless Cosplay Theater Troupe were especially generous with their time and their guidance. I must also thank all the *tongrennü* who shared their *Axis Powers Hetalia* (APH) fan fiction and art, the designers and collectors of deity toys, and the workers at temples throughout Taiwan who generously accepted my interviews.

I have been lucky to have many wonderful research assistants over the years whose contributions have been tremendous, helping me contact people for interviews, transcribing interview tapes, organizing archival materials, and helping organize conferences. I can thank only a few of them here, but I am grateful to them all. I could not have done my research on Pili without Huang Lingyi, who was both my research assistant and an expert informant for several years, introducing me to members of the Pili production team and the leaders of different fan clubs and helping me set up and facilitate an online discussion group. Ellie Huang also served this dual role for me, introducing me to many APH fans. I am especially grateful to both of them for the insights and delight I got from many discussions over the years of BL (boys' love) aesthetics, the dynamics of fan culture, and many other topics. Chang Chun-ying, Chen Ru-han, I-yi Hsieh, and Wen-yi Huang also worked on several of the projects that went into making this book.

One might think that writing is a more solitary pursuit than fieldwork, but luckily for me, it has not been, and I have many people to thank for improving my arguments and how I present them. First, I must thank two people above all. Without Ilana Gershon and Paul Manning, this book simply would not exist. Paul, as the editor of the *Journal of Linguistic Anthropology*, first solicited the article that became the framework for this book (thanks also to Rupert Stasch for recommending that article to him), and he and Ilana have read multiple versions of every chapter since then. Their engagement and encouragement over many years was the fuel that kept this project (and me) going. I also want to especially thank my go-to guides to all things Japanese, especially animation—Laura Miller, Shunsuke Nozawa, and Debra Occhi—and Hsun Chang, DJ Hatfield, and Wei-Ping Lin for sharing their expertise in Chinese folk religion in Taiwan.

Naifei Ding, Chien-ting Lin, and Amie Parry not only contributed their readings of various versions of the chapters but also have, over many years, provided me with the kind of good fellowship and intellectual stimulation that make it worth it to get out of bed and turn on the computer every day. My colleagues in the "Starting from the Voice" research group at the Institute of Ethnology—Chu Ruey-ling, Heidi Fung, Pei-yi Guo, Fei-wen Liu, and Jenyu Peng—also deserve many thanks for their helpful comments and for constantly pushing me to get this book finished.

I was able to present early versions or parts of most of the chapters at conferences. I want to thank the following institutions for invitations to present my research in workshops, conferences, and lectures: the University of South Carolina, Columbia; National Tsing Hua University Department of Anthropology; the University of California, Berkeley; the Kaohsiung History Museum; the University of Texas at Austin; the University of Leiden; and National Taiwan University. I am grateful for the helpful feedback I got from the organizers of these events, and from their colleagues and students who attended. I was also privileged to organize four conferences of my own at the Institute of Ethnology, Academia Sinica, while I was working on the book, and out of these an interdisciplinary network of friends interested in questions of animation has emerged that has provided me with all sorts of inspiration. I want to thank all of the participants in those conferences, along with others who gave me valuable feedback on my presentations at various conferences. I am grateful for comments both challenging and encouraging from Anne Allison, Meghanne Barker, Christopher Bolton, Allen Chun, Kerim Friedman, Helen Grace, Fabio Gygi, Ari Heinrich, Ts'ui-ping Ho, Tai-Li Hu, Lucifer Hung, Earl Jackson, Kajri Jain, Andrew Jones, Hirofumi Katsuno, Jen-peng Liu, Petrus Liu, Fran Martin, Toshio Miyake, Marc Moskowitz, Peng-yi Tai, Youngie Wuo, and Irene Yang Fang-chih. Thanks are also due to the anonymous reviewers of my manuscript for the University of Hawai'i Press for their helpful suggestions.

I am grateful to my parents, my aunt Jody, and my brother Jay and his family for their patience and for giving me some real breaks from work, and to Wu Jingru for her impatience, for challenging me to make my writing more accessible, and for her support over so many years. Thanks to Ru-hong Lin for asking questions that pushed me past stumbling blocks.

Allison Alexy was the best series editor one could hope for, and I am grateful for her careful readings, forbearance, and encouragement. Many thanks also to Rosemary Wetherold for the long hours and attention she put into copy editing the manuscript. I am grateful to Long-chun Ang for his help with the glossary of Holo terms and to Allison Alexy for her help with the Japanese. All translations from oral and written sources are my own, unless otherwise indicated, and all mistakes are my own.

Much of the funding for the research and writing for this book was provided by Taiwan's National Science Council (now the Ministry of Science and Technology), and I gratefully acknowledge the following grants from that institution: [NSC 92-2412-H-001-035-SSS/NSC 93-2412-H-001-002], [NSC 94-2412-H-001-011], [NSC 97-2628-H-001-005-MY3], [NSC 101-2410-H-001-034-MY2].

Several chapters in this book include substantial revisions of previously published material. The introduction and chapter 1 together are an expansion and reworking of my article "Animation: The New Performance?" *Journal of Linguistic Anthropology* 20, no. 2 (2010). Revised parts of "Pop Culture Icons: Religious Inflections of the Character Toy in Taiwan," *Mechademia* 3, edited by Frenchy Lunning (Minneapolis: University of Minnesota Press, 2008), appear in chapter 2. Chapter 4 reworks and updates "Remediation and Local Globalizations: How Taiwan's 'Digital Video Knights-Errant Puppetry' Writes the History of the New Media in Chinese," *Cultural Anthropology* 22, no. 2 (2007); and chapter 5 draws on

"Informationalized Affect: The Body in Taiwanese Digital-Video Puppetry and COSplay," in *Embodied Modernities: Corporeality, Representation, and Chinese Cultures*, edited by Fran Martin and Larissa Heinrich (Honolulu: University of Hawai'i Press, 2006).

# Note on Language

In this book I use terms in Mandarin, Holo (Taiwanese Hokkien or Min-nan), and Japanese. For Holo terms, I use the Peh-oe-ji romanization system developed by Christian missionaries, which is still used by the Presbyterian Church and many others. For Mandarin, I use the pinyin romanization system. For terms that exist in both Mandarin and Holo, I provide both romanizations for the first use, with the Mandarin first. For terms that are used frequently in both languages, I generally use the Mandarin pronunciation after the first use. I use the Holo for terms that have no Mandarin equivalent (such as *ang-a*) or for terms that are specific to the local context and where the Mandarin is adopted from the Holo (such as *po-te-hi* and *koa-a-hi*). I use Mandarin for all terms within quotes from written sources and for proper names. I use the standard spellings in Taiwan for place-names and well-known historical figures (such as Taipei and Sun Yat-sen). For Japanese, I have used the Hepburn romanization system. For personal names, I have used the person's preferred spelling if known; otherwise their names are written in pinyin. Japanese and Chinese names are generally written with the surname first, unless the person publishes in English with the surname last. To clear up any confusion and to help any readers who read Chinese or Japanese and want to pursue further research, I provide glossaries at the end of this book with the Chinese characters and Japanese kanji and kana for proper names and for terms used in the text. Diacritical marks for tone in Mandarin and Holo are not included in the chapters, but they are provided in the glossary.

Also please note that I use "they," "them," and "their" for non-gendered singular pronouns, rather than "he/she," "him or her," or other phrasings.

# Welcome to the Age of Animation

It's early in the twenty-first century in Taipei, Taiwan, and I find myself surrounded by animated characters—virtual personalities that live within bodies made of ink and paper, wood and cloth, vinyl and metal, pixels and code. The movie theaters are showing the latest blockbusters from Pixar and Studio Ghibli. Millions of gamers sit in front of screens in their bedrooms or in Internet cafes, making virtual elves, orcs, and legendary Chinese generals fight their way through MMORPGs (massively multiplayer online role-playing games). There are three cable channels showing nothing but animated cartoons and another one dedicated to puppetry; even the TV news channels illustrate the day's events with 3-D animation reenactments. At the universities, students in the engineering departments are making humanoid robots that can sing, use sign language, and bathe hospital patients, and they're holding cosplay contests in the gym. There are experimental animation festivals at the art museums, an Osamu Tezuka exhibit at the Chiang Kai-shek Memorial Hall, and displays of ornately handcrafted action figures at the Taipei Toy Festival. People are sending text messages punctuated with winking, bowing, or roaring emoticons on phones that can talk. My bus card has the image of Shrek on it, and my ATM card features Astro Boy. A poster of a smiling cartoon policeman reminds me that my alley is covered by surveillance cameras. Above the check-in counter for China Airlines at Taoyuan International Airport, there's a video loop in which puppets demonstrate how to go through the security check, stow one's carry-on luggage, and buckle one's seat belt. And the mouthless visage of Hello Kitty is ubiquitous—on clothing, handbags, cellphone covers, stationery, waffles, trash cans, and even cars and airplanes.

Of course, virtual personalities have always been around. In Taiwan, more traditional non-flesh-and-blood persons include gods, ghosts, and ancestors, as well as the frequently represented heroes of the *Romance of the Three Kingdoms* and *Journey to the West*. When I first started doing fieldwork in Taipei in the early 1990s, there were already stores in every neighborhood where students could rent translated Japanese manga, and some companies, such as Tatung Electronics, had cartoon mascots. Japanese anime and local puppetry were popular at VHS video rental outlets and on television.

Nonetheless, a quantitative change, a population explosion in virtual personalities, seems evident. Taipei may be an extreme city in the number of animated characters inhabiting it, but it is by no means unique. Since the 1990s, there has been a similar population explosion of animated characters throughout the postindustrial world and in metropolitan centers from Rio de Janeiro to Jakarta.

This proliferation of animation has been facilitated by several transformations taking place on a global scale, notably the development and spread of digital technologies, the development of new and old creative industries, the increasing size and power of multinational corporations (especially media conglomerates), and the increasing flow of people and products across national borders.

Much of the animation that surrounds us is created directly through digital technology—for example, the computer-generated characters that populate PC and online games of all sorts, as well as the annual blockbusters from Pixar and DreamWorks. Digital transfer has also allowed for older, analog forms of animation—for instance, Walt Disney's and Miyazaki Hayao's hand-drawn cell animation and Aardman Animations' Claymation features—to more easily reach a global audience and for fan communities to spread both fan-subtitled canon clips and their own textual, graphic, and animated productions via the Internet. Digital technology also lies at the heart of other types of new virtual personalities, such as interactive robots.

Animated characters are being produced and circulated not only through digital technology but also within new industries that are largely dependent on that technology. It is no coincidence that the countries that are the largest producers and consumers of commercial animation—Japan and the United States—are among those where, since the 1980s, traditional manufacturing and agriculture have been declining, while the high-tech, information, and service sectors have been growing and also converging. One of the effects of the movement of traditional manufacturing out of Europe, North America, and the wealthier parts of East Asia has been that the so-called creative industries or content industries (cinema, television, publishing, software design, advertising, etc.) have become increasingly important there, accounting for a growing portion of national GDPs every year. These industries are often supported by government policies aimed at projecting soft power (Iwabuchi 2010). Cartoon characters have become "cultural ambassadors" and sources of national pride not only in the United States and Japan but in several other countries whose international standing rests on economic rather than military strength, such as Finland and South Korea.

The growth of large multinational corporations facilitates the spread and diversification of cartoon characters through what businesspeople in North America sometimes call "synergy" and in Japan is referred to as the "media mix." Industrial structures and marketing strategies that bind video animation with comics and graphic novels, figurines, games, and other tie-in products have emerged from the dialogue between American and Japanese entertainment industries and spread throughout the postindustrial world (Allison 2006; Jenkins 2006).

The increasing mobility of both the workforce and the audience has also helped pave the way for the international flow of animation commodities. The range of animated characters found in cosmopolitan centers mirrors the limited diversity of animation studio and robotics lab staffs. Immigrant communities in North America played an important role in the importation of Japanese anime and character goods there, and fans with experience working or studying overseas have been responsible for much of the translation of manga and anime (both official and unofficial) in various countries (Patten 2004; Allison 2006; Kelts 2006; Yano 2013; Hsiao 2014).

It would be easy to perceive the proliferation of cartoon characters (and talking phones, robot pets, etc.) as a mere side effect of the development of digital technologies, economic restructuring, and globalization. But what I argue in this book is that the rise of animation is by no means trivial. Rather, the quantitative increase in animated characters indexes a qualitative change, a paradigm shift. We are entering an Age of Animation. What I mean by this is not simply that we are increasingly surrounded by virtual worlds and virtual entities. I mean that our attention is increasingly turned toward the *idea* of animation. Animation in the narrow sense (a kind of cinema or video) is popular because animation in the broad sense (giving objects lives of their own) is good to think with—specifically, to think through what is happening right now in the intersections of technology and capitalism, of the global and the local, of the human and the nonhuman.

That animation is good to think with is evident in the content of much recent animation art, especially in Japan, where cyborgs and robots with borrowed minds and lives of their own are prominent in both art-house and popular anime. We see it in children's play with interactive digital technology, when questions about what can be considered alive, or what can be considered sentient, almost always arise (Turkle 1984). We can see it in the returning interest of anthropologists in recent years to the topics of animism and the fetish, and in the recent turn in religious studies and art history toward the materiality and agency of objects of worship.

This book brings together insights from a variety of fields—anthropology, sociology, cinema and media studies, science and technology studies, psychology, religious studies, and art history—as well as my own ethnographic research, to construct an anthropological theory of animation, a theory of animation not as a specific technology but as a broader category of human, cultural action. The book looks at a wide variety of virtual beings, and objects invested with agency, which includes cartoon characters but also puppets, dolls, robots, images of gods, brands, and nations. What does it mean to make such things, to invest them with their own agency, and what is it like to live among them?

I propose animation here as a concept in opposition to, but also as a complement to, the concept of performance. Over the course of the twentieth century, a concept of performance developed in which the embodiment of roles came to be seen as a kind of action that linked human behavior across a range of social fields, a trope that could be extended from the field of professional entertainment to religion, politics, economics, kinship, and all the social interactions of everyday life. By the end of the twentieth century, performance studies was established as an academic field, and "performance" was a ubiquitous keyword in academic writing, not only in the humanities and social sciences, but also in science and engineering departments and in business schools. Performance had also become a common term in all kinds of popular discourse, used to analyze everything from pop star wardrobes to presidential campaigns to sexuality to war.

The performance paradigm arose in its own context of a quantitative increase in visible yet intangible characters, also facilitated by then-new technologies and transformations in the structure of global capitalism. Raymond Williams noted in 1974:

> In most parts of the world, since the spread of television, there has been a scale and intensity of dramatic performance which is without any precedent in the history of human culture. . . . [I]t seems probable that in societies like Britain and the United States more drama is watched in a week or weekend, by the majority of viewers, than would have been watched in a year or in some cases a lifetime in any previous historical period. (Williams 1990:59)

In other words, like today's digital media, television produced its own population explosion of virtual personalities—the difference being that these characters (nonfictional "television personalities" as well as purely fictional ones) were photographic images of real human beings.

Performance turned out to be an extremely productive concept for thinking through the transformations of the twentieth century. What I hope to show in this book is that animation has the same potential as a structuring trope in the age of digital media and the rise of the creative industries that performance had in the age of broadcast media and the rise of the service industries and consumer culture.

The idea of theorizing animation in relation to performance was inspired by my own research experience. My PhD dissertation project was squarely within the anthropology of performance. In the 1990s, I did fieldwork on the practice of women's cross-gender performance in Taiwanese Opera (koa-a-hi; in Mandarin: gezaixi or gezixi) and on how this practice related to the way that actresses and their mostly female fans, as well as Taiwanese society more broadly, performed and thought about offstage gender roles. When I took up a research position at the Institute of Ethnology, Academia Sinica, in Taipei in 2002, I decided to make my second project about puppetry, in part because in Taiwan the hand-puppet theater, po-te-hi (in Mandarin: budaixi), was a genre performed and watched primarily by men, and studying it would let me explore how masculinity was performed in Taiwan.[1]

As it turned out, I was wrong about a lot of things. For one, I was wrong about the gender of puppetry audiences. When po-te-hi was adapted to the new medium of television in the 1970s and then to digital video in the early twenty-first century, women came to make up almost 50 percent of the audience and became the most active fans. (Several chapters in this book discuss how the meaning of gender changes when we start thinking in terms of animation rather than performance.)

Another mistake I made was in directly applying performance theory to puppetry. This led me, at first, to miss what was most important about the genre to its fans, both male and female. Opera fans focused on specific actresses; characters were, for them, merely vehicles for the actress to express herself. Puppetry fans, in contrast, were fans of specific characters, rather than of specific puppeteers. When I asked puppeteers or fans cosplaying puppet characters questions like "How do you get into character?" or "Do you identify with the character?"—questions that had elicited detailed and enlightening answers from opera actresses and fans—I got answers that I found confusing, or, even more often, I just got blank looks.

I gradually realized that the differences between opera and puppetry ran much deeper than technique.

The concept of performance is often used to describe many of the phenomena I have called animation above. The creation and manipulation of cartoon avatars in various online virtual environments is commonly analyzed in terms of performance (e.g., Peachey and Childs 2011; Meadows 2005; Heng 2003; Dibbell 1998). Cinema and video animators themselves claim to be "just very shy actors."[2] But there are ways in which the concept of performance seems to fall short when we are talking about animated characters. Using the concept of performance to talk about Pixar's production process or avatars in MMORPGs highlights what makes virtual personhood in the digital age similar to pre-digital forms of virtual personhood, but it also obscures what makes them different. For instance, as Hastings and Manning (2004) have pointed out, the concept of performance has become so tied to the expression of self-identity that it has tended to deflect scholarly attention from the fact that many speech acts are, in fact, "acts of alterity." The concept of performance, in other words, tends to obscure all the ways in which animation is *not* self-expression, leading us to ignore both the material and ontological differences between animated characters and the people who create, use, and interact with them. We lose sight of the uncanny illusion of life that makes animated characters fascinating in a way that movie stars, for instance, are not.

One of the things that has made the concept of performance such a powerful analytical tool is its association with the ideas of embodiment and mimesis, making the concrete micro-processes of identity politics—socialization, habitus, the management of stigma—visible. To see animated characters as just disembodied performance, then, also weakens the political potential of the performance concept.

In *Perform or Else: From Discipline to Performance*, Jon McKenzie argues that "performance is the stratum of power/knowledge that emerged in the United States in the late twentieth century" and that "performance will be to the twentieth and twenty-first centuries what discipline was to the eighteenth and nineteenth" (2001: 18). While I think that McKenzie's historical analysis of the power effects of performance discourse is right on target, I also think that the ubiquity of animation in the twenty-first century should make us suspicious of his projection of these power effects into the future. I would suggest that we are already seeing the emergence of animation as an alternative model of and model for human action in the world, one that, like performance and discipline, is compelling in every sense of the word.[3]

I do not propose that animation should replace performance any more than performance replaced discipline. Rather, like discipline and performance, performance and animation intersect and complement each other. Each may be seen as simply a version of the other, but separating them as heuristic tools allows us to focus on aspects of the postindustrial condition that might otherwise escape notice. What I am suggesting here is that the concept of animation, more than the concept of performance, might capture something particular to the early twenty-first century, by locating the commonalities among such diverse phenomena as World of Warcraft and the US Supreme Court's *Citizens United* decision, emojis and climate change activism, the Marie Kondo Method of tidying your home and zombie movies, Hello Kitty and drone warfare.

This book is an exploration of what it means to live in the Age of Animation, primarily through an ethnographic study of various animation practices within a specific cultural and historical context. My aim is not only to show how connections among religion, entertainment, politics, and labor are being redrawn in twenty-first-century Taiwan but also to demonstrate how an anthropologist might make use of the animation model to illuminate cultural logics anywhere, and to see how specific local cultural traditions make sense of and contribute to global transformations.

## Why Taiwan?

Many, if not all, cultures have some historical traditions of animation practice, and ethnographic studies focusing on, for example, puppetry and animism have been (and hopefully will continue to be) done in many places. But these studies have usually been limited to one specific genre or set of ritual practices. There are some reasons why I think that Taiwan is a particularly interesting place to do a study that covers animation more broadly right now. For one thing, as I noted above, Taiwan is probably one of the most "animated" (in the narrow sense) places in the world; Taiwan is probably rivaled only by Japan for the ubiquity of cartoon characters in daily life. But it is also an excellent place to look at the contemporary Age of Animation because it is thoroughly penetrated by American and Japanese comics and animation and also has its own Chinese heritage of animation practices.[4]

Nearly all attempts in recent years to theorize animation in the digital age have been based on studies of comics, cinema, television, and online games produced in either the United States or Japan. These include the work of film and media studies scholars interested in what makes animation different from live-action cinema and television (e.g., Cholodenko 1991, 2007; Lamarre 2009), studies of how digital technology has changed the relationship between animation production and consumption (e.g., Jenkins 2006; Azuma 2009; Malaby 2009; Condry 2013), and studies of the psychology and sociality of game play through animated avatars (e.g., Boellstorff 2008; Nardi 2010), as well as many studies of specific works, genres, and fandoms. There is by now a fairly large body of research that looks at the globalization of animation, and almost all of it focuses on the circuit between the United States and Japan (e.g., Patten 2004; Kelts 2006; Allison 2006; Napier 2006; Yano 2013). A lot of powerful insights have come out of this research, and I engage with them in this book. But I also try to pull the conversation around contemporary animation out of what Roland Kelts calls "the Mobius strip of . . . Japanamerica" (Kelts 2006:69). We seem to be stuck at the moment in a loop in which the Age of Animation is widely seen as the product of a circuit between two countries, and the rest of the world merely adapts to or remains outside it. Taiwan offers both the opportunity to engage in direct dialogue with recent theories developed in Japan and the United States and to expand the concept of animation culture beyond their industrial and fan networks.

One thing Taiwan provides is a postcolonial perspective on the animation practices of Japanamerica. Taiwan was a Japanese colony from 1895 to 1945. After World War II, the island was handed over to the Chinese Nationalist Party (KMT). When the KMT was defeated by the Chinese Communist Party on the mainland in 1949, Chiang Kai-shek and his army retreated to Taiwan and militarized the island as a base for recovering China. The United States had military bases on Taiwan during the Korean and Vietnam Wars, which were closed only when the United States officially recognized the People's Republic of China (PRC) in 1979. From the end of World War II to the present, Taiwan has been dependent on US military aid and protection. Taiwan is more isolated politically now that the Cold War is over. It is excluded from the United Nations, the World Health Organization, and other global governmental organs. Taiwan was, however, admitted to the World Trade Organization in January 2002. Taiwan's ability to maintain any kind of voice in the emerging world system is predicated on success in the narrow field of economics.

Both Japan and the United States have had profound impacts on Taiwanese popular culture. It was under the Japanese regime that Taiwanese people first experienced urbanization, industrialization, railroads, indoor plumbing and electricity, and the systematization of education, policing, and medicine. This period also saw the introduction of a wide array of new media, commercial entertainments, and public venues, including the first commercial theaters, newspapers, magazines, radio, cinema, music recording, coffee shops, and dance halls. For older Taiwanese who grew up during the Japanese occupation, Japan is intimately tied to ideas of the modern, the developed, and the sophisticated.

After the end of World War II and Taiwan's handover to KMT rule, American products began to enter Taiwanese popular culture. Japanese cultural products were officially banned or restricted by the KMT between 1946 and 1965, and Japanese media products were again banned after Japan recognized the PRC, from 1972 to 1993. Nonetheless, Japanese books, music, and films were still regularly available during these periods through black and gray market channels (Lee 2004:61–86) For the generation born during the Cold War, youth culture was largely dominated by American products—rock-and-roll music on the United States military's radio station (which remains today under local ownership), American fashion and fashion magazines, Hollywood movies in the rapidly proliferating cinemas, and imported American programming on television after it was introduced in 1962.

The end of martial law coincided with a concerted push by the Japanese entertainment industries to expand their market in Asia, especially the former colonies of Taiwan and Korea (Iwabuchi 2002; Lee 2004). The 1990s saw a resurgence of the influence of Japanese pop culture among Taiwanese youth, with the "Japanophile tribe" (harizu) becoming even more visible than what one of my students called the "fake American-Born Chinese [jia ABC] subculture."

The influence of Japan is especially prominent in the field of animation. J-pop must share the Taiwanese music market with American pop, K-pop, Canto-pop, and homegrown Mando-pop and Holo music, and the same largely holds for live-action television drama. But Japanese manga and anime completely dominate the Taiwanese markets for printed comics and television animation. By the early 1990s, when I began doing fieldwork in Taiwan, a wide variety of Japanese manga were available in bookstores and rental shops, and were extremely popular among students of all ages. Today, over 90 percent of the comic books on sale at the annual Taipei Comics Mart, and in the numerous chain manga stores throughout the island, are Japanese works.[5] Many are available in both the original Japanese and Chinese translation, and many of the young manga/anime fans I have interviewed learned to read Japanese for the purpose of reading their favorite comics in the original language. Until recently, American comics have been largely unavailable in Taiwan, although since the release of a spate of recent live-action Hollywood films based on Marvel and DC superhero comics, their fandoms have begun to grow.

Video animation in Taiwan is also dominated by Japanese anime. Cable television was legalized in 1993, and with it the importation of Japanese programming. There are now hundreds of stations available in various packages in Taiwan. Almost all of these packages include both the Japanese anime channel Animax and the American Cartoon Network, and Japanese and American cartoons are regularly broadcast on many other stations, both domestic and international, as well. A 2011 survey on children's television by the National Communications Commission found that almost 93 percent of all commercial children's programming in Taiwan was Japanese anime (National Communications Commission 2011). DVDs are another channel through which anime are imported to Taiwan, and even more people watch through the Internet. Taiwanese now in their twenties and thirties grew up on Japanese animation, and a few American animated shows (such as *The Simpsons*) have had periods of popularity.

The flow of animation between Japan, the United States, and Taiwan is also facilitated by an increasing flow of Taiwanese bodies. Taiwanese elites began sending their children to the United States for university education from the start of the KMT's rule, and as Taiwan's economy has grown, the number of Taiwanese studying, working, and living in the United States has also grown. According to Taiwan's Overseas Compatriot Affairs Council, in 2012 "55 percent of all emigrants from Taiwan [were] living in the United States" (Overseas Compatriot Affairs Council 2012). Since the end of martial law, Japan has become the second most popular destination for study or work abroad and the number one overseas travel destination for vacationing Taiwanese. It is quite rare for me to meet anyone in Taipei who does not have at least one relative currently living in either the United States or Japan.

This frequent border-crossing between Taiwan and Japanamerica is one reason that it is not only manga and anime that have been imported into Taiwan but also the fan practices that have grown up around them as well. These include the production of *dōjinshi* (amateur comics, novels, and art using characters from mass media franchises, primarily Japanese manga and anime; called *tongrenzhi* in Mandarin), the collection of tie-in products, and cosplay (dressing up as animated characters). Taiwanese animation fans' vocabulary is mostly borrowed directly from Japan, with the Japanese kanji pronounced in Mandarin. The Comic World Taiwan (CWT) *tongrenzhi* market, modeled on Tokyo's Comiket, began in 1997. There are currently at least three CWT conventions per year in both Taipei and Kaohsiung, in which hundreds of individuals or small groups of fans rent booths to sell printed copies of their original stories and drawings and participate in cosplay contests. The August 2013 CWT/Fancy Frontier convention in Taipei featured over 1,300 booths and drew more than 50,000 visitors in a weekend (*Apple Daily*, August 11, 2013). Hundreds of smaller *tongrenzhi* markets and cosplay events also take place every year in Taipei alone, organized by school clubs, publishing companies, and private fan networks. There are also thousands of Internet fan discussion groups, as well as sites where fan art and fiction (including pieces translated from Japanese or English) and fansubs (videos with subtitles translated and added by fans) can be shared.

Recent theories of animation coming out of Japan and the United States are also known and discussed in Taiwan. Writers such as Azuma Hiroki, Otsuka Eiji, Scott McCloud, and Henry Jenkins are taught in social science and humanities departments (by myself among others), as well as animation production departments. Azuma's *Otaku: Japan's Database Animals* (2009), first published in Japan in 2001, was translated into Chinese and published in Taipei in 2012, and according to my students, it quickly became the book everyone wanted to be seen reading in the bohemian cafes around the National Taiwan University campus, just as it had been in the cafes around Tokyo University ten years earlier.[6]

Taiwanese manga and anime fans and scholars are, in other words, deeply engaged in the global conversation on what the Age of Animation means. Some take a subaltern position, focusing on differences between Taiwanese and Anglophone or Japanese readings of manga and anime; most see themselves as part of a global subculture and present their views as part of a common conversation. But, postcolonialism being what it is, they are rarely heard outside Taiwan. So part of this book will look at how Taiwanese people read manga and anime, and "Japanamerican" theory, through the lens of their own traditions of animation.

Another major focus of the book is on how Taiwanese people are combining their own Chinese animation traditions with digital technology. This involves the selective use of various aesthetic styles from Japanese and American comics and animated cinema, video, and games, as well as ways of interacting with animated characters that originated in Japanese and American animation fandoms. But what I am most interested in is how recent transformations of Taiwanese animation practices offer alternative (and not just reactive) concepts of animation in the broader sense and, thus, alternative ways of imagining and bringing into being the Age of Animation. Taiwanese people are not passive players in the transition from the Age of Performance to the Age of Animation but are actively engaged in bringing that transformation about, at both the local and the global scale.

I will be focusing on two traditional practices of animation, the Chinese folk religious practice of worshipping gods through statues and the artistic tradition of *po-te-hi* (hand puppetry). Chinese folk religion was brought to Taiwan by the first settlers from Fujian in the seventeenth century. The first written records of puppetry performances on Taiwan date to the nineteenth century and indicate that they were already popular at this time. In both of these traditions, which are historically related, small wooden anthropomorphic figures are invested with vitality, personality, and power.

Both Chinese folk religion and *po-te-hi*, along with *koa-a-hi* (opera), were perceived as "backward" but were tolerated during most of the Japanese colonial period and then suppressed during the war as markers of Chinese identity. From 1936 to 1945, puppeteers and opera performers were forced to perform in Japanese, to Western orchestral music, with characters in kimono or Japanese army uniforms. Religious festivals, puppetry, and opera all saw a revival after the end of Japanese rule. The KMT, however, saw them as markers of Taiwanese identity, polluted by Japanese influence and potentially in conflict with the Chinese cultural identity the party promoted, which was largely based on elite northern heritage. Folk religion was denigrated as superstition, and contemporary forms of *po-te-hi* and *koa-a-hi* were seen as "chaotic" and "vulgar" mixtures of Japanese, Western, and Chinese pop cultures.

With the rise of the Native Soil Consciousness literary movement and opposition politics in the 1970s, folk religion and *po-te-hi* were revalorized and came to play an important role in the construction of Taiwanese identity and in the projection of that identity into the global arena. Folk religion, particularly the worship of Mazu, the goddess of the sea, is seen as one of the main cultural practices making Taiwanese culture distinct from that of the Communist mainland. After the lifting of martial law in 1987, politicians, including members of the KMT, began making public shows of worshipping Mazu. *Po-te-hi*, along with *koa-a-hi*, is now considered a national folk art, promoted in government publications, museums, and tourist attractions. Local scholars portray the development of *po-te-hi* on the island as a synecdoche for the "Taiwanization" of Chinese culture (Chen Longting 1991, 2007; Wu Mingde 2005). Hou Hsiao-hsien's award-winning film *The Puppetmaster* (*Xi meng ren sheng*, 1993), based on the autobiography of *po-te-hi* master Li Tien-lu, uses the ups and downs of the puppet theater as a parable for the fate of ordinary Taiwanese people through the political and economic upheavals of the twentieth century. The qualities that formerly made folk religion and *po-te-hi* abject—working-class roots, syncretism, lack of restraint—are now seen as the source of their vitality (*shengmingli*), as animating Taiwanese culture as a whole (Silvio 2009).

In the twenty-first century, as I've mentioned, among the booming population of animated characters inhabiting Taiwan, the vast majority are immigrants. The manga, anime, and game programming industries in Taiwan are all quite small. The government has begun to encourage the use of "local culture" within the cultural creative industries, but most of the workers I have interviewed within these industries agree that Taiwanese-produced manga, anime, and games are still dominated by techniques and visual styles developed in Japan, North America, and Europe.

But within the field of animation in Taiwan, there is one genre that draws explicitly on Taiwanese/Chinese traditions, not only in its content, but in its technological and aesthetic structures. This is the genre of "digital knights-errant puppetry" (*shuwei wuxia budaixi*), which blends *po-te-hi*, action-film-style cinematography and editing, and computer-generated animation.[7] There are a few studios producing this genre now, but the longest-running (over thirty years) and by far the most popular digital knights-errant puppetry series is produced by the Pili International Multimedia Company.[8]

The Pili producers often describe the series as "between traditional *po-te-hi* and anime," but it is far more than a simple combination of the two, and it looks nothing like either. The narratives fall within the *wuxia*, or knights-errant, genre, but with added elements from fantasy and science fiction. Pili characters include two-hundred-year-old sword-wielding Buddhist monks who fly, vampires who dress like eighteenth-century European aristocrats and play the saxophone, gender-bending Japanese wizards, Tang-poetry-quoting Chinese literati, poison-spitting lizard-men, murderous elf-eared queens, and demonic clowns. The pace varies from slow scenes of the heroes drinking tea and discussing strategy to frenetic battle scenes involving dozens of puppets, which may feature two or three shots per second, all from different angles. Wooden puppets, photographs, computer-generated images, and brush paintings sometimes occupy the same screen.

The Pili serials are seen as a form through which traditional Taiwanese culture both absorbs the global and globalizes itself. The Pili Company has been celebrated as one of the great success stories within the "traditional culture creative industries" (*chuantong wenhua chuangyi chanye*), an example of how a traditional art can be revitalized through new technology in such a way as to become marketable not only to a new generation of Taiwanese but also (potentially) throughout the world. The Pili Company has, with varying success, attempted to expand its market into Japan, the United States, and the PRC (these attempts are detailed in chapter 4), and scholars, business reporters, and bureaucrats have expressed high hopes that Pili will lead the way in replicating the global success of the Japanese and South Korean content industries.[9] It was my fieldwork at the Pili studios and among Pili fans that first inspired the argument of this book, and the Pili series is a major focus of most of the chapters.

## Methodology

This book is based on several research projects undertaken in Taiwan between 2002 and 2015. I conducted my first fieldwork with the Pili Company production workers and Pili fans from 2002 to 2005. Although I moved on to other projects, I kept up with new developments there, occasionally watching new episodes, attending fan events, and meeting with scriptwriters, marketing directors, and other Pili Company employees. My early work with Pili fans brought the importance of their interaction with puppets and tie-in figurines to my attention. For my next project, I conducted a one-year study comparing the collectors of different types of figurines, including Pili puppets and figurines but also antique icons, antique and contemporary handcrafted puppets, and manga and anime character figurines. While doing this fieldwork, I began attending the annual Taipei Toy Festival, the largest exhibit of designer figurines and toys in Asia. I met some of the designers, and from 2009 to 2012, I did an ethnographic study of commercial character designers, including vinyl art toy designers, handicraft and souvenir figurine designers, comics artists, logo designers, and character designers for online games, in both Taiwan and Hong Kong.

This book is thus based on many years of interviews (with artists, entrepreneurs, members of temple committees and worshippers, collectors, and cosplayers) and participant-observation (at television studios, puppet theaters, temple festivals, museums, marketing expos, licensing firms, design studios, antiques markets, boutique toy stores, and fan conventions), as well as a lot of informal get-togethers with Pili fans, character designers, and puppet and toy collectors and sellers. I have been a judge for cosplay contests, a translator for the Pili Company, a speaker at conferences on the development of the creative culture industries, and in 2013 the curator of a museum exhibit entitled "Go, Figures! The Culture and Charisma of

Statues, Puppets, and Dolls."[10] And I have spent over a decade listening to my students, friends, and colleagues in Taiwan discussing specific works of animation, trends in animation, and theories of animation.

One advantage of doing research in the same place over many years is that I've been able to follow informants as they have moved from fan fiction writers to professional scriptwriters to series supervisors, from amateur cosplayers to professionals, from nonfans to fans and agnostics to worshippers (and vice versa). I have observed how slowly or quickly particular media franchises reach a peak of popularity and fade and how these trends relate to what is happening in the broader society, such as changes in the labor market and emerging political movements. Hopefully, this gives the ethnography in this book a deeper historical perspective and a sense of how industry and fandom, imagination and lived experience, are actually intertwined in the careers and lives of individuals.

## The Structure of the Book

Chapter 1 outlines a general anthropological theory of animation as a kind of social action. I define animation in contrast to performance, compare them in terms of the contexts under which each paradigm emerged and developed, and show how concepts from different fields—art and media studies, anthropology and sociology, religious studies, psychoanalysis, and labor studies—contributed to the creation of comparative frameworks. I also outline some of the consequences of looking at social action in terms of animation as opposed to performance and suggest some of the questions we might ask about how performance and animation are interwoven in practice.

Chapter 2 makes the transition from general theory to the analyses of ethnographic material in later chapters. Here I describe what I call a mode of animation that Taiwanese people might see as unique to Han Chinese culture. A mode of animation is a sort of meta-genre, a collection of practices bound together by the types of objects seen as animatable, the kinds of human characteristics with which they are invested, and the kinds of actions through which this investment is accomplished. I posit a Taiwanese/Chinese mode of animation that centers on a specific type of object called *ang-a* in Holo or *ou* in Mandarin, a small, three-dimensional, anthropomorphic figure. The *ang-a* is invested with specific human qualities (personality, affect, and charisma) through specific types of actions (ritual, iconographic, and communicational practices). I compare the *ang-a* mode of animation with modes of animation theorized for Japan.

Chapters 3 and 4 explore the implications of the *ang-a* mode of animation in different social fields. Chapter 3 looks at the recent craze for cute cartoon figurines of Buddhist and Daoist deities in Taiwan. While chapter 2 focuses on how religious conceptions of what it means to ensoul an *ang-a* inform the production and consumption of puppetry and commercial animation, chapter 3 looks at the connection between religion and popular culture from the opposite direction, focusing on how styles and modes of interacting with intangible characters move from Japanese manga/anime industries and fandoms into local religious practice.

Chapter 4 considers what globalization might look like as seen through the lens of animation. This chapter focuses on the strategies used by the Pili International Multimedia Company to expand its market beyond Taiwan. I compare Pili's various globalizing projects in terms of how it negotiates between the *ang-a* mode of animation and aesthetic systems and business models developed in North America and Japan. I argue that Pili has been most successful when it has emphasized overlaps between modes of animation and when its video content reflects an implicit historiography connecting contemporary digital technology with preindustrial Chinese aesthetic traditions.

Chapters 5 and 6 take up the question of what happens to identity politics when we approach identity through the lens of animation. Chapter 5 looks at the practice of cosplay, focusing on fans who dress as Pili puppet characters. I look at how cosplayers tend to fall along a continuum, from those who see cosplay as performance to those who see it as a kind of animation using the human body as a medium. Most cosplayers are women, and among Pili cosplayers, most of the characters they embody are male. I place the particular appeal to women of using the body to re-present animated characters in the context of changing gender expectations in both the labor market and the family, arguing that using the body to animate virtual personalities is one way of negotiating between the demands of embodied affective labor and the intellectual demands of working and playing within digital environments.

Chapter 6 examines another mostly female fan practice, the creation of amateur fiction, manga, and artworks using characters from media franchises. Here I focus on the Taiwanese fandom of a Japanese manga/anime franchise, *Axis Powers Hetalia*, in which all of the characters are personifications of nations. Most of the fans of *Axis Powers Hetalia* identify as *funü* (*fujōshi* in Japanese, "shippers" or "slashers" in English)—that is, women who produce and consume the genre of BL (boys' love), which focuses on romantic and/or sexual relationships between male characters. I argue that

the ways in which both the original *Axis Powers Hetalia* and *funü* fans'
amateur works combine genres and modes of characterization challenge
some of the assumptions about national identity and national belonging
that currently underlie identity politics throughout the world. Animation
fans' queer practices of personification provide a model of anti-branding, a
model in which the anxieties provoked by the process of branding in neoliberal capitalism are transformed into pleasures.

   This book is meant to be the start of a conversation rather than a conclusion. My hope is that you will find the concept of animation presented
here good to think with and therefore worth applying to places, genres, and
practices not covered here—that you will take it in new directions, transform it, or deconstruct it.

# CHAPTER I

# Animation versus Performance

As we have moved from the twentieth century into the twenty-first century, we have also been moving from an Age of Performance into an Age of Animation. Not only is animation in the narrow sense (a genre of cinema and video art) becoming more ubiquitous, but animation in the broader sense is becoming an important, if still mostly implicit, trope for describing what human beings do in the world. The purpose of this chapter is to get a handle on this broader sense of animation. In the introduction, I relied on dictionary or commonsense definitions—animation as investing something with life or the appearance of life. Now it's time to get more technical and to try to come up with a specifically anthropological concept of animation.

In order to do that, I am going to explain what I mean by animation by comparing animation with performance. Because I want to arrive at an anthropological concept of animation, I want to start with an anthropological concept of performance, one that has proved extremely useful for making connections between different areas of social life within a given society at a given time and for facilitating comparisons across historical periods and across cultures. Many scholars have used the concept of performance, and each provides an explicit or implicit definition with different emphases. I think it's best for my purpose if I provide my own definition, synthesizing the aspects of the concept that I see as most important in the particular tradition of scholarly writing that I want to outline here. So let me define performance this way: *Performance is the construction of social selves (individual or group identities) through the introjection of qualities from exterior models (roles, images) and the expression of those qualities through the medium of the body (speech, gesture, etc.).*

In this chapter, I will first provide a history of how theoretical interventions in several different areas of study—the arts, religion, psychology, labor, and politics—contributed to the development of this concept of performance. Then, following that history, I will outline how other theoretical interventions in those same fields of study might be combined to come up with a complementary definition of animation: *Animation is the construction of social others through the projection of qualities perceived as human—life, soul, power, agency, intentionality, personality, and so on—outside the self and into the sensory environment, through acts of creation, perception, and interaction.*

This definition is anthropological in that each term within it can be defined only within specific cultural contexts. What a social other is and what qualities are perceived as human are culturally specific, although there are many overlaps among different societies and social contexts. I should explain that qualities perceived as human are not necessarily uniquely or exclusively human; rather, an action/act of perception can be considered animation only if the object onto which it is projected is culturally defined as not having those qualities. Thus, in a technocratic society like contemporary Taiwan, treating, or perceiving, a rock as "alive" is an act of animation. But perceiving a cat as being alive is not, because it is, in such societies, generally agreed that "life" is a quality shared between people and animals. Talking to your cat, however, or ventriloquizing what you think your cat is thinking/saying is an act of animation, since it is not generally accepted that animals have thoughts, language, and personalities in the same way human beings do—even people who believe that their pets do have their own humanlike thoughts and personalities know that they are, to some extent, projecting when they imagine what their pets are thinking. On the other hand, in animist cultures such as that of Heian-era Japan or of Amazonian tribal societies before contact with Europeans (at least, as historians and anthropologists imagine these cultures)—where all natural objects were generally agreed to have a *kami*, or spirit, or where animals were believed to have their own languages and cultures—perceiving a rock as having a spirit or talking to a leopard would not be acts of animation.

After historically contextualizing and explicating my definitions of performance and animation, I will list some of the consequences of using these different models as an approach to research both within and across academic disciplines, social fields, and cultures. Finally, we will explore some of the ways that we might look at how these two models are combined in actual cultural practice.

In defining performance and animation in this way, I am of course picking and choosing from among a wide variety of conceptualizations of both performance and animation that have been articulated over the years and am exaggerating the differences between them. There are many ideas that are important parts of the discourses of both performance and animation—communication, mimesis, play, and liminality, for instance—and a great deal of overlap between them. This is why they are suitable for comparison; they occupy the same conceptual space, so to speak, where the conscious practices of artists serve as metaphors for social action in general. I think it is worthwhile, however, to set out the differences between performance and animation as starkly as possible before getting into the complexities of how they are intertwined in both theory and practice.

## The Performance Model of Social Action: Art and Technology

The *theatrum mundi* metaphor ("All the world's a stage, and all the men and women merely players") goes back at least to the Roman Empire, and underlies all iterations of the performance model to some degree. What "the world" and what "men and women" or "people" mean in different interpretations of the *theatrum mundi* are dependent on what "the stage," "players" or "actors," and "acting" mean. Thus, one of the main conditions for the emergence of the particular model of performance I am talking about here was the emergence of new technologies of dramatic representation, and the new theories and practices of professional acting that came along with them.

If we want to understand the contributions that the arts have made to our particular model of performance by defining the *theatrum* in the *theatrum mundi* metaphor, we need to pay attention to the process that Jay David Bolter and Richard Grusin call remediation. Bolter and Grusin define remediation as "the representation of one medium in another" (1999:45), when a new technology "appropriates the techniques, forms, and social significance of other media and attempts to rival or refashion them in the name of the real" (65). The process works in both directions—"What is new about new media comes from the particular ways in which they refashion older media and the ways in which older media refashion themselves to answer the challenges of new media" (15). In other words, when media technologies are first introduced, people tend to use them for purposes modeled by media with which they are already familiar and to repurpose content from those older media. At the same time, older media redefine themselves in relation to the new, either absorbing new content, styles, and functions from the new medium or emphasizing affordances that distinguish them from the new medium.[1]

Several scholars have pointed out that Bolter and Grusin's view of the goal of remediation as always being "the real" is problematic—realism is not a universal aesthetic, and there are other values that might influence people's adoption of new media (beauty, for instance) (Silvio 2007:286; Gershon 2010a:99–100). I think that the concept of remediation works quite well cross-culturally, however, if we say that remediation happens when the affordances of a new medium offer a way to capture some aspect of people's lived experience (including emotions) that other media do not provide, or that they better capture some aspect(s) of people's experience. Still, in Europe and North America, the drives toward and away from realism have characterized the introduction of every new media technology. New media adaptations tend toward visual (and/or aural) mimesis, and older media in response develop nonrealist or antirealist aesthetics.

For instance, when the first cameras were invented, photography was largely seen as a remediation of painting. The most popular genres of photography were (and remain) the same as the most popular genres of painting in the early nineteenth century—landscapes and portraits. These were genres that, since the Renaissance, had aimed to capture how human eyes see the material world, and the camera was seen as accomplishing this in a more precise way than hand and brush ever could. After the popularization of photography, painters responded by developing a wide variety of nonfigurative styles (Surrealism, Cubism, abstract art, etc.). In other words, Modernist painters redefined "art" as "not photography," as capturing psychic or spiritual truths that photography's direct impressions of light bouncing off surfaces could not.

Since we want to analyze the development of the *theatrum mundi* trope in the twentieth century, let us focus on the remediation of drama, starting with the invention of the movie camera in 1895. Early cinema was widely experimental, including many styles of both live action and animation, but by the 1920s, cinema was primarily a more immersive (to use Bolter and Grusin's term) format for the realist drama that had emerged in European theaters in the late nineteenth century. The screen took the place of the proscenium arch, reinforcing the "fourth wall" and the positioning of the audience as unseen voyeurs observing real-seeming social interactions. The development of shot/reverse shot and continuity editing also made psychic identification between spectators and characters more fixed.

The realist theater and cinema required a new style of acting, which was largely defined during this period by Konstantin Stanislavski. Stanislavski's system established several of the aspects of acting that would form the basis for the anthropological concept of performance later in the twentieth century: working from both the "outside in" (introjection of the role) and the "inside out" (physical expression), mimesis, and physical discipline. When the Stanislavski system was adopted in the United States, particularly at Lee Strasberg's Actors Studio, Freudian theory was introduced and psychological introjection and projection were emphasized over physical training.

Once the aesthetics and acting practice of realism were well established within Hollywood, a new generation of directors and playwrights redefined theater as "not cinema," creating new genres of antirealist theater, from Antonin Artaud's metaphysical Theater of Cruelty to Bertolt Brecht's political Epic Theater.[2] The acting practices developed for these antirealist theaters would provide another set of characteristics attached to performance more broadly as the performance model developed, including liminality and reflexivity. This tension between realism and antirealism in theater and cinema, between the function of drama as re-creating material and psychological realities and exposing spiritual or social structural realities, between identification and alienation effect, set the stage (so to speak) for new interpretations of the *theatrum mundi*.

Television turned out to be the media technology that provided the conditions for the development of a specifically anthropological performance concept. Television remediated cinema and its realism but also remediated radio (especially in its business model and programming schedules) and theater.[3] As with cinema, the first decades after television was popularized in the United States in the late 1940s were characterized by experimentation and a range of adapted performance styles. Here I want to focus on two important ways in which television performance differed from cinema performance, stemming largely from television's remediation of radio. First, television brought drama directly into private homes, now with the bodies of the performers visible. Second, it created a new kind of performer, one who, in one way or another, was seen (and not just heard) to be "playing themself."

Lynn Spigel notes that, in the early days of commercial television, its promotion as a domestic technology was facilitated both by advertising that represented the television set as bringing the experience of going to the theater into the home and by programming that presented domestic space as a literal stage. *The Burns and Allen Show* was typical of early sitcoms in this sense.

> At the level of content, this program was based on the premise of a real life couple (George Burns and Gracie Allen) who played themselves playing themselves as real-life performers who had a television show based on their lives as television stars. If this is a bit hard to follow, it should be, because the fundamental principle of this program was a *mise-en-abyme*

structure, an endless stage within a stage, a bottomless pit of representation. (Spigel 1992:16)

Apart from sitcoms, actors playing themselves, or playing themselves playing themselves, also appeared in soap operas (where actors who played one role over many years were often assumed by the press and the audience to be typecast) (Jeremy Butler 1991), in variety and talk shows, and of course in advertisements ("I'm not a doctor, but I play one on TV").

For people living in North America in the 1950s, who were presented daily with virtual personalities playing themselves in all kinds of convoluted ways, certain questions almost inevitably arose: What was the relationship between public and private space? Between public and private selves? What did it mean to "play oneself"? Thus, it is not at all coincidental that Erving Goffman's seminal sociological theorization of performance, *The Presentation of Self in Everyday Life*, was published in 1959, at the end of the golden age of American television.[4]

For Goffman, every social interaction was a kind of performance, in which participants rotated between the roles of actor and audience, with individuals switching roles constantly as they moved from one context to another. While social actors are like professional actors in that they enact roles through speech and gesture, the stage and the real world differ in how roles are defined and where they come from. Goffman defines roles, or social identities, as the "rights and duties attached to a given status" (1959:16), as sets of communal expectations for how someone in a given position should act in different contexts. In everyday life, roles do not come from scripts, from the imaginations of individual authors, but from social structure.

The way that Goffman defines a successful performance is closely related to the context of the golden age of television. The realist acting tradition that came to dominate cinema's remediation of theater, especially Strasberg's Method acting, defined successful performance as that which revealed internal conflict. Successful performance was based on showing inconsistency. As James Naremore puts it, "We could say that realist acting amounts to an effort at sustaining opposing attitudes toward the self, on the one hand trying to create the illusion of unified, individualized personality, but on the other suggesting that character is subject to division or dissolution into a variety of social roles" (1988:72). The Brechtian acting tradition that arose in response to the dominance of realism made contradictions and inconsistencies visible—in this case, the dichotomy between actor and role, between positions within and outside social structure. Goffman, in contrast, defines a successful performance in terms of consistency. For Goffman, since roles are defined by conventional expectations, a successful, or believable, performance is simply one that does not break convention, that does not reveal the self in a different role that would be inconsistent with the context. The goal of coherence or consistency is also characteristic of the acting practices developed in the stage genres that the television soap opera and sitcom remediated: melodrama and vaudeville. The *mise-en-abyme* structure of shows like *The Burns and Allen Show* and *I Love Lucy* combined a dichotomy between contexts (stage versus living room, public versus private) with a stress on the continuities of the self across these contexts.

By the mid-1960s, this kind of reflexive yet consistent performance on television had become rare. A certain type of homogenized naturalism took over in television drama, partly influenced by the trend toward a universalist psychological realism on Broadway and in Hollywood (Spigel 1992). The naturalized naturalism of later television dramas provoked many in the avant-garde, from Jerzy Grotowski to the San Francisco Mime Troupe, to relocate the real of the theater in precisely what was lost in the transition to television—the performers' and audience's sharing of time and space, interactive and direct communication between performers and audience, and the material presence of the actor's body. As cinema increasingly defined itself as more psychologically real than television, and theater defined itself as more spiritually or politically revealing than television, academics in psychology, religious studies, politics, and economics, as well as activists, began to take up the concept of performance. As the newness of the idea of "playing oneself" faded into the background, Goffman's model of all interpersonal interactions as self-performance came to seem overly conscious or cynical, and scholars began to focus on aspects of performance that Goffman had ignored or left in the background—emotions and the subconscious, embodiment and mimesis, collaboration and complicity, and the replication and transformation of social structures.

These aspects of performance had long been the focus of studies of religious ritual, and in the 1970s, anthropological studies of religion began to intersect with concepts of performance developed in theater studies and sociology.

## Contributions of Religious Studies to the Performance Paradigm: The Ritual Model

In the 1970s and 1980s, a new group of anthropologists began developing the performance concept by applying it to religious ritual and then taking religious ritual as the ideal type of performance. Switching the model of performance from professional acting to ritual participation allowed theater scholars and anthropologists to expand the concept of performance by focusing on several aspects of performance neglected by Goffman.

First, drawing on a long tradition in anthropology (e.g., Durkheim, Malinowski), they focused on performance as a communal, rather than individual, activity. In 1959, Milton Singer had linked Indian "weddings, temple festivals, recitations, plays, dances, musical concerts, etc.," under the rubric of "cultural performances": discrete units with "a definitely limited time span, a beginning and end, an organized program of activity, a set of performers, an audience, and a place and occasion of performance" (Singer 1959, cited in MacAloon 1984:4). He noted that "Indians, and perhaps all peoples, think of their culture as encapsulated in such discrete performances, which they can exhibit to outsiders as well as to themselves" (ibid.). Following Singer, the symbolic anthropology that developed in the 1970s saw cultural performance as the means by which individuals occupying a wide variety of social positions were unconsciously drawn into shared semiotic systems and group identities.

Second, ritual tied the idea of performance to larger social structures and, beyond those, to cosmologies. Thus, where Goffman focused on roles that were largely voluntary and enforced only through social contract (e.g., doctor, salesman, girlfriend), anthropologists of ritual focused on roles perceived as assigned by forces outside society itself. Sometimes these roles came from outside the self in the most literal sense, as in spirit possession; sometimes they were roles simply seen as natural or predestined—for example, man and woman, child and adult. Performance thus established relationships not only among humans but also between the human and the beyond-human.

Third, while Goffman focused on speech, these scholars focused on nonverbal communication as well. And where Goffman's everyday performances were largely calculated and aimed at the audience's conscious perception, ritual studies focused more on how performances aroused, sustained, or altered emotional states, in both performers and audiences.

Finally, ritual studies focused on performance as a means of both maintaining and transforming social structures over time. Most influential here was the cooperation between anthropologist Victor Turner and theater director Richard Schechner, which led in 1982 to the founding of the first performance studies program in the United States, at New York University. Turner and Schechner expanded on Arnold van Gennep's concept of liminality, a state "betwixt and between" social roles (e.g., child and adult), during which the individual is literally or figuratively separated from society (e.g., Turner 1967; Schechner 1985). While van Gennep saw the liminal as simply a passage between stable social roles, for Turner and Schechner it became a space for reflection on and critique of structure. As the field of performance studies developed, liminality became a characteristic of ritual itself, not just a phase in specific rituals, and then became a defining characteristic of all performance. Performance thus provides a feedback loop between the virtual and the actual, the potential and the realized (McKenzie 2001:49–50, 88–94).

Because most of this work was done by anthropologists and Western theater practitioners working in non-Western sites, a cross-cultural perspective became an explicit part of the performance model, and most of the axes of analysis that come out of studies of religious ritual as performance are applicable to the animation model as well.

## Political and Economic Contexts for the Emergence of the Performance Paradigm

I have focused on the dialogue between theater and anthropology, but of course this dialogue and the performance concepts developing within it were deeply entwined with broader transformations, not only in the media landscape, but also in economic and political formations. In the United States, these included the development of marketing and the service industries, as well as the rise of the civil rights and feminist movements. In the spheres of both work and democratic politics, empowerment and oppression took on new forms, centered around the ideas of representation and identity. From the 1960s on, culture and performance became increasingly important terms in the discourses of both business managers and political activists.

According to Michael Omi and Howard Winant (1986), until the 1960s the black civil rights movement in the United States had worked within what they call an "ethnic" racial formation. That is, the movement had been fighting for black Americans to be granted equal rights as citizens, just as members of European immigrant groups had been granted. But in the 1960s and 1970s, faced with conservative whites' backlash against the gains made in political representation and institutional integration, more radical activists argued that the ethnic model perpetuated an inherently exclusive system. The alternative politics of radical antiracism included what Omi and Winant call cultural nationalism, a politics that drew explicitly on the concept of cultural performance developed in the scholarship that came out of the study of religious ritual:

> Cultural nationalism found expression in every minority community. This was an explicit critique of the dominant Eurocentric (i.e., white) culture, understood to pervade both everyday life and "high culture." Cultural nationalists sought to redefine and recapture the specificity of their minority cultures. . . . Painting, theater, dance, music, language, even cars and clothes, all became media through which a new style could be developed, and through which "genuine" oppositional culture could be distinguished from assimilationist practices. (1986:105)

A similar trend emerged in the feminist movement in the 1980s, with what is sometimes called difference feminism. Scholars such as Carol Gilligan argued that women had distinctive traits—moral values, aesthetics, modes of speech and action—based on shared experiences, which challenged the norms of a dominant (masculine) society. While some strains of difference feminism, like some strains of African American cultural nationalism, saw these differences as innate (based in biological differences), many focused on shared cultural experiences, such as childhood socialization (e.g., Gilligan 1982) or subcultural practice (e.g., Smith-Rosenberg 1975). Black cultural nationalism and difference feminism opened the way for performance to be seen not only as a means for expressing political ideas, but as a means for maintaining politicized identities and creating solidarity and emotional attachment to those identities.

In the economic sphere, the sociological concept of performance had been tied to the field of wage labor since Goffman. *The Presentation of Self* focuses on "the individual in ordinary work situations" (Goffman 1959:xi), and the vast majority of Goffman's examples are of men working in the service and marketing sectors (e.g., salesmen, hotel workers). Sociologist Alvin Gouldner writes that Goffman's theorization of performance "marks the transition from an older economy centered on production to a new one centered on mass marketing and promotion, including marketing of the self," and "resonates the sentiments and assumptions of the new middle class: of the 'swinger' in the service-producing sector of the economy, of the status-conscious white-collar worker, professional, bureaucratic functionary, and of the educated middle class" (1970:381).

As the US economy began to deindustrialize in the 1970s and 1980s, "performance" became a key term in business discourse. Here, of course, it generally meant "getting things done" rather than having any association with theatrical performance. But some management gurus in the 1980s and 1990s did cite Goffman. Jon McKenzie traces the shift in business management philosophy from the 1950s to the 1990s from the focus on discipline within Fordist scientific industrial management to a performance management paradigm in which proactive performance, rather than obedience, was seen as the mark of the ideal worker. Although "organizational theorists often describe this change . . . as moving the managerial emphasis from controlling workers to empowering them, from giving orders to creating participatory interactions" (McKenzie 2001:57), the goal was the same: "working better and costing less," or efficiency (56). And as anyone knows who has undergone a work performance evaluation in the past fifty years, failure to perform (in an empowered, participatory way) has the same consequences for workers that failure to be disciplined did in the Fordist era.

McKenzie notes that the change in emphasis within management discourse from discipline to performance was partly a response to legal victories by the civil rights and feminist movements, which resulted in the diversification of the American labor force. Although racial diversity within workplaces was a goal of the affirmative action programs established in the 1960s (including the creation of the Equal Employment Opportunity Commission in 1965), and some industries did see an increase in formerly excluded racial and ethnic minorities, the group whose workforce participation increased most dramatically over the course of the 1960s–1980s was white women. The percentage of women sixteen and older who worked for wages increased from 33.9 percent in 1950 to 51.6 percent in 1980 (Fullerton 1999:4). Working women during these decades were largely segregated into female-dominated occupations. "Pink-collar" jobs, aside from being significantly less well-paid than male-dominated white- or blue-collar jobs, were also primarily service jobs—nursing, teaching, secretarial and clerical work, cleaning, and so on. It was in the pink-collar sector that performance as presentation of self and performance as worker efficiency were most entangled.

In her classic 1983 study of airline stewardesses, *The Managed Heart*, sociologist Arlie Hochschild argued that one of the chief characteristics of pink-collar labor was the emphasis on "emotional work." Emotional work is the labor of managing the emotional states of service consumers through speech and bodily performance. For the women whom Hochschild interviewed, Goffman was already common sense; they talked about their jobs explicitly as "acting a role." The stewardesses' training incorporated

the principles of Method acting; controlling the emotional states of pas-
sengers was accomplished through the conscious control of one's own
emotional states.

Hochschild was especially disturbed by the psychic effects of Goffman's
model *of* performance/acting becoming a model *for* performance/efficiency.
She found that stewardesses often became alienated from their own emotional lives, no longer able to determine which emotions they were authen-
tically experiencing, even outside of work hours. In both the discourse and
practice of labor management, Goffman's construction of performance as
an explanatory model of social action was transformed into a model for
worker behavior, one enforced with various degrees of threat and violence
and with oppressive consequences.

## Judith Butler's Synthesis: Performance = Psychic Introjection + Mimetic Embodiment = Identity

In the 1980s and 1990s, the performance paradigm developed in new directions under the influence of post-structuralist theory. In articles and the
books *Gender Trouble* (1990) and *Bodies That Matter* (1993), Judith Butler
articulated the concept of performance that has remained the most influential ever since within performance studies, anthropology, and cultural studies. Butler complicated and combined the various aspects of performance
already developed within theater and anthropology with J. L. Austin's concept of linguistic performativity, Michel Foucault's concept of social identity
as constructed through discourse, and Jacques Lacan's description of the
mirror stage in the individual's ego formation.

Butler's model binds the concept of performance to embodiment
and to identity in new ways. It was an extremely appealing formulation for
American feminists at the time, as it managed to steer a clear path between
the Scylla of biological essentialism (the dangers of which had become
amply clear with the emerging critique of American mainstream feminism
by women of color) and the Charybdis of purely discursive constructions of
female identity, in which, as Simone de Beauvoir had pointed out, "Woman"
is always defined negatively, as only what the unmarked term "Man" is not.

In her first publication on performance, in *Theatre Journal* (1988),
Butler makes this phenomenological argument:

> Gender is in no way a stable identity or locus of agency from which vari-
> ous acts proceede [*sic*]; rather, it is an identity tenuously constituted in

> time—an identity instituted through a *stylized repetition of acts*. Further, gender is instituted through the stylization of the body and, hence, must be understood as the mundane way in which bodily gestures, movements, and enactments of various kinds constitute the illusion of an abiding gendered self. (519)

In other words, Butler argues here that the individual's sense of self as a woman or as a man cannot be taken for granted as preexisting their presentations of self, as not only Goffman but most feminist theorists at the time did. Rather, it is continual everyday performances that create that sense of self. Butler's model thus makes moot the debates around cynicism versus sincerity that had characterized reactions to Goffman's work by erasing the ontological difference between onstage and backstage. For Butler, the actor's "real" (backstage) self is as much an effect of embodied, mimetic performance as is the onstage persona.

In the 1998 article, Butler cites anthropologists and performance theorists, including Goffman, Turner, Schechner, and Bruce Wilshire, and although she frames her argument mostly through Maurice Merleau-Ponty's phenomenology, her debt to ritual studies is clear in her emphasis on embodiment, mimesis, and continuity. In her later work, as she further explicates and expands on these ideas, Butler reframes her argument more in the vocabulary of linguistic philosophy and psychoanalysis.

Butler explains her thesis that performances of masculinity and femininity do not simply express preexisting social roles but constitute gender identity itself, with reference to the linguistic philosopher J. L. Austin's concept of performativity. In *How to Do Things with Words* (1962), Austin argues that certain types of utterance—for instance, the making of a promise—are not denotative but performative. That is, they do not refer to or describe reality but, rather, bring a new reality into being. His most memorable example is that of a clergyman saying, "I now pronounce you man and wife." But performatives work only under what Austin calls "conditions of felicity." That is, "I now pronounce you man and wife" creates a marriage only when the speaker is authorized to marry people (e.g., is a clergyman). If the frame (as Goffman would call it) of the speech act is not perceived by the witnesses as "real" (e.g., if the pronouncement is made onstage as part of a play), neither is the marriage.

In Western societies, the "felicitous" conditions that render gender performances performative are thought to be biological and therefore "natural"—but, as Butler argues, this perception is ideological and enforced by institutional practices both subtle and violent. In order to understand the depth of biologistic ideology, we need to look at embodiment in two senses. First, there is embodiment in the sense of what anthropologists call habitus, the unconsciously reproduced styles of movement that are the result of constant mimetic physical action. Second, we must also see embodiment in the sense of the placement of the ego sense, of subjectivity, within specific physical bodies.

For Butler, psychoanalyst Jacques Lacan's description of the mirror stage provides the model for embodiment in the second sense. In the mirror stage, when the infant first sees its reflection in a mirror, it misrecognizes the image as an idealized self and feels that it can control what it sees through its own movements. The mirror image here does not have to be an actual mirror; in fact, it is most often another human body—for instance, that of the mother. In Butler's model, individuals throughout their lives continually misrecognize external images as idealized selves and embody gender and other roles through continually imitating these models. But the adult's feeling of subjective control over the body and its movements, like the infant's, is illusory—the image of the other is never internalized or (re)externalized perfectly. It is Lacan's idea of *méconnaissance*, or misrecognition—the idea that the mirror image the self perceives might not match the way that others see the same body—that allows for the possibility that performance might transform, as well as maintain, culturally constructed identities.

Butler argues that what we might call "infelicitous" performances, such as drag, can work to denaturalize gender as a system. Infelicitous performances can make audiences question what it is that makes gender real and thus can expose the concept of biological, essential gender identity as ideological. Butler developed her concept of gender performance during the worst years of the AIDS crisis, and it is not surprising that a theory that denaturalized the relationship between bodies and selves, challenging the boundaries between "normal" and "abnormal" gender identities and sexual orientations, was taken up eagerly by feminist, queer, and AIDS activists. McKenzie notes that after Judith Butler, performance studies came to be seen as virtually synonymous with gender/queer studies in the American academy. This is not simply because Butler herself identifies as a butch lesbian and focused her research (at the time) on gender and sexual identity, but because there was a high degree of overlap between performance studies academics and activists in the queer identity political movements in the US and the UK. Performance studies scholars such as Sue-Ellen Case, Peggy Phelan, and anthropologist Esther Newton not only focused their research on the radical political potential of cross-gender theatrical performance, but were also active in queer art and social movements. Public performance was taken up, with much success, as a major tactic by ACT UP, the Lesbian Avengers, and many other activist groups.

While Butler's synthesis of concepts of performance from theater studies, anthropology, sociology, psychology, and linguistics—the idea that identity is performance—was taken up most enthusiastically within gender and queer studies, it was also applied quite effectively in studies of other types of identity: racial, ethnic, national, regional, class, subcultural, and so on. Brechtian, self-reflexive performance became an important strategy within many different social and political movements. Despite its emergence within a particularly North American, late twentieth-century set of ideologies about the body, the psyche, and representation, the performance model has proved useful for scholars and activists within a wide variety of cultural contexts and for cross-cultural comparison. Performance allows for comparisons across many axes: the content of habitus, which aspects of embodiment (form, movement, aging, decoration, etc.) are bound to identity and which are not, what constitute felicitous conditions for performative acts, the degree to which mimesis is enforced or flexible, and so on. As Butler's theories were translated and applied by academics working outside Europe and North America, they were modified and challenged through encounters with cultures in which gender (and other) identities were not necessarily naturalized through the discourse of scientific biology, or where realism was never a goal of theatrical or ritual performance, or where selves were not conceptualized as independent or necessarily coherent across contexts.

In sum, over the course of the twentieth century, the performance paradigm emerged in response to developments in media technologies and economic restructuring but also participated in those structural transformations. The concept of performance as the construction of social selves through the introjection of qualities from exterior models and the expression of those qualities through the medium of the body both developed within and transformed a number of dialogues over the course of the twentieth century—dialogues between artists and academics, business and politics, the West and the Rest.

The conditions that made performance such a productive trope have not gone away, just as the conditions that made discipline a productive concept did not disappear as the performance model emerged. Live performance and live-action cinema and television are still flourishing. The service sector is still the fastest-growing part of the labor market in the United States, as well as in many other postindustrial societies. Resources and recognition are still distributed unequally based on identity categories everywhere, and identity-based activism is still necessary.

But we are seeing new developments in media technologies and in global political and economic structures that are raising new questions. These developments include, as I mentioned in the introduction, the growth and spread of digital technologies, the formation of new economic classes both within and among geographical regions, climate change, and a range of new or transformed activist movements in response to all of these.

Over the past few decades, a number of scholars and artists have been thinking through these changes in terms of what I call animation, some explicitly, some implicitly. In the next section, I outline the concepts that have developed in different fields of study and provide some context for their emergence. Following in the footsteps of performance studies, I interweave approaches from the arts, anthropology, and psychology. All of these approaches retain something of the etymological sense of animation as investing a thing with life, but each defines "life" and "thing" in a slightly different way.

## Digital Remediations: From Performance to Animation

If the performance trope starts with the work of the performing artist, we can start our definition of animation with the work of the animating artist— the artist whose work involves creating characters out of inanimate materials. And if the context for the emergence of a new sociological version of the *theatrum mundi* was television's remediation of theater, the context for the emergence of a new trope of animation as cultural action is the development of computer-generated animation and its remediation of cinema animation and puppetry.

Computer-generated animation seems to be reaching the kind of golden age that television had in the 1950s, when certain ways of using the new media technologies, certain genres and formats, are becoming established as standard, and an industrial structure is becoming more or less stable. As with television, the mainstream of digital media is defined by a trend toward increasing verisimilitude and immersive effects. This is especially apparent in online games, where the goal of creating increasingly lifelike images (more detailed texturing, smoother movement, 3-D) is taken for granted by programmers and designers in large companies such as Blizzard Entertainment.

The most common contemporary use of the term "animation" refers to a genre of film or video, and most academic theorizing of animation has taken place within film and media studies. The concept of animation within cinema and media studies largely follows the focus of industry practitioners. Animation in this sense is defined in opposition to "live action" cinema or television. Non-digital cinema animation is created frame by frame and includes two-dimensional (e.g., hand-drawn cel animation, paper cutout animation) and three-dimensional (e.g., stop-motion photography of dolls or other objects, Claymation) techniques.

The history of digital animation can be traced back to the 1940s, but until the 1980s it was primarily used for scientific purposes, for special effects in live-action cinema and television (such as moving titles), or for making short experimental films. In the 1980s a number of new programs were developed for both 2-D and 3-D digital animation that remediated cinematography techniques (such as panning and zooming) and allowed both for more realistic movement and texturing and for more fantastic effects (such as the morphing of one photographic image into another). Many of these techniques were introduced to the general public through music videos and science fiction films.

According to the detailed Wikipedia entry on the history of digital animation, "1991 is widely considered the 'breakout year'" for digital animation in cinema, with the release of *Terminator 2: Judgment Day* (featuring the liquid-metal T-1000 robot) and Disney's second fully computer-generated feature film, *Beauty and the Beast* (the first came out in 1990, Disney's *The Rescuers Down Under*).[5]

Not coincidentally, 1991 also saw the publication of the first book within academic philosophy and cultural studies dedicated entirely to cinema animation, edited by Alan Cholodenko, the result of a 1990 conference he organized. A major rewriting of the history of animated cinema from within cinema studies began. This begins by tracing the transformation of still images into moving ones through devices such as the stereopticon and Muybridge's stop-motion photography.[6] Cholodenko (1991, 2007) makes the compelling argument, based on this technological history, that all cinema is in fact animation, because film itself is a technology whose primary effect is the illusion of movement created through the rapid sequence of still frames. In cinema and video studies, then, animation is defined in terms of techne—a set of technologies and techniques for using them—and in terms of creating, as the title of Cholodenko's conferences puts it, "the illusion of life."

Avant-garde performance artists and theorists in the 1960s and 1970s challenged the naturalist conventions of television drama by emphasizing the nonrealist and corporeal elements of live theater and ritual, rather than the verisimilar and mechanical, drawing on pre-realist and non-Western theater practices. Similarly, avant-garde animators and animation theorists today are emphasizing the reflexive effects of earlier, especially preindustrial, technes of animation, such as puppetry. While cinema historians focus on the techne of the animator, these reflexive works tend to focus on the objects of animation and their apparent autonomy. Here the focus is less on movement and more on other human qualities, such as sentience and will. This type of reflexivity can be seen in some of the earliest cinema animation, such as Winsor McCay's *Gertie the Dinosaur* (1914) and the Fleischer brothers' *Out of the Inkwell: Koko the Clown* (1921), in which the live-action animators drawing the character are placed in conflict with the character they have animated, who claims their freedom through mischievous or rebellious action. The locus classicus of this type of reflexive animation is no doubt Chuck Jones' 1953 *Duck Amuck*, in which the animating hand stretching, erasing, displacing, and otherwise tormenting Daffy Duck turns out to be the hand of another cartoon character, Bugs Bunny. Where performative reflexivity focused on the split between actor and role, animative reflexivity focuses on the split between animator and animatee, on questions of uncanny ontology—not just the illusion of autonomous life but also the possibility that it might not be illusion.

One of the most influential animators exploring the relationship between technology and ontology is Japanese auteur director Oshii Mamoru. Oshii's oeuvre (especially the *Ghost in the Shell* series) explores the nature of the human and the nonhuman through dense narratives about a future world in which human souls are "hacked" into a wide range of media/objects—mechanical bodies, prostheses, puppets, cyberspace itself. As in early television programs like *The Burns and Allen Show*, we are presented with *mise-en-abymes*, where automatons turn out to be manufactured by cyborgs, who may themselves be controlled by "ghosts" that float between various material hosts and a disembodied state. Oshii cites a wide range of academic theory in his art (one of his characters is named after Donna Haraway, for example), and some of the most interesting academic cultural contextualizations and elaborations of the puppetry trope come out of critical studies of Oshii's work (e.g., Bolton 2002; Steven Brown 2008; Orbaugh 2008).

Not only avant-garde but recent mainstream cinema animation also contains a strain of reflexivity. There are 3-D digital movies about toys with lives of their own (Pixar's *Toy Story* series), and video games featuring cute animated corpses (Plants vs. Zombies). We might see the recent epidemic of live-action zombie movies as the old media's critical reflection on the advent of the digital network society.

In the mid-twentieth century, television presented us with star actors playing themselves playing themselves playing themselves, which raised questions about the relationship between individuals and society and about the nature of self-identity. In the early twenty-first century, we are presented with animated images of animated objects animating other objects and images. As we are increasingly surrounded by this new type of *mise-en-abyme*, different philosophical questions have become newly urgent: What makes something alive? What is the boundary between the human and the nonhuman? What is the relationship between the material body and the mind? It is again no coincidence that several recent trends in academic research and theory are focused on these questions. These include not only the work of Donna Haraway and others on cyborgs and human-animal relations but also actor network theory (e.g., Latour 1993, 2005), what is often called the "ontological turn" in anthropology or "new animism studies" (e.g., Descola 2013; Viveiros de Castro 2012; Bird-David 1999), work in anthropology and science and technology studies on artificial intelligence and artificial life (e.g., Hayles 1999, Helmreich 1998), and work in literary criticism and philosophy on materiality (e.g., Bill Brown 2001; Bogost 2012). There is too much of this literature now for me to summarize here, but I do want to focus briefly on how a concept of animation is emerging within some of the fields that contributed to the development of the performance paradigm.

## Religious Concepts of Animation

With the move from Goffman's sociological interpretation of the *theatrum mundi* to Turner's, Schechner's, and others' study of religion, we moved from a focus on the presentation of self to the process of becoming the self. When we move from the study of animation as art and techne to the study of animation as religious practice, we make a parallel move from the illusion of life to the investment and perception of agency.

Where the anthropology of performance focuses on religious ritual, an anthropology of animation would focus instead on the investment of icons, effigies, talismans, fetishes, and natural objects with divine power or agency, what Victoria Nelson refers to as "practices of 'ensouling' matter" (2001:30). Within anthropology, the foundational text here is James Frazer's formulation, in *The Golden Bough* (1925), of magic as the investment of power within objects through either similarity or contagion (the sharing of appearance or the sharing of substance). To date, one of the most well-articulated theorizations of religious animation, which draws on Frazer, is probably Alfred Gell's (1998) analysis of how sacred objects are invested with their own agency—both through formal qualities that abstractly represent cultural concepts of personhood and through human interaction with the objects. It is perhaps not surprising that the anthropology of religion has in the past twenty years made something of a turn from analyses of ritual to studies of materiality (e.g., Keane [2007] and the online journal *Material Religion: The Journal of Objects, Art and Belief*, which began publication in 2005).

Mauss' theorization of the gift as a part of the self invested in an object and Marx's theory of the commodity fetish might both be seen as expansions of the anthropological model of animation beyond the overtly religious sphere. William Pietz' historical study of the origin of the concept of the fetish in the meeting of Catholic Portuguese traders and West Africans in the sixteenth to eighteenth centuries and its subsequent rearticulations by Marx and Freud is an excellent example of how the concept of animation itself travels across both cultural/historical contexts and spheres of social and intellectual endeavor (Pietz 1985, 1987; see also Graeber 2007; Masuzawa 2007).

Given the long history of comparisons between animation in the narrow sense and religious animism (e.g., Eisenstein 1986 [1940–1941]), an anthropology of animation should also include the study of cosmologies in which nonhuman entities are seen as being or having spirits or souls. Recent anthropology that focuses on animism demands that animist ontologies be respected, and my placing animism within a definition that includes techniques of illusion might be seen as reinscribing animist cosmologies within a scientist worldview. My purpose is not to do this. But I do intend an anthropological theory of animism to be geared toward the twenty-first century, and in this century, indigenous peoples with animist traditions live in worlds that are as much the products of colonialism as their own cultural traditions, where they must deal with national legal and education systems, and they are familiar, whether they want to be or not, with scientistic ontologies. Since most people now negotiate between simultaneously existing cosmological systems (and have been doing so for centuries), I have included "*acts* of perception" in my definition of animation; perceiving souls in nature, like refusing to see them, requires effort.

## The Psychology of Animation: Projection and Transitional Objects

If performance studies took its psychological model from Lacan's mirror stage, animation studies has looked more to object-relations theory. In particular, D. W. Winnicott's concept of the transitional object provides a way of thinking about animation as a psychic process, one that is as crucial to the process of socialization and individual development as performance, from which it is inseparable. Winnicott has been cited both in self-reflexive comics (Alison Bechdel's *Are You My Mother?* [2012]) and by anthropologists working on Japanese animation culture (e.g., Yano 2013; Allison 2006).

Technically, transitional objects are the blankets and soft toys that infants tend to become obsessed with, carry around, and use for self-comfort. For Winnicott (1971), what is most important about transitional objects is the role they play in the infant's developing ability to establish a relationship between self and environment. Transitional objects, according to Winnicott, are neither subjective nor objective—neither pure projections of the child's psyche nor purely external objects. Infants' play with transitional objects occurs in a space that is neither me nor not-me, a space of allowed illusion, which he argues is crucial for the development of the creative capacity and the ability to enjoy life. Like the mirror stage, this transitional space cannot be seen as a developmental stage that the infant passes through (see also Stern 1985). Rather, transitional space is important throughout life, since "the task of reality-acceptance is never completed" (Winnicott 1971:13). Winnicott sees religion, art, creative scientific work, and indeed "cultural experience" in general as taking place within this transitional space between individual subjectivity and the objective existence of social structure and inherited tradition.

Like the image in the mirror, the transitional object is a point of friction and therefore of potential social change. When infants look in the mirror, they may not see what others see. Thus, the self-image becomes a site where the socially sedimented (objective) role resists the subject (a resistance often experienced as oppression), but at the same time, performance becomes a means whereby subjects may try to reconstruct social roles to match their own imagination. Winnicott points out how the transitional object is a similar point of friction when he distinguishes object usage from object-relating. Object-relating involves only projection by the subject, without resistance from the object. He notes, however, that "the object, if it is to be used, must necessarily be real in the sense of being part of shared reality, not a bundle of projections" (Winnicott 1971:88). This recognition of the object's externality is predicated on the object's psychic destruction and its survival of that psychic destruction: "It is the destruction of the object that places the object outside the area of the subject's omnipotent control. In these ways the object develops its own autonomy and life, and (if it survives) contributes-in to the subject, according to its own properties" (Winnicott 1971:90).

Subjectivity and objectivity, introjection and projection, are flip sides of the same coin. It is when the social objectivity of the role runs up against individual subjectivities that social identities change; it is when individual subjectivities run up against the objectivity of the environment that stereotypes (socially sedimented figurations, imaginings of otherness) change.

## The Labor of Animation: Branding

If the performance paradigm was institutionalized during a period when the service sector, especially pink collar labor, was expanding, the newest part of the current "new economy" is what is often called the creative industries, the content industries, or the IP (intellectual property) industries. This includes, of course, the work of producing manga, anime, and computer games but also design and advertising, which have been moving closer to the model of animation over the past thirty years.[7] Like service work, work in the creative industries is emotional work. But because the medium of communication is not the body, this labor cannot be accomplished through interpersonal micro-interactions; it must take place through nonsimultaneous, mediated interactions between designers, or networks of designers, and anonymous masses. This kind of labor is exemplified by the work of branding.

One of the most prominent uses of animated cartoon characters today is as brand logos or mascots, personifications of corporations and other organizations. This may be particularly true in East Asia. In Taiwan, for example, the list of entities represented by cartoon characters includes banks, life insurance companies, gas companies, restaurant chains, snack foods, electronics manufacturers, real estate agencies, agricultural associations, temple alliances, urban neighborhoods, the 2010 International Floral Expo, and the national postal service. These cartoon characters are designed to attach the consumer's positive feelings both to the products or services produced by an organization and to the organization itself. Paul Manning, summarizing recent work on the semiotics of branding, writes that in some contemporary brand discourse "the pervasive associations based on the role brands play in consumers' lives are transformed into actual anthropomorphic characteristics imputed to brands understood as holistic, organic, living, growing entities with which consumers can form actual social relationships directly" (2010:36).

If there is an equivalent in the animation model to the punitive power that McKenzie finds in the business model of performance as efficiency ("Perform or else!"), it probably lies in the command to brand. Branding makes the value of nonmaterial labor legible, by turning abstract qualities—goodwill, recognition, affect—into products that can be sold. Not only corporations but also individuals and nations are coming to see the brand as the primary repository of value and self-branding as a precondition for action in the world.

Ilana Gershon has found that in the United States, job seekers are urged constantly to construct personal brands by management gurus and by employment retraining and assistance programs run by local governments and nongovernmental organizations (NGOs), even though the employers she interviewed were all more focused on applicants' skill sets. Gershon argues that self-branding is part of a neoliberal twist on the idea of the self as property—the idea of the self as a financialized business, "a collection of skills, assets, and alliances that must be continually maintained and enhanced" (2014:288). Self-branding is appealing to (some) job seekers and their helpers because it seems to provide a way to negotiate between the contradictory demands for constant flexibility—movement between short-term contracts, upgrading skills—and for enough consistency to be legible. But self-branding, animating oneself as if one were a thing, can prove to be just as self-alienating and exhausting as the performance of service worker roles (Gershon 2014, 2016).

## The Politics of Animation

As I noted earlier, the performance paradigm was intimately bound up in identity-based political movements. Identity politics have by no means disappeared; feminist, queer, and antiracist movements and their performance-based strategies are still essential. But now we are also facing political challenges that might be described as struggles over environment rather than identity. They include, obviously, the devastation of the natural environment but also the erasure of people's affective relationships with both the natural and the built environments through forced displacement of poor, indigenous, and old people from their homes and the replacement of environments saturated with local memory with dams, high-tech parks, generic shopping malls, and luxury apartments (i.e., "development"). We might see these disparate cases as parts of a massive assault on the idea of animation in the broad sense. If the struggles of identity politics are against the coercive ways that "human nature" is defined, we might see many current political struggles as fighting hegemonic definitions of "thing nature."

The concept of animation as a model of and for action may provide one approach to this problem. Starting with Weber, there is already a large amount of scholarship that criticizes disenchantment, or what we might call the de-animating strategies of capitalism (the discursive thing-ifying of the material world), as well as a large anthropological literature that turns to indigenous people's animistic ontologies for inspiration as to how we might reanimate the world.

Miyazaki Hayao's oeuvre is a good example of animation that reflexively combines these political discourses. His films are noted for their environmentalist ideology. *Princess Mononoke* (1997) and *Spirited Away* (2001) draw explicitly on Shinto animist imaginaries (Napier 2005; Thomas 2012:105–107). Thomas Lamarre (2009) has looked beyond the content of the films to the production process. He sees the effect of layered, shifting planes of images that results from the animation stand technology used to make most Japanese anime as offering an alternative to the target-vision perspectivalism of most cinema, which Paul Virilio links to militarism—an offer Lamarre sees auteur animators, especially Miyazaki, as taking up quite consciously. The perspective of shifting, layered planes, according to Lamarre, allows for a vision of less violent and hierarchical interaction between self and environment, the human and the nonhuman.

This concern with the nonhuman environment, and with how human subjects live in it and interact with it, is not limited to the content and style of specific works of animation. It is, in fact, built into the way that the entire entertainment industry has been restructured around digital technology. The fact that huge numbers of professional animators spend much of their work lives creating virtual environments for online games or social platforms is one index of the connection emerging between the ideas of animation and environment. Participants in these virtual reality platforms also often see constructing the built environment as a part of the appeal of playing there—for example, the popularity of building houses and other spaces in Second Life (Boellstorff 2008; Malaby 2009). Henry Jenkins notes a recent shift in the structure of the global entertainment industry toward "world-making"—rather than producing just films or games or comic books, networks of artists, corporations, and fans are collectively producing transmedia environments in which characters and narratives continually evolve (Jenkins 2006:113–122).

If television's remediation and ubiquitization of drama, along with the growth and feminization of the service industry, pushed scholars to explore the relationship between performance and identity, this trend toward world-making as both work and entertainment is a sign that it might be time for anthropologists to start exploring the relationship between animation and environment. Performance studies taught us that "acting" is not just something set apart from reality but a model of and for the process through which real identities are constructed. What I suggest here is that we can begin to think of animation as more than an entertainment medium, as a possible mode of performative (real, social) world-making.

Having briefly discussed some of the ways that animation differs from performance as a model within different spheres of social endeavor—art, religion, labor, and politics—I will now discuss a few general differences between animation and performance. We might think of the characteristics of animation outlined here as axes along which cross-cultural comparison can be done.

## Creator/Character Ratio

Although performance and animation overlap in many ways, a noted difference between them is the ratio of creator(s) to character(s) (Kaplin 2001). In performance, whether it be theatrical performance, the performance of ritual, or the performance of self in everyday life, one body can inhabit only one role at a time. There are forms of puppetry in which one puppeteer voices and manipulates a single character, but these are rare. More usual are forms like *wayang kulit*, in which one puppeteer moves and voices all of the characters, or bunraku, in which several people are responsible for creating a single character. Both ends of the puppeteer-to-character ratio continuum have their parallels in contemporary digital culture.

On the one hand, many analyses of the experience of working on computers, especially of participating in virtual communities, note that one individual playing multiple roles is very common. As Allucquère Rosanne Stone notes, in early discussions of American online communities, the trope of "multiple personalities" or "split personalities" was often used to describe the effect of working in several windows at the same time, creating a different persona in each one—what Kate Bornstein and Caitlin Sullivan call "splattering" identity (Stone 1995; Bornstein 1998:212–225). It may be that this sense of newness, of exhilaration and terror, that many experienced while creating multiple characters in online space was at least in part related to their reading of their online action as performance. (It is perhaps no accident that both Stone and Bornstein have long been involved in trans-gender activism and are also performance artists.) Thinking of online role-playing as animating rather than performing might help us localize these experiences in place and time. We might ask, for instance, whether young people who grew up doing much of their communication through MSN and cell-phone texting or who grew up in Java, where master *wayang kulit* pup-peteers are powerful social and religious figures, experience having multiple online personae in the same way.

On the other hand, the animation of one character by many people is the norm within the entertainment industries. Contemporary manga, anime, and logo characters are often acknowledged as the creations of col-lectives rather than creations of auteurs.[8] Manga/anime fans and scholars often argue that the sense that these characters have lives of their own comes not only from the professional animators but also from the charac-ters' re-creation in numerous media and styles by hundreds or thousands of fans. Animated characters "belong" to fans in a way that is different from the way embodied human stars like Marilyn Monroe or Mick Jagger do.

Digital technology has increased this focus on the collective nature of character creation. Media fans were writing their own stories and making artwork based on their favorite characters back in the days of the mimeo-graph, but the Internet has increased the range of media through which fans re-create characters and has intensified the replication of images and narratives. In the age of what Jenkins (2006) calls convergence culture, even characters originally embodied by human actors are becoming like ani-mated characters in this sense of being collective works.

## Organic versus Striated Personhood

Roland Barthes, in his influential essay on bunraku, spoke directly to the difference between animation and embodied performance, defining "the Western conception of the theater" as one in which the character's coher-ence ("the illusion of totality") is modeled on the presumed organic coher-ence of the human body. In bunraku, by contrast, the character is composed of separated media—the puppet itself, its manipulation by actors visible behind and beside it, the voice of the singer who sits by the stage and recites the dialogue. Barthes observed that "by the discontinuity of the codes, by this caesura imposed on the various features of representation, . . . the copy elaborated on the stage is not destroyed but somehow broken, striated, with-drawn from that metonymic contagion of voice and gesture, body and soul, which entraps our actors" (1982:54–55). I believe it is no coincidence that he wrote this essay in the early 1970s, at the dawn of the information age, for bunraku provides a meta-perspective on the body as a semiotic medium that is very similar to that provided by electronic media. Although Barthes' fascination with bunraku is often read as Orientalism, we could also see it as an early harbinger of the more idealist readings of the potential of the digital media for deconstructing the Western concept of the individual, and of our current fascination with post-organic bodies of various sorts, from cyborgs to Vocaloids.

Many scholars see the striation of codes as a defining characteristic of puppetry in general, and Steve Tillis classifies puppetry forms based on the technologies and styles of "the three sign-systems of the puppet": design, movement, and speech (1992:118).[9] The question of whether puppetry is therefore a unique form of expression or merely a particularly pure example of the construction of character through systems of code that are characteristic of all performance has been a fraught one since the debates between Prague School semioticians Otakar Zich and Petr (Peter) Bogatyrev in the 1930s. Scott Cutler Shershow (1995) has shown that this debate was irresolvable, since it never escaped a fixed ideological opposition between high culture (drama) and low culture (puppetry).

An anthropology of animation could retain the basic insight that the difference between embodied performance and media-striated animation matters, but could treat the question of *how* it matters as an ethnographic problem rather than a philosophical one. In other words, we can see specific animation practices as microcosmic instantiations of broader "media ideologies" (Gershon 2010b). Thus we could, for example, move beyond critiques of Barthes' Orientalism to ask how Japanese artists and audiences talk about the differences between bunraku and kabuki and how this discourse might relate to Japanese philosophies of personhood.[10]

The striation of different media has also been noted as one of the characteristics of communication through digital media. Paying attention to how different sign systems and media are organized in relation to each other in, for example, the design of online games or social networking sites can tell us something about contemporary concepts of the sign. For instance, Manning suggests that comparing how characters are voiced—through which medium (as in the debates in Second Life over the introduction of voice technology versus text chat) and in what linguistic registers—might be "revelatory of our own complex and fraught actual world semiotic ideologies about the category of the voice, so often a proxy for notions of authentic self" (2009:318).

## Fleshing Out versus Stripping Down

What are the axes that animators themselves use to compare different styles of animation? One axis used by animators in many media is to place animated characters (or scenes) along a continuum of dimensionality, between the fleshed out and the stripped down. Fleshed-out characters are created by adding detail—features, shading, texture, and so forth. Stripped-down characters are created by removing detail, by creating empty space.

This may seem very similar to the axis along which we can see theatrical performances as ranging from realist to stylized. Method actors striving for psychological realism, for example, flesh out the bones of a script by adding layers of idiosyncratic detail—gestures, vocal range, costume—and adding interior layers that are not directly visible to the audience by creating backstories for characters and using their own emotional memories as the basis for getting into character. Brechtian Epic Theater, on the other hand, works through erasing these individualizing touches.

What is interesting, however, is that actors and animators tend to see fleshing out and stripping down very differently, in terms of their effects on how viewers identify with characters. Most professional actors (even if they work in nonrealist traditions) believe that fleshing out increases audience identification. In realist theater, the more multidimensional the character seems, the more he or she can serve as a mirror, the more aspects there are for a viewer to latch onto as parts of themselves or as parts of selves they would ideally like to be. Stripping down is the audience's work here, in their selection of dimensions with which they identify. The performer's stripping down, as in Brechtian theater, is assumed to create an "alienation effect." The audience should see the character, not as a mirror of the self (either real or ideal), but as an other, an explicitly stereotypical social-historical subject position to be evaluated from the outside.

In animation, however, paring down is a means to increase audience identification and emotional involvement. Cartoonist Scott McCloud puts it this way: "When you look at a photo or realistic drawing of a face, you see it as the face of another. But when you enter the world of the cartoon, you see yourself. . . . The cartoon is a vacuum into which our identity and awareness are pulled" (1993:36). Ivan Koos of the Budapest State Puppet Theatre makes the same point about puppetry:

> The most important thing in the visual representation of the puppet stage is that it sets something going in the spectator's imagination without finishing the process. At a certain point the idea is left open to be completed

by the spectator. . . . Take a familiar example: some of the puppets have no mouths, yet the spectator has the feeling that at certain appropriate moments the puppet smiles or gives expression to its sentiments by facial mimicry. (Cited in Tillis 1992:116)

Fleshed-out animation is associated with the aesthetics of what Bolter and Grusin call immediacy—making the animated environment feel more tangible, more real, to viewers. This is the goal of much mainstream 3-D digital animation for cinema and games. But this is not the same as creating psychological identification. In 3-D animated first-person shooter games, for example, the avatar is nothing but a point of view. When fleshed-out animation characters are designed to invite audience identification (as in Disney movies), it is the characteristics they share with embodied performances—voice, script, habitus—rather than the realism of their visual style (shading, texture, smoothness of movement) that makes them so.

Let me sum up the argument so far in a table:

| Performance | Animation |
| --- | --- |
| Embodiment | Materialization |
| Identity | Alterity |
| Self | Environment |
| Becoming | Making |
| Ritual | Ensoulment of matter |
| Introjection | Projection |
| Mirror stage | Transitional objects |
| Service industries | Creative industries |
| Emotional labor | Branding |
| Organicity | Striation |
| Role | Stereotype |
| One creator–one character | Many creators–one character or one creator–many characters |
| Fleshing out | Stripping down |

## Performance and Animation Together

Thus far, I have been exaggerating the differences between performance and animation—performance involves embodiment, introjection, and self-identity; animation involves materialization, projection, and environment; and so on. Even theoretically, these differences are tenuous; in practice, performance and animation are even harder to separate.

Here I want to outline some of the ways that anthropologists might analyze how animation and performance interact in practice, at different levels. I focus on the semiotic and media ideologies in play in different situations, particularly on how different interactions between performance and animation are structured by, and serve to construct, other social formations such as gender, generation, and class.

### Discursive Distinctions between Performance and Animation

Performance and animation are not objective categories but heuristic ones. The same practices can be seen as either performance or animation, as either constructing selves or constructing worlds—indeed, it is impossible to do one without doing the other. The distinction between animation and performance is made through discourse as much as, if not more than, through practice. One task for the anthropologist, then, is to look at which practices are linguistically coded as performance and which as animation, by whom, and how ideologies are encoded in the distinction. Scott Cutler Shershow's *Puppets and "Popular" Culture* (1995) is an excellent example of this type of analysis, done on historical materials.

As I've noted, in the United States, the dominant discourse around participation in digitally created virtual worlds is one of performance. In online platforms such as Second Life and World of Warcraft—which are usually called, tellingly, role-playing games—the participant/player must represent themself through an animated character. The software for these platforms was developed in California alongside New Age ideology, and the name for such a character is taken from the Hindu/Buddhist religious vocabulary—"avatar," the embodied form of a deity. In much (I would venture to say most) American discourse about participation in online virtual worlds, it is taken for granted that the avatar is an extension of the self, that manipulating an avatar is performing identity. Perhaps the most explicit use of the performance metaphor to frame the digital avatar is Mark Stephen Meadows' *I, Avatar*, in which he compares the virtual community of Second Life and similar online social spaces to Hollywood in the 1920s. Both communities, he argues, were driven by work in the newest medium of mass communication, and both attracted huge numbers of new immigrants seeking to live out their fantasies and construct new identities for themselves

(Meadows 2005:7–8). For Meadows, what digital animation remediates is cinema's remediation of the actor. Although the actor's physical body is no longer the medium of expression, the cinematic performance and the avatar both carry on two of the functions of performance—constructing and presenting a public self and (potentially) making a living. For Meadows and others (e.g., Dibbell 1998; Rehak 2003), the avatar also works as a sort of Lacanian mirror image that is imagined and then constructed by the user but in turn can also transform the user's/performer's experience of self-identity.

When Americans do use terms for animation to describe participation in online virtual worlds, there is often a negative implication, as when the term "sock puppet" is used to describe an online alias designed for the purpose of deception. Ilana Gershon has found that the discourse of performance is so pervasive in the United States that even when people know from personal experience that digitally mediated communication may have more in common with animation than embodied performance—for example, that several people may work together to write messages sent from a single Facebook or text-messaging account—they receive messages as if they were the self-expressions of a single, coherent author and feel surprised and deceived if they find out otherwise (Manning and Gershon 2013).

In Taiwan, however, the dominant discourse frames participation in digital virtual worlds as animation. Although the majority of Taiwanese people worship Buddhist deities and are well aware that "avatar" is the preferred term in English for online characters, the term is rarely used in that sense by gamers.[11] Instead, Taiwanese gamers usually refer to the characters they are playing as simply "characters" (*jiaose*). One of my Taiwanese graduate students who was an occasional gamer put it this way: "We always use the possessive—'my elf,' 'my wizard,' etc. We think of them as sort of like pets." Pets, unlike avatars, are not extensions of the self (or at least, not only extensions of the self)—pets have lives of their own.

I am merely painting the broad strokes of dominant discourses here. Analyses of how performance and animation are distinguished within a specific subculture can be much more complex. For example, Paul Manning outlines an animacy continuum (see Mel Chen 2012) of character types in the discourse of gamers in the MMORPG Ryzom, ranging from "main" avatars, which represent/perform the self, to "alt" (alternative) avatars, which perform roles different from the usual or authentic self, to fully or partially automated characters, which are seen as being animated (either by the program or by players) rather than performing (Manning and Gershon 2013).

## Interactions between Performance and Animation Genres

One way that anthropologists can study culturally and historically specific conceptions of performance and animation, and the relationship between them, is to look at how genres coded as animation remediate genres coded as performance, and vice versa. Throughout South, East, and Southeast Asia, traditional genres of human performance and puppetry share narratives, characters, gestures, music, costumes, and makeup—for instance, *kathakali* and *pavakathakali* in Kerala, India; kabuki and bunraku in Japan; *wayang orang* (human theater), *wayang kulit* (shadow puppetry), and *wayang golek* (marionette theater) in Bali and Java; and *koa-a-hi* (opera) and *po-te-hi* (hand-puppet theater) in Taiwan. These genres are almost always studied separately, but a comparison of the different contexts in which it is considered appropriate to perform a human genre versus a puppet genre, and what performers and audiences feel makes them different, might reveal a great deal about how people conceive of the relationship between body and soul and between the human and nonhuman worlds.

With digital technology, such remediations have become even more widespread. In the contemporary cinema, for example, live-action films are full of animated special effects; human embodiment is critical to the process of motion capture, a key technique in digital animation; the same stories and characters are transferred constantly between live action and animated film (live-action remakes of *The Flintstones* and *Blood: The Last Vampire*, a cartoon version of Rowan Atkinson's *Mr. Bean*, etc.). Cosplay, the practice in which fans dress as animated characters, photograph themselves, and sometimes perform dances or skits, is another example (see chapter 5).

Yet another example is the emoticon, a simple form of cartoon that remediates some of the conventions and functions of embodied performance within digital communication networks. In East Asia, what started as simple facial expressions represented through common keyboard symbols (e.g., :) for a smile) have now developed through more elaborate keyboard cartoons (e.g., (оДо) for surprise) to emojis, graphic images, and sometimes moving images of complete cartoon characters such as Claire Belton's Pusheen the Cat or Taiwanese designer Wan Wan's Wan Wan character.[12] These characters are developed by individual designers and used in their blogs to illustrate and create affect as they narrate their daily lives. Others can download these character-emoticons for use in their own online communications. These figures are, like the logo characters discussed above, drawn extremely simply, and the cartoon images are often framed in boxes and captioned (e.g., "Go go go!" "Angry!" "Happy!").

The emoticon or emoji is an icon of generic affect rather than individual identity, and it remediates the pose. The conventionalized, held pose is a key part of the structure of such traditional East Asian performance genres as Peking Opera and kabuki, where it condenses the character's emotional state and often signals a narrative climax. Conventionalized poses are also a common way that manga and anime characters are invested with affect. The emoticon images of Wan Wan and Pusheen serve the same function, allowing individuals to narrate their own emotional lives through the medium of animation.

The conventional poses of emoticons and manga/anime characters are also re-embodied as part of the performative style of *kawaii* (cuteness) within pan–East Asian youth culture (Kinsella 1995). Some of these poses incorporate conventionally iconic elements. For example, Japanese and Taiwanese young people, during the course of a conversation, may hold up three fingers of one hand and move their hand in a downward motion beside their face. This gesture imitates the downward lines that are drawn in manga beside a character's face to indicate extreme stress or embarrassment (///), often said to be an abstracted icon of sweat running down—making the gesture an embodied remediation of what is already a conventionalized icon of embodied affect. The convoluted travels of the pose—from theater to manga and anime, from manga and anime to emoticons and cosplay, from emoticons and cosplay to everyday comportment—reflect long and continuous histories in which human theater and puppetry, performance and animation, have been intertwined.

### How Performance and Animation Are Mapped onto Social Distinctions

Finally, an anthropology of animation should pay close attention to how performance and animation are mapped, through both discourse and practice, onto social identity categories (e.g., gender, race, ethnicity, nationality, class). Who does work coded as performance, and who does work coded as animation?

In postindustrial economies, the dominant form of work now is what has been called immaterial labor. As Michael Hardt and Antonio Negri point out, immaterial labor is divided into two categories: "the immaterial labor of analytic and symbolic tasks" and "the production and manipulation of affect [that] requires (virtual or actual) human contact, labor in the bodily mode" (2000:293). We might see the first, analytic and symbolic tasks, as including such world-making animation practices as computer programming, branding, architecture and city planning, and of course labor within the animated cinema, television, and comics industries. The second, affective embodied labor, is, as I have argued above, often seen as performance work by those who do it. These two types of immaterial labor are (still) largely divided by gender, with men doing the majority of (paid) animation labor and women doing the majority of affective, embodied performance work.

While sociologists might focus on how performance and animation labor is divided, anthropologists and cultural studies scholars might want to focus more on the cultural logics behind the division of labor. Why, for example, are women considered "better at" affective labor? How are men and women educated (formally and informally) and channeled into different types of labor? Why are women's practices of ensouling the material environment of the home (Gordon 2006) usually coded as "consumption" rather than "production" (Graeber 2007)?

The mapping of animation and performance onto gender and labor practice moves continuously from popular culture to social fact and back again. One good example of how the cultural logics of the gendered division of animation and performance labor are both revealed and promoted within popular culture is the online novel/manga/film *Densha otoko* (Train Man). Alisa Freedman (2009) has noted that *Densha otoko* elicited more discussion of changing gender roles in Japan than any other piece of pop culture in the mid-2000s, with the protagonists being held up as model marriage partners as well as model consumers. We can also read this story as a fantasy about the complementary, heterosexualized union of performance and animation. In *Densha otoko*, an unnamed twenty-two-year-old "typical Akihabara *otaku*" falls in love with an older OL (office lady) after rescuing her from an abusive drunk on the train. The term *otaku* generally refers to young men who are seen as "obsessive" fans of manga and anime and, more generally, digital technology. The hero of *Densha otoko* works as a computer technician for a business firm. He spends his nights in an anonymous online forum where participants chat and exchange ASCII art (cartoon images created with keyboard symbols). The OL's work involves dealing with her firm's foreign clients. Speaking English is, of course, a sign of the woman's upper-class status, but it is also significant that her work is a kind of emotional labor, having something in common with the facilitation of communication between men done by bar hostesses (Allison 1994). The course of the romance consists primarily of the woman, aided by the *otaku*'s virtual network of anonymous friends, teaching the *otaku* literally how to act—how to play the role of boyfriend, how to dress and order in a restaurant, how to express his feelings verbally. In exchange, the *otaku* helps her navigate technology. In the film, the OL reveals that one of the things that most moved her was when the *otaku* rearranged her sugar cubes into a pyramid—an act with dollhouse-play overtones, which might be seen as an act of animation, of re-enchanting the real world by creating a separate, miniature fantasy space within it.

As Manning and Gershon (2013:110) point out, although I have classified the woman's work as performance, the *otaku*'s final embodied persona might also be considered the result of her animation (and that of his online friends of both genders). Indeed, when one looks further, the gendered division between animation and performance breaks down. At the end of Ocha Machiko's *shojo manga* (girls' comic) version of the *Densha otoko* story (Ocha 2006), the only commercial version created by a female artist that I could find, the female lead (drawn much younger than the actress in the movie) reveals her huge collection of dolls, character figurines, and stuffed toys to the *otaku*. From their own perspective, women mediate competencies in both performance and animation, both in their work and private life, rather than embodying a pure performance model.

I have defined animation as *the construction of social others through the projection of qualities perceived as human—life, soul, power, agency, intentionality, personality, and so on—outside the self and into the sensory environment, through acts of creation, perception, and interaction.* In this chapter, I've tried to explicate that definition through a comparison with performance, showing how these two different models of human action in and on the world have emerged over time, inspired by overlapping but diverging artistic practices and intellectual concerns and under changing technological, economic, political, and social conditions. I've also outlined some of the questions that anthropologists and other researchers might be able to ask through the frame of animation or by looking at how performance and animation are mediated in actual practice.

My aim has been to set up animation as a platform for comparisons across cultural fields within a particular time and place and for comparisons across cultures and historical periods. In the rest of this book, I demonstrate how an anthropology of animation could work through my own research on Taiwan and make comparisons among Taiwan, China, Japan, and North America.

# CHAPTER 2

# The *Ang-a*

## A Taiwanese Mode of Animation

I have defined animation as the process of projecting qualities perceived as human, such as life, soul, and personality, outside the self
and into the sensory environment. As an anthropologist, one of the things
I am most interested in doing with this definition of animation is looking
for the threads that bind different kinds of animation together across social
fields. In other words, I want to see if the concept of animation can help us
see particular kinds of cultural logic. In this chapter, I trace the contours of
a specific mode of animation that links the fields of religion, play, politics,
commerce, and art in Taiwan.

First, let me explain what I mean by a "mode" of animation. A mode is
something like a meta-genre. A mode of animation connects specific forms
of animation art, ritual practice, scientific project, and so on by virtue of
what they share in the different parts of my broad definition of animation.
In other words, the forms within a mode of animation may be connected by
which qualities of human existence they treat as projectable, by how projection is accomplished, and/or in terms of what kinds of nonhuman objects
are taken to be animated or animatable. Modes of animation might also be
characterized in terms of what Raymond Williams (1986) calls "structures
of feeling," by the affects they conjure—by the specific fantasies and nightmares they evoke, and the particular ways they expose, resolve, or suppress
contradictions within the broader historical-cultural field.

Modes of animation, like genres, can be thought of as assemblages of
traits, and like genres, they are fuzzy things. They can be defined, not by
boundaries, but by relative closeness to ideal types, which may be rare or
even nonexistent in actual practice. Just as almost every movie considered
a western lacks some element we think of as quintessential to the genre (a
hard-bitten gunslinger, Sioux warriors on horseback, a saloon, a Morricone
sound track) and almost every western contains some elements we associate

with other genres (a film noir mystery that slowly unfolds, a family melo-drama conflict, musical numbers), so no particular instance of animation will have all the qualities that characterize a given mode of animation, and each instance will have some qualities that link it to other modes. Modes of animation coalesce around key concepts, more or less explicit and more or less diffuse, and they are always changing. Different modes of animation converge and diverge, both within and between social groups and histori-cal moments.

Let me give a couple of examples of what I mean by modes of anima-tion from Anglophone culture. The English term "animation" comes from the Latin *anima*. In the original Latin, *anima* contains the concepts of both life and soul, but in English these concepts are differentiated. The separation of life and soul, body and mind, is foundational to Christian metaphysics. It is integral to the concept of animation in the Abrahamic traditions—God breathed both life and soul into Adam and Eve simultaneously, and the split between the mortal material body and the immortal soul came with their fall. Thus, it is not surprising to find divergent modes of animation in Europe and North America today that project life on the one hand and soul on the other.

The dichotomy might be clearest in the fields of science and engineer-ing, where artificial life and artificial intelligence are two separate projects, so I will refer to the two modes of animation I outline here as AL and AI. AL invests inanimate objects with the properties of biological life—movement, growth, eating and excreting, and reproductive capacity. Technically, "AL" usually refers to computer programs that simulate the growth and evolu-tion of biological organisms and species.[1] We can also include the kind of robotics for which the MIT labs are famous, which focuses on reproduc-ing organic motion (especially of insects). There are also long traditions in the arts in which objects are made to seem alive in this sense. The illu-sion of biological life is the mode of automata—for instance, Jacques de Vaucanson's famous eighteenth-century Digesting Duck, which appeared to eat corn and then defecate—as well as pre-cinema technologies such as the zoetrope, which creates the optical illusion of movement.

AI, on the other hand, simulates "intelligence," defined in terms of capabilities for logic and language. Histories of this engineering project usually start with Alan Turing's 1950 article "Computer Machinery and Intelligence," in which he described his test for AI—if a machine can con-vince a person having a purely textual conversation with it that they are conversing with another human being, it may be considered to have its own intelligence. We can see many developments in computer technology, including virtual personal assistants like Siri and Alexa and poetry-generating programs, as falling within the AI mode of animation. In the field of art, the qualities projected often go beyond the narrow scientific definition of intelligence to include emotions, habitual attitudes, and personality more broadly—that is, "mind" or "soul." We might see the technology of writing itself as falling within the AI mode as a technology for reproducing the manifestations of an author's mind or soul separable from their biological being.

In many animation practices, of course, AL and AI are not separated. In terms of scientific practice, there are strong historical and ongoing connections between AL and AI. In Japanese roboticist Mori Masahiro's famous formulation of the "uncanny valley," based on people's reactions to different types of humanlike objects, the least uncanny are bunraku puppets and anthropomorphic robots—nonbiological beings that give the impression of both independent life and distinctive personalities (Mori [1970] 2010). If we look at speculative fiction, most utopian fantasies of animation combine these two modes (e.g., *Pinocchio*, the *Toy Story* movies).

It is when artificial life and artificial intelligence are most separate that they become uncanny and even frightening. Thus, at the nadir of the uncanny valley we have the zombie, the human body with life but no soul. On the other hand, the figure of the completely disembodied, unalive mind or soul is equally uncanny—poltergeists, for instance, or HAL in *2001: A Space Odyssey*. What makes AL potentially creepy, in other words, is quite different from what makes AI creepy.[2]

AI and AL are modes of animation quite familiar to Taiwanese people. Taiwanese engineers and scientists are involved in many international AI and AL projects, and ordinary Taiwanese people know them both well through American and Japanese science fiction. But science fiction is a genre often noted for its late arrival and comparatively minimal development within the Chinese literary field. What I want to do in this chapter is to outline one mode of animation that Taiwanese people might recognize as their own. I am asking, What genres of animation (as I've defined it) do Taiwanese people see as uniquely Taiwanese or Chinese, and what might make these genres similar to each other in their eyes?

I posit a mode of animation that centers on a specific type of object called *ang-a* in Holo or *ou* in Mandarin, a small, three-dimensional, anthropomorphic figure. *The ang-a is invested with specific human qualities (personality, affect, and charisma) through specific types of actions (ritual, iconographic, and communicational practices).* This mode of animation assembles a set of concepts about body and soul, resemblance, reproduction, and power and resonates across the fields of religion, entertainment, politics, and business.

All modes of animation emerge from within specific worldviews. What anthropologists call ontologies or cosmologies set the limits and possibilities for modes of animation. AL and AI developed within the context of the history of struggles and accommodations between science and Christian theology since the Renaissance; it is this background that gives them both their utopian and dystopian edges. In contrast, the foundational model for the *ang-a* mode of animation emerges from Chinese folk religion—not from an origin myth or any written or oral text but from practice.[3] Taiwanese ideas about what animation means are modeled on the act of *pai-pai*, a term that is usually translated simply as "worship."[4] *Pai-pai* is a basic ritual, performed daily in temples and households throughout the island, in which people communicate with gods, ancestors, and other supernatural beings through their images, especially small wooden sculptures.

I was first alerted to the importance of *pai-pai* as a background to how Taiwanese people conceive of animation in general by fans of the Pili International Multimedia Company's digital video puppetry series. Fans of Pili puppet characters often joke that they "worship idols" (*chongbai ouxiang*), as do fans of human pop stars. They usually mean, as do most people anywhere who use this metaphor, that they idealize the characters and are "fanatically" emotionally attached to them. But Pili fans also often used the metaphor that puppets are like religious icons in more concrete and more positive ways.

In some cases, the link between puppets and religious icons is not metaphorical but literal. A story I was told several times during my first few years of fieldwork by people both inside and outside the Pili Company claimed that a criminal gang had once stolen the puppet of Ye Xiao Chai (a mute swordsman known for his loyalty), placed it on an altar, and made offerings to it. This story may well be apocryphal, but puppets have, historically, often served as objects for worship. Icons (*shenxiang*) with moveable limbs have been found in temples throughout China, and puppets of Tian Du Yuan Shuai, a god that protects puppeteers and actors, are worshipped by puppeteers in Fujian to this day.[5] In Taiwan, the traditional marionette theater (Mandarin: *kuileixi*; Holo: *ka-lei-hi*) was used primarily for ritual purposes, especially exorcisms and funerals. Glove-puppet theater (Mandarin: *budaixi*; Holo: *po-te-hi*) is still performed as an offering to the gods at temple festivals, and some taboos apply to the handling of the puppets of the gods and immortals who perform the *ban xian/pan sian* ritual during temple festivals. Many carvers of religious icons in Taiwan are also puppet carvers. So there is a historical association of puppets with worship.

There are also linguistic connections. In both Mandarin and Holo, the same measure word is used for puppets and for statues of gods for worship—*zun/chun*, a character that when used as a verb means "to honor." In Holo, puppets are often called *ang-a-sian*, or doll immortals.[6]

When I was doing fieldwork with Pili fans, I was even more struck by the similarities between how fans interact with puppets and how worshippers interact with icons. I began to wonder what it actually meant to say that puppet, manga, and anime characters are "like idols" in a place where "idol worship" is not some long-ago and faraway form of heresy but an accepted and common part of everyday life.

In positing a Taiwanese *ang-a* mode of animation, with *pai-pai* as its primary model, and focusing on the parallels between religious icons and puppets, I am not claiming that there is a single Taiwanese mode of animation reflecting some essential Taiwanese or Chinese culture. People in Taiwan juggle multiple modes of animation, and multiple modes of animation could certainly be traced throughout Chinese history (although that is not within the scope of this book). I simply want to describe one way that Taiwanese people relate to animated characters and that they explicitly see as drawing on specifically Chinese religious traditions. I want to use the *ang-a* mode of animation as a heuristic concept, a thing to think with, but as my ethnographic descriptions will show, in practice it is no more separable from other modes of animation than animation is separable from performance.

My main purpose in delineating the *ang-a* mode of animation is to explore its similarities to and differences from other ways that animation has been theorized, particularly in studies of European puppetry and Japanese manga and anime. Scott Cutler Shershow (1995) argues that puppetry has been a "theological theater" throughout Western history, tracing how the metaphor of puppetry has functioned in religious, artistic, and philosophical discourse from Plato through the twentieth century. Although the meanings and values of puppetry vary greatly over time, the idea of the act of puppeteering as a human reconstruction of the divine act of creation seems to always underlie the metaphor.

In contrast, running through much of the research on Japanese manga and anime today is the idea that cartoon characters and robots are in some ways like *kami* (in Shinto, the animating spirits of elements and forces of nature, also ancestral spirits). As Anne Allison summarizes, "Fed in part by folkloric and religious traditions, an animist sensibility percolates the modern landscape of Japan today. . . . [I]n postwar properties like *Tetsuwan Atomu*, for example, one sees a universe where the borders between thing and life continually cross and intermesh" (2006:12–13).

Chinese folk religion is neither monotheistic nor animist but, rather, is multitheistic and anthropocentric. I propose the *ang-a* mode of animation, for which Chinese folk religion provides the cosmological grounding, as an alternative to the model of animation as "playing God" on the one hand or as a manifestation of the idea that *all* things have souls on the other.

## The *Ang-a:* A Schematic Genealogy

No direct equivalent for the verb "to animate" exists currently in Mandarin, Holo, or Hakka. This doesn't mean, of course, that the concept is not express-ible in Chinese. In Mandarin, one can say, for example, "*rang ta kanqilai huo sheng sheng de*," meaning "make it appear to be alive." There are plenty of verbs for specific kinds of animating action: one can draw (*hua*) or produce (*zhizuo*) manga and anime; one can make (*zao*) a robot; one manipulates (*cao*) a puppet and plays with (*wan*) a doll. But the idea of making some-thing come to life as a general type of action is not formalized within the language(s). If the types of actions that animate are not linguistically related in Chinese, however, there is a character, *ou*, that unites many of the types of objects that can be animated. An *ou* is a small, three-dimensional image of a person or sometimes an anthropomorphized animal or object.

The earliest meaning of the character *ou* was an even number, and the current meaning came out of the sense of a double.[7] One of the earliest references to *ou* as human-form figures comes from the Confucian *Book of Rites* (*Li ji*), compiled during the Han dynasty (202 BCE–220 CE). The prac-tice of placing figurines of people in tombs to accompany the dead to the afterlife probably originated around the time when Confucius lived, some-time from the sixth to the fifth century BCE. According to the compilers of the *Book of Rites*, Confucius was afraid that the new practice of making clay and wooden figures with faces and moveable parts, which he called *ou ren* (*ou*-persons, which Patricia Berger translates as "body double"), would incite people to revive the custom of human sacrifice (Berger 1998). Over the centuries, varieties of *ou* proliferated, including military decoys, autom-ata, toys, and decorative statues, although the character *ou* was not always part of the most common name for them.

Two of the most important forms of figure that I will be discuss-ing in this chapter are the religious icon (*shenxiang*) and the puppet. The practice of worshipping statues of gods came to China from India with Buddhism, beginning in the Han dynasty. The practice was quickly adapted from Buddhism to the worship of local Daoist gods as well (Li Song 2006). The first textual records of puppet theater performances come from the Tang dynasty (618–907), although legends trace the origins of puppetry back to at least the Han. By the Song dynasty (960–1279) there are reliable records of puppeteers performing in several different genres throughout China, for audiences of all social classes (Stalberg 1984; Ruizendaal 2006). Icons were brought to Taiwan by Chinese settlers in the seventeenth century, and there are written records of village *po-te-hi* performances by the mid-nineteenth century.

In Taiwan today, the most common meaning of *ou* is "puppet," which is usually called *mu ou* (wooden *ou*) or sometimes *xi ou* (theater or drama *ou*) in Mandarin. *Ren ou* (person *ou*) and *wan ou* (play *ou*) refer to plastic figurines of Japanese anime and manga characters, which are sometimes also called by the Cantonese term *gongzai* or the English "figure."

The Holo term *ang-a* also refers to a three-dimensional image of a person (or anthropomorphized entity) and covers a similar range of objects as *ou*. As with *ou*, its most common referent is the puppet. The category of *ang-a* brings together a number of different kinds of objects that have separate names in Mandarin (or are called by loanwords from Japanese, English, and Cantonese). These include not only mass-produced character toys but also baby dolls (called *yangwawa* in Mandarin), plush toys (*bu wawa*), decorative statues (*diaoxiang*), and icons that have been desacralized or have not yet been sacralized. In comparison with *ou*, *ang-a* emphasizes aspects of playfulness, attractiveness, and childishness—for instance, *ang-a-mi* means a toy, and a girl with an *ang-a-bin* has a "doll face." Also, *ang-a* can sometimes refer to stylized graphic images, as in the term *ang-a-chhe* for illustrated storybooks or manga.

I will use the term *ang-a* throughout this book, for the sake of convenience, but I want to include the associations of *ou* as well. I use *ang-a* to refer to anthropomorphic images that range from religious images to mass-produced toys, a category that gathers together the ideas of personality, replication, companionship, attractiveness, stylization, and play.

Below, I outline the characteristics of the *ang-a*, the things that hold the continuum from religious images to toys together. I will focus here on the overlapping characteristics of Daoist and Buddhist icons and puppets, which constitute the ideal type of the *ang-a* mode of animation. Other Taiwanese forms of human-form figure (such as funerary effigies) share some of these traits as well, but I should emphasize that no single type of figure, not even the icon or the puppet, has all the traits I list. I will also try to show how the *ang-a* mode of animation is sometimes extended in Taiwan to include imported objects, especially Japanese manga/anime character toys.

## Characteristics of the *Ang-a*

*The ang-a is a material representation of a character, or a virtual personality.*

Different types of *ang-a* represent very different types of characters—deities, historical figures, fictional human characters, and fictional nonhuman characters. When I categorize them all as "virtual personalities," I am not arguing that gods are "just as fictional" as manga characters. What holds these characters together is not ontology (how real they are) but epistemology (how we know them). All types of *ang-a* represent intangible entities; people know them all through narratives and material representations rather than through face-to-face, embodied interaction.[8]

Different *ang-a* of the same character may emphasize, or better capture, specific aspects of the virtual personality. Nevertheless, all instances of *ang-a* of the same character represent the same personality. Individual *ang-a* do not have their own distinctive personalities, like the Thai icons of the Buddha, which are said to have quirks (such as the Emerald Buddha icon's taste for duck eggs) that other icons of the Buddha lack (Robert Brown 1998).

*The character is conceived of as existing in an intangible but imaginable world that is encountered through narrative and material/visual representation.*

*Ang-a* and narratives are mutually animating. There are cases in which a narrative about the characters is produced before the *ang-a*, and cases in which the *ang-a* is produced before any narrative. Nevertheless, the mere existence of an *ang-a* implies and calls forth potential narratives, and vice versa. Gods could not be worshipped if they existed only in texts. The toy industry looks first to characters already popular through various storytelling media. When appealing characters appear without stories (e.g., mascot/logo characters), producers are often pressured to create narratives for them, or fans take on the task of telling their stories themselves. To ask which came first, the story or the *ang-a*, is a chicken-or-egg paradox.

The interaction of narratives and material representations creates the sense of worlds that exist "somewhere out there," separate from the one we live in. Chinese gods are believed to exist in several different places or states simultaneously. They are said to be "all around," watching over the human world. Daoist gods exist in a parallel world of the dead, where they are officials in a hierarchical imperium, and buddhas and bodhisattvas exist in their own transcendent realm. Fictional characters live in fictional worlds, with their own rules and special atmospheres, be it an imagined Ming dynasty or Middle Earth. Although fans are quite aware that these worlds are created by authors, they also often feel that these worlds have an existence beyond canonical texts. Hence, fans often claim to know the characters and their world better than some of the canon writers and say that the canon writers can get characters "wrong."

*Characters and their worlds are always transforming and are potentially infinite. The evolution of characters and worlds is a collective process.*

Prasenjit Duara argues that the cults of Chinese gods expand through the accretion of overlapping, sometimes contradictory narratives, a process he calls superscription:

> In this process, extant versions are not totally wiped out. Rather, images and sequences common to most versions of the myth are preserved, but by adding or "rediscovering" new elements or by giving existing elements a particular slant, the new interpretation is lodged in place. Even if the new interpretation should become dominant, previous versions do not disappear but instead come into a new relationship with it, as their own statuses and roles within what might be called the "interpretive arena" of the myth come to be negotiated and redefined. (1988:780)

Duara's "interpretive arena" of myth that characterizes the cults of Chinese gods is very similar to how several theorists have described the role of narrative in the fandoms of mass media characters and worlds. Both American media theorist Henry Jenkins (1992, 2006) and Japanese manga/anime theorist Otsuka Eiji (2010) have argued that contemporary producers of media franchises focus on constructing complex fictive worlds, rather than closed narratives, and that fans participate in the construction of these worlds. Both Jenkins and Otsuka see this development as having roots in pre-twentieth-century folk cultures. Otsuka distinguishes the individual works of manga/anime artists and fans ("variations") from the collectively recognized and produced "grand narrative" or "world" on which they are based, which includes what literary theorist M. M. Bakhtin calls the chronotope (time-space setting), as well as the major characters and their relationships. Otsuka writes that this structure has precedence in Japanese history, and he takes the terms "world" and "variation" (*sekai* and *shukō*) from kabuki and puppet theater (*ningyo joruri*), where settings are often taken from mythology, popular history, and folk tale cycles (Otsuka 2010). The same structure applies to Chinese folk theaters and vernacular literature, as well as to religious mythology. We could say that the *San guo* (Three Kingdoms) and the *Xi you ji* (Journey to the West) are Chinese interpretive arenas or "worlds." Just as Japanese manga and anime draw on the world/variation tradition of theater and puppetry, contemporary Taiwanese commercial animation draws on a similar tradition in Chinese fiction and performance genres. The Pili puppetry serials, with their increasingly complex world of *wulin*, the "martial forest" of wandering swordsmen, is an excellent example.

The shared imagination of media characters' personalities and relationships and the worlds in which they act are abstracted not only from the original comics and videos (the canon) but also from fans' own circulating narratives and images (the "fanon") as well. Pili fans who create *tongrenzhi* (the Mandarin pronunciation of the Japanese *dōjinshi*, referring to amateur manga, novels, and art using characters from published works), like Japanese manga/anime fans, are constantly adding new variations to the world of Pili's *wulin*, making it an increasingly dense interpretive arena.

*The ang-a is one material medium within a network of media platforms for representing the same characters.*

*Ang-a* are representations of characters that exist, at least potentially, within a field of representations in different media. Buddhist and Daoist deities, for example, have been represented in a wide range of aesthetic styles, from ornate to abstract, and in almost every material medium imaginable, from solid gold to cookie dough. Taiwanese temples are filled with images of gods and immortals—not only dozens of carved wooden icons but also ceramic and stone friezes, mosaics, paintings, paper lanterns, and so on. Statues of gods made for worship circulate in a world in which the same deities are also ubiquitously represented through the human body—by spirit mediums in trance and in theater, film, and television dramas—as well as in novels, in manga and anime, and as graphic images printed on stationery, mugs, T-shirts, towels, and on and on.

The same density of media networks occurs in Pili puppetry fandom, where, aside from the wooden puppets used to make the videos, the characters are represented, by both the Pili Company and by fans, in a wide range of styles and in a wide range of media, including through the human body in cosplay, through the voice in amateur radio dramas, in writing (novels), as graphic images (in comics, posters, and on products), and in three-dimensional form (as stuffed toys, plastic dolls, beaded keychains, etc.).

Again, this is a phenomenon that has been well noted by scholars of contemporary media culture in North America and Japan. Henry Jenkins (2006) has noted the rise of "transmedia storytelling" interweaving film, comics, games, websites, toys, and other media as a marketing strategy within the American content industries, and in Japan this type of networking is well known as "media mix." Marc Steinberg has argued that the manga/anime character toy played a particularly important role in Japan, constructing relationships between material and visual media platforms and between fictional characters and fans' daily lives: "The manga and anime series gave the toy a personality, a narrative setting, a group of characters, a series of set poses, and a voice. . . . [T]he toy gave the character matter, narrative openness, and movement" (2012:122).

Although the *ang-a* seems to have a particularly prominent place in Taiwanese religious and popular culture, the *ang-a* mode of animation may at this point appear to be just as Japanese as it is Chinese or even to be a global "folk" mode of animation. The characteristics of the *ang-a* I have listed so far—that the *ang-a* is a material representation of a virtual personality, collectively imagined as living in an intangible elsewhere, represented via a network of media—are easily found in many places outside Taiwan, and not only in East Asia. So now I'll move on to some of the ways in which the Taiwanese *ang-a* embodies a more specifically Chinese way of thinking about animation.

### The ang-a is an artifact; it is an object designed and crafted by people.

The *ang-a* is never a natural object such as a stone or a tree. Perception alone is not enough to make an object an *ang-a*.

### The ang-a is basically human in both form and content.

The character *ou* is composed of the "person" radical and a sound radical, and the human form of the *ou* is part of its definition. The virtual personality represented by the *ou* or *ang-a* is also conceived of as essentially humanlike, even though it may be divine or immortal.

As David Jordan (1972), Arthur Wolf (1974), and others have long noted, in Chinese folk religion the boundaries between gods, ghosts, and ancestors are porous. Many of the gods worshipped in Taiwanese temples, both Buddhist and Daoist, are historical persons who were deified after their death, including Mazu, Guan Gong, and Guan Yin. Most (male) gods are thus also ancestors, and ancestors may become gods. Ancestors may become ghosts if worship is discontinued; ghosts may become ancestors again if they are rediscovered (e.g., through dreams or divination) and worship is resumed. The Earth God (Tudi Gong) and the City God are actually bureaucratic positions, but although worshippers do not know who is occupying those positions at any given time, they assume that these gods are someone's ancestors. Not all gods were historical persons, but even "heavenly gods" (*tian shen*), those who were always gods and were never born as humans, such as the Jade Emperor (Yu Huang Da Di), are, like the others, always represented in human form. When animals or forces of nature become gods, they are anthropomorphized when icons are made for their worship (Wei-Ping Lin 2015:74; Hansen 1990:34).[9] In general, Chinese folk religion is not animist but anthropocentric.

To an extent, this human-centered orientation is reflected in the landscape of *ang-a* in Taiwan. While there are certainly many nonhuman characters that are popular in Taiwan (Doraemon the robot cat and Snoopy, for example), most of these are imported. Locally produced nonhuman characters (especially if they are not anthropomorphized in any way) tend to remain in the realm of corporate logos and institutional mascots rather than becoming characters around whom dense narrative arenas emerge. Nearly all the main characters from locally produced animation franchises (such as the Pili series) are human.

### The ang-a is a vessel; it has internal agency.

Let me now turn to the processes by which the *ang-a* may be animated. Alfred Gell (1998) distinguishes two strategies by which nonhuman objects are animated. The first strategy, which he calls externalist, consists of treating the object as if it were human, "simply stipulating for it a role as a social other," and the second, which he calls internalist, consists of positing some kind of mind or soul that resides within the object. Gell sees the externalist strategy as emerging from a sociological theory of agency, one that focuses on the idea that social interaction is the source of social personhood. In other words, people attribute agency, and often intentionality, to things with which they can interact in predictable ways, even in the absence of any objective proof of a "mind." The internalist strategy, in contrast, is linked to a psychological view of agency, one that focuses on the idea of person-hood as individual subjectivity. Gell writes, "It seems that ordinary human beings are . . . inclined, more or less from day one, to believe in some kind of 'ghost in the machine' and to attribute the behaviour of social others to the *mental representations these others have 'in their heads'*" (1998:127). I would rephrase this distinction in terms of two separate aspects of humanity that may be projected onto the animated object, social agency (the capacity for interaction) on the one hand and what Gell, following Boyer (1996), calls intentional psychology (mind or soul) on the other.

As Wei-Ping Lin (2008, 2015) has noted, both externalist and inter-nalist strategies are used to animate the Taiwanese icon. I will first discuss how the icon is invested with internal agency, how it comes to have a soul inside. Gell notes that although the attribution of internal agency theorized by psychologists and philosophers is potentially applicable to any kind of nonhuman thing, religious images often encourage the attribution of inter-nal agency through their form, which thematizes the division between exte-rior and interior.

The discourse and ritual practice around Taiwanese icons likewise emphasizes this type of distinction between exteriority and interiority, body and soul. The word for "icon" in Holo is *kim sen*, or "golden body." Liu Wensan, author of the only book-length study of Taiwanese *shenxiang*, writes: "The icon [*shenxiang*] is the god's body-shell [*shen ke*], where the god's soul [*linghun*] resides. The same god can have many icons because divine power/efficacy [*shenling*] is limitless. Gods can divide their divine power [*shen li*] from their souls and send it into their icons to protect and bless worshippers in every district" (1981:10).

The rituals that give the golden body its soul/internal agency and its efficacy vary from place to place, but the process always includes these two steps:

1. *Ru shen/jip-sin*, "bringing in the god." In this ritual, done after the icon is completely carved, a number of objects are sealed into a hole in its back. This ritual brings the god's *ling* (power or efficacy) into the icon. If the icon represents an already existing god, the incense ash from the burner of another icon of that god is placed in the hole; if the god is a new one, the ash is replaced with a *fu*, a paper Daoist charm. Other items symbolically give the god in the icon life force. These items may vary for different gods and in different places but often include raw grain and a live wasp or the fresh blood of a rooster.

2. *Kai guang dian yan/khai-kong*, "opening the light by dotting the eyes." This ritual is performed at the installation of the icon on a temple or home altar. Again, while the ritual varies, it generally involves dipping a writing brush in fresh rooster's blood and dotting critical points on the statue's body (the joints, over the heart), ending with the dotting of the eyes. If the *ru shen* ceremony imbues the *ang-a* with life force, the *kai guang dian yan* ceremony makes the body functional, giving it *qi* (breath, energy), hearing, and sight. Only after its eyes have been opened is the statue said to "have a god" (*you shen/u sian*).[10]

When an icon has not been worshipped for a long time, people say the god will leave it. If one is not sure whether a god is inside an icon or has left, and one does not intend to worship it (for instance, when one wants to sell it as an antique), a ritual may be performed inviting the god to leave.

Other types of *ang-a*, such as puppets and manga/anime character toys, are often perceived as having internal agency, although they do not (indeed, must not) go through the above rituals. Gell argues that one of the reasons that idols are anthropomorphic is because human forms "render [the idol] more spiritual, more inward, by opening up *routes of access* to this inwardness" (1998:132), especially through the eyes. Like sacralized icons, human-form puppets and figurines are often perceived as endowed with sight and hearing. Fans and carvers often told me that the difference between a well-made puppet and a bad one is that a good puppet has *yan-shen*. The term *yanshen* is composed of the characters for "eye" and "god" and refers to a gaze, the expression of the eyes. When a puppet head does not have *yanshen*, it is often said to look *dai dai*—stupid, in the sense of blank or empty.

It is the status of the *ang-a* as a body-shell that is the source of the particular brand of uncanniness in the *ang-a* mode of animation. Several members of temple committees I spoke to told me that it would be dangerous to dot the eyes of a puppet or a character toy. The fear here is that any human-form figure is potentially a vessel for any kind of soul; if the *ang-a* is not specifically carved to be the vessel for a particular god, dotting the eyes is an open invitation, and a ghost or other malevolent spirit may take up residence within it. Many older Taiwanese believe that the human form, with its routes of access to interiority, is enough to allow disembodied entities to take up residence, even without dotting the eyes. Several collectors of puppets and character toys told me that their parents or grandparents would not let them display their puppets or Japanese manga/anime tie-in toys in the living room, where family altars to gods and ancestors are located, since their simply being near the incense lit to legitimate gods and ancestors would attract unwanted spirits to them. One young man told me that his parents made him give away all his character toys after the family experienced a series of economic setbacks and health problems. They thought that "something unclean" might have entered one of the toys. An icon that is known to have a particular god inside is not uncanny, nor is an icon, puppet, or character toy that is known to be empty. The *ang-a* is uncanny whenever one cannot know for sure whether something is inside or not, and if so, what.

### The ang-a acquires agency by being embedded within social networks.

Let me now deal with how agency is attributed to the *ang-a* externally, by making it into a social other/actor. One of Wei-Ping Lin's spirit-medium informants was quite explicit that the purpose of making an icon is to allow bonds to form between the god and the temple community. The same rituals performed to introduce a newborn child into the community are performed for a newly carved and sacralized icon. Families often invite icons from the temple to be placed on their home altars for important events (such as weddings) or "to worship it for protection during a long-distance trip, success in business, a cure for long-term illness, or the reform of a disobedient child" (Wei-Ping Lin 2008:471).

As with icons, bringing a puppet home and displaying it allows the character to become embedded in personal and communal relationships. One Pili fan wrote the following on a website I set up (January–December 2004):

> My first puppet was an 18 inch "White Knight" [one of a series of mass-produced Pili puppets sold through 7-Eleven convenience stores in 2004] . . . When I first saw it I was surprised by its beauty. It was like the original, but even more slim and handsome! I used to feel that people who bought an "*ou*" and brought it home were really crazy, a friend of mine even described it . . . it's carrying a miniature "*shenxiang*" (the kind that go through the streets in processions) home to worship! (I hope this doesn't offend anyone.) But, after I got my 18-inch "White Knight," it gave me a kind of "tasteful collection" pleasure! [Ellipses and quotation marks in the original]

Another fan responded: "Actually, I also feel that when we buy a puppet and place it in our home, taking care of it in all sorts of ways, it really does

feel a bit like an icon." Although I have never heard a collector of manga/
anime character toys make an explicit analogy between toys and icons, they,
like puppet collectors, often refer to buying character products as "bringing
Doraemon (or whatever character) home."

Members of temple committees in Taiwan often address each other
using kinship terms. Similarly, fans tend to use the trope of fictive kinship
to define their community, calling their fan friends "sister" or "brother."
The puppet or character toy brings the character into this fictive kinship
network. Both Pili puppet and character toy collectors often say that "the
White Knight (or Doraemon) is a member of the family." Pili fans even
jokingly call their puppets "my daughter" or "my son" or, more commonly,
"our family's [women jia de] White Knight." Just as important icons from
temples will be moved to the home of whichever member is elected to be
the "master of the incense burner" (luzhu) each year, Pili fans will send their
puppets and dolls to visit other members of their friendship/fictive kinship
circle for days, months, or years.

Several scholars have noted the similarities between how religious
icons are handled and doll play (not just Chinese icons but also those of
ancient Egypt and Greece, as well as in Eastern Orthodox ritual; see Gell
1998; Belting 1994). The same similarities hold in Taiwan. Both icons and
puppets are regularly dressed in new clothes. Some female Pili fans hold
and cuddle their puppets and character dolls like babies. I have heard that
a separate ticket is often purchased for icons when they are taken on overseas pilgrimages, and I have seen men holding icons of Mazu in their laps
on airplanes. Most fans carry their large puppets in specially made carrying
cases, but I have seen them propping puppets on their laps or giving puppets their own seats on buses for fan pilgrimages to the Pili studios as well.

### The ang-a is a medium for communication between living persons and a virtual personality.

Another important aspect of the external agency of the ang-a is that one
can communicate with or through it. Once an icon has been installed on
an altar and its eyes have been ritually opened, people can access the god
through ritual—that is, they can pai-pai. To begin the basic ritual, one lights
one, three, or another odd number of incense sticks, depending on the occasion, and holds them in front of one's face while making three shallow bows.
The worshipper may then speak directly to the god (usually this speech is
internal, not out loud). As I have been told when performing pai-pai at

temples or in the homes of friends, the worshipper should begin by stating their name and residence and may then proceed to ask the god for blessings or specific forms of aid or to simply pay their respects. Once the worshipper has finished speaking, they place the incense sticks in the burner at the icon's feet and bow three times again, with hands folded in front of the chest. This may be a daily practice (as in home altars to Guan Yin, the Buddhist Goddess of Mercy, or in shop altars to Guan Gong), according to lunar calendrical rituals (as in major temple festivals), or irregular (e.g., requests for a sickness to be healed or for a child to pass her exams).

Gods reply through divination. The most common divination method performed in front of icons is the throwing of moon-shaped blocks (*poah-poe*), which answer "yes," "no," or "laughing," depending on how they fall. Another method is picking a divination stick from a jar; the stick is engraved with a number, and the worshipper may then take a sheet with an answer in classical Chinese (usually obscure) from a cabinet drawer marked with that number.

For fans of the Pili puppetry serials, puppets and dolls may likewise serve as a medium for communication with fictional characters. For example, Xiao Hong was one of the officers of a fan club dedicated to one of the Pili stars.[11] When I interviewed her in 2006, she was twenty-nine years old, living with her parents and working as the secretary for her family's small retail firm. Around three years earlier, she had started to collect Pili character "Xiao Yu dolls"—plastic dolls around eight inches tall, with oversized heads, huge round eyes, and tiny O-shaped mouths, fitted with specially made costumes, wigs, and accessories to look like various Pili heroes.[12] At the time I interviewed her, Xiao Hong had purchased nine of the dolls, each one a different character. She and her friends tried to buy different characters so that they could create a wide variety of scenarios with them, and they frequently sent their dolls to each other's homes to "stay over."

I asked her how she interacted with the dolls. She said:

> I kiss each one every night, only then can I sleep. I used to sleep holding my Yi Ye Shu doll. . . . Yes, I talk to them, I tell them everything. They watch the Pili videos with me. If the plot of the video makes me angry, I'll scold them for their bad behavior. If they do cute things in the videos, I'll kiss them. . . . I don't really do voices for them, it's more like I'm teaching a child, I tell them what to do. . . . I really like the one of Ao Xiao Hong Chen, because in some ways he's really stubborn, stubborn to the point that you just want to bully/tease [*qifu*] him. He always gets tricked, and

then I think that in some ways his personality is really adorable—everyone just fools with him and he gets all confused. It's really cute. And he's also an upright hero. I just think it's really fun to tease that kind of person.

Xiao Hong's interactions with her dolls layer many of the functions of the *ang-a* within the *ang-a* mode of animation. The doll is simultaneously a materialization of the character, a vessel for the character's personality, a companion, and a medium for communicating directly with the character. What is particularly interesting here is that the doll brings the character into Xiao Hong's daily life, rather than bringing her into the Pili world, and that the doll's form allows for a kind of intimacy in which Xiao Hong has a sort of parental authority—a kind of intimacy that the characters cannot have with each other within the canonical Pili world.

### The ang-a is part of a lineage of replicas that can be traced back to an original.

Both academic and folk theories of how objects are invested with agency, presence, efficacy, or aura revolve around the ideas of mimesis and the sharing of substance, what James Frazer, in *The Golden Bough* ([1911] 1925) called the Law of Similarity and the Law of Contact or Contagion (see, e.g., Taussig 1993; Gell 1998; Belting 1994). In other words, animated objects or images may derive their humanlike qualities or supernatural powers (which are often extensions of human capacities, such as vision or psychosocial influence) from either looking like an original object or sharing some material substance passed on from an original object. In many cases—including "voodoo dolls" and similar magical images, as well as many types of religious icons—mimetic and contagious connections are combined. I will discuss how mimesis works specifically in the representation and reproduction of personality in Taiwanese *ang-a* in the next section. Here I want to look at how the passing of substance (contagious magic) invests both icons and Pili puppets with aura. One thing that is specific to the *ang-a* mode of animation is that this process is framed in kinship terms, so that the presence and power of a specific *ang-a* derives from its place within a genealogy.

In Chinese folk religion, lineages of icons of the same deity are created through the sharing of incense ash. As I noted earlier, when a new icon of a deity is sanctified, incense ash from the burner in front of an older icon of that deity is placed inside it during the *ru shen* (bringing in the god) part of the ritual process. This process is called *fen xiang/hun hiu$^n$*, or "dividing the incense." The relationship between the original icon and those that contain its incense ashes, at least for Mazu icons, is described in terms of a matrilineal metaphor; they are "mother" and "daughter" icons (Chang 2003:2–4). The term for a "parent" icon is *benzun/pun-chun*, the "original"; the term for its "children" is *fenshen/hun-sin*, or "divided bodies" (Sangren 2000 translates *fenshen* as "branch bodies").

Pilgrimages are organized around this matrilineal metaphor, and several anthropologists have described how icon genealogies are reanimated through pilgrimage (Sangren 1987, 2000; Chang 2003; Yang 2004; Hatfield 2010). In annual Mazu pilgrimages, held in the period leading up to Mazu's birthday on the twenty-third day of the third lunar month, worshippers carry *fenshen* icons from their local temples to cult center temples to visit the older icons from which the incense ash within them came. In these pilgrimages, Mazu *fenshen* are said to "return to their mother's house" (*hui niang jia*), and they "visit their sisters" when they stop at temples housing other *fenshen* of Mazu. The efficacy, or *ling*, of the *fenshen* is "recharged" by mixing the incense ash from the *benzun* with that of the *fenshen* and passing the daughter icon through the smoke of the mother icon's burner.

The Mazu cult is said to have originated in Meizhou, Fujian Province, where Lin Moniang, the historical woman who was deified as Mazu, was born. According to oral history, the oldest icons of Mazu—the original originals, so to speak—were carved from Lin Moniang's coffin in Meizhou. The power of Mazu icons in Taiwan is intimately linked to their substantive proximity to these Meizhou *benzun*. Several temples in Taiwan have been in fierce competition over the authenticity of the claims of their Mazu icons to direct descent from Meizhou, claims whose verification is particularly open to interpretation because the *benzun* icons left in Meizhou were destroyed during the Cultural Revolution. Since the legalization of travel between Taiwan and the PRC, pilgrimages between Mazu temples in Taiwan and Meizhou have been frequent and highly politicized events, at both the local and national levels (Hatfield 2010).

The idea of descent from an original crosses in Taiwan from the sphere of religion to the sphere of entertainment. One of the most distinctive aspects of Pili puppetry fandom, and one of the most explicit ways in which religious icons and puppets are linked, is that Pili producers and fans divide *ang-a* of the fictional characters into *benzun* and *fenshen*. Fans of the Pili serials refer to the puppets used in the videos and films as the *benzun*; all other *ang-a* of the same character can be called *fenshen*.[13]

Before 2009, fans could purchase *fenshen* puppets through a few individually owned boutique stores. Heads carved by the same carver who created the *benzun* were highly valued and more expensive than others. Fans also went to great lengths to get cloth from the same batch used by the Pili costume bureau, sometimes scouring cloth markets throughout the island. In 2009 the Pili Company decided to enforce its intellectual property rights. Its legal department drew up exclusive contracts with both the carvers and the boutique owners; those who were not willing to sign the contracts were shut down. The Pili Company now sells *fenshen* puppets at a much higher price than the boutiques used to, but fans are still willing to buy them in order to guarantee a lineage, not only of mimesis and production (a replica that is almost exact but just different enough to show that it was hand-carved by the same person) but also of substance (the same bolt of cloth, the same paint, the same hair).

Although they are not seen as possessing supernatural efficacy (*ling*), the Pili *benzun* puppets definitely have aura. Like Mazu worshippers, Pili fans take their *fenshen* puppets and dolls on pilgrimage to refresh the presence of the character through visual and physical contact with the *benzun*. On most weekends and vacation days, busloads of fans arrive at the Pili Company's studio in Huwei to tour the studio and small museum. The highlight of these trips is when the puppeteers bring out the *benzun* puppets, and the fans and their *fenshen* are allowed to shake the puppets' hands. Fans also bring their own puppets or dolls to performance events organized by the Pili Company and/or fan clubs. The emotional highlight of these events is always when the puppeteers come out with the *benzun* puppets to demonstrate their technique. When the puppets are brought out, fans shout excitedly and hold up their own puppets and dolls to see the *benzun*. Fans highly prize photographs of themselves and their *fenshen* puppets and dolls posed with the *benzun*.

On September 30, 2010, a fire at the Pili studio destroyed hundreds of the puppets stored there. Fans were truly distraught. They updated "lists of the deceased" throughout the day, wept, and wrote commemorative poetry. One fan wrote on her blog:

> The puppeteers' sweat, the carvers' skill, the costume makers' hard work, the persistence of the whole work team, and also . . . the living soul [*ling-hun*] of each character. . . .
>
> Seeing the scene of the fire from a distance, it seemed like the puppets were walking into the fire of battle, turning their heads to look back at us, and leaving. I cried. . . .
>
> Perhaps you are not a Pili fan, you might think I'm crazy, but for us, these characters are alive, because they live in the hearts of every fan. . . .

Fans hold up their *fenshen* dolls to see a *benzun* puppet during a puppeteering demonstration at an animation convention in Hangzhou, 2012. Photograph by the author.

> After the final assessment, [I found out] Wu Jun's literary puppet [*wen xi ou*] was destroyed . . . but his military puppet [*wu xi ou*] survived!!! The literary puppet is the *benzun*, the military puppet is the secondary [*fuzun*], that is to say, [also] a *benzun*.[14]

In some ways, the *benzun* of Pili characters are even more closely linked to the characters than *benzun* icons are to gods, since gods are seen as preexisting their icons, while the Pili characters fully come into being only when their *benzun* are presented on screen.

The idea of the original *ang-a* and its lineage of descendants is one of the things that distinguishes the *ang-a* mode of animation from other modes. The idea of an "original" materialization of a character does not, as far as I know, exist in other puppet theaters or in cinema and television animation. While hand-drawn cels by auteurs such as Disney, Tezuka, and Miyazaki and first-edition comics and toys can fetch high prices in the art market, it is doubtful that any fan would feel as though the characters had in some sense died or would mourn for them if these objects were destroyed. To the contrary, both Azuma's (2009) and Steinberg's (2012) analyses of contemporary media-mix manga/anime franchises and fandoms apply Baudrillard's theory of the simulacrum, arguing that the proliferation of tie-in products, as well as the blurring of the boundary between canon and fanon, have rendered distinguishing between an original and copies of characters fruitless. Both authors have their critiques and adjustments of Baudrillard's conceptual framework, but they both dispense with the idea of the original.[15]

Although Taiwanese fans of American and Japanese animation generally treat their characters in ways very similar to those of Japanese fans, there are some instances in which the idea of substantive genealogy is applied to imported cartoon characters. For instance, copyrighted (*zhengban*) character toys are more valued than pirated (*daoban*) ones. This is not because fan collectors are concerned with the intellectual property rights of the original artists. Rather, copyrighted toys are most valued, not only because the copyright is seen as a guarantee of quality, but also because it is seen as guaranteeing both a mimetic closeness to the original (canon) images and, in some cases, a shared substance. Xie Yuqi, the author of *The Doraemon Collector's Set*, describes copyrighted Doraemon toys as "products with a Japanese bloodline" (*riben xuetong de shangpin*) (2002:48).

Taiwanese fans of imported animated characters may also engage in pilgrimage practices that are closer to those of Pili fans (and Mazu worshippers) than to those of Japanese manga/anime fans. Fans of Japanese manga/anime (including Taiwanese fans) visit real sites depicted in the canon work or sites said to have inspired canonical settings (sites that look like images in the canon) (Thomas 2012:31). But sometimes Taiwanese fans of non-Taiwanese cartoon characters are more focused on origin sites and on renewing contact between their own toys and some ancestral image. For instance, Leng Bin's second book on her Snoopy toy collection is the record of an international tour that included visits to Charles Schultz' birthplace (St. Paul, Minnesota), the Camp Snoopy theme park in California, and the Snoopy Town store in Osaka. The book includes photographs of Leng's own Snoopy toys at several of these sites (Leng 2003).

I have never heard the terms *benzun* or *fenshen* applied to any puppets other than those made by the Pili Company and its rival video puppetry series producers. This similarity between Pili puppets and religious icons is thus not "traditional" but arises in the context of the media-mix business model and the broader rethinking of animation as it is remediated through digital technology and the globalization of multiple modes of animation.

*The number of ang-a that replicate and materialize a virtual personality is an index of that personality's influence—its efficacy or charisma.*

Contrary to Walter Benjamin's description of the religious work of art or relic before the age of mechanical reproduction, the aura of the Taiwanese *benzun* icon comes not from its uniqueness but from its ancestral status. As many scholars have pointed out, the proliferation of *fenshen* enhances the power of the *benzun*. P. Steven Sangren summarizes the logic here in this way: "One worships a god because it is powerful; one knows a god is powerful because it is worshipped" (Sangren 2000:73). *Fenshen* are made because people want to worship; the more *fenshen*, the more people worshipping; the more people worshipping, the more powerful the god must be, and thus the more efficacious (*ling*) their *benzun* must be.

Most temples in Taiwan are dedicated to a main god (*zhu shen*), whose oldest icon is placed in the center of the altar at the back of the main hall, but accompanying gods (*pei shen*) are also represented through icons placed beside the main god and on other altars. There are usually many *fenshen* of both the main and accompanying gods crowded together. It is striking how similar fans' home displays of animated characters resemble these temple altars. The favorite character's *ang-a* is usually given the central place on

Icons of the same god in a temple. Photograph by the author.

A manga/anime toy collector's home display. Photograph by the author.

the shelf, but it is often surrounded by other *ang-a* of the same character and of the supporting characters. The point of such displays, in both homes and temples, seems to be the same: to concentrate a sense of the god's or character's presence.

This may be one reason that the popularity of star characters matters so much to Pili fans. Popularity contests for the characters are held regularly. I was struck, in listening to conversations among fans, by how seriously they take the competition between supporters of different stars. One reason is that if a character is popular, he or she may have a better chance of getting more time on screen (although script writers claim the popularity of characters with fans has no influence on the plot) but an even more certain chance of having his or her image reproduced in a wide assortment of tie-in products. As I learned to my dismay when I wanted to buy a puppet of a "retired" character, the carvers commissioned by the Pili Company to make puppets for sale make heads only for characters that are currently the most in demand. The Pili Company produces images of the characters because they are popular; fans know which characters are popular because their images are reproduced.

*The form of an ang-a is a visual objective correlative of the virtual personality that animates it. Both the form and the content of the ang-a are modular assemblages of features.*

As I have mentioned, the *ang-a* is one medium within a network of media, and popular characters (and popular gods) are represented in many media.

They are also represented in a wide variety of styles within each medium, ranging from the farcical to the tragic, from the abstraction of a few suggestive brushstrokes to photographic realism. How do people in Taiwan recognize such different *ang-a* as being the same character? Shunsuke Nozawa (2013) has argued that in Japan's media mix, characters must be malleable enough to cross media and styles yet maintain "(non-in)consistency." What Nozawa means by the double negative here is that characters may be considered "the same" across media platforms and styles so long as they are not perceived as being "out of character" in how they look, speak, or act.

In the *ang-a* mode of animation, (non-in)consistency of look is maintained by each instantiation of the character having a minimal number of core identifying features. Some of these features cannot be left out without the deity or character becoming unrecognizable, while others may be left out or altered in individual *ang-a*, so long as at least some appear.

For icons and puppets, these features are divided into the *zaoxing* (outward appearance), which includes clothing and accessories such as hats and swords, and the face. The *zaoxing* and the face are usually produced by separate artists and represent different aspects of the *ang-a*'s persona. The *zaoxing* generally indexes the character's social status; the face, their individual personality.[16] I will focus on the face here, but the same aesthetic principles apply to elements of the *zaoxing* as well.[17]

Many Chinese art historians have noticed a long tradition of folk portraiture that exists separately from the history of trends within literati or high-art painting and sculpture. Within this folk tradition, which includes ancestor portraits as well as religious images and puppets, the face is modular. Faces are constructed by selecting features from taxonomies of types (Kesner 2007; Siggstedt 1991). In Taiwan, from the late Qing dynasty through the Japanese colonial era, craftsmen who often had to paint posthumous ancestor portraits carried books with drawings of different types of noses, eyes, lips, and so on to show to relatives (Su 2012).

Mette Siggstedt (1991) has argued that this modular style of representing the face was strongly influenced by the practice of face reading (*xiangxue* or *xiangshu*), used for fortune-telling and what we might call interpersonal reconnaissance. In *xiangxue*, each feature (e.g., eye shape, height of cheekbones, skin tone, and placement of moles, dimples, and wrinkles) is read as the outward expression of an inner trait or disposition. *Xiangxue* manuals give examples of different types for each feature and the traits they index. Here is an example from a relatively recent Taiwanese popular *xiangxue* how-to book: "A chin that is round and full with healthy muscle reveals that this person is full of kindness. A person with this kind of face is practical and reliable and won't pick at other people's faults or coldly criticize others" (Chen Qiufan 1993:202).

This type of one-to-one correspondence between facial features and personality traits is at its most rigid and abstract in the *hualian*, the "painted-face" makeup patterns used for certain characters (mostly generals) in many genres of both Chinese opera and Chinese puppetry, including traditional *po-te-hi*. In the *hualian*, colors and designs are symbolic of moral qualities in particular (e.g., red for loyalty, black for integrity).

Some older Taiwanese icons carvers are also face readers (*kan xiang*). Carvers of Pili puppet heads and the creators of other types of animated characters in Taiwan today do not, in general, use the traditional *hualian* patterns, nor do they use *xiangxue* manuals when designing faces or even claim to believe in the accuracy of these folk systems for revealing personality traits. Nonetheless, *xiangxue* does influence the carvers, consciously and unconsciously. For example, one of the younger Pili puppet carvers told me that he had given two of the characters pointy chins because Chris Huang, the CEO and script supervisor of the company, "heard that people with pointy chins are sneaky." More often, an indirect influence operates, evident in the fact that the majority of the script group usually agree on which faces "fit" which new characters.

The idea of the face as an objective correlative of personality, and as a modular construction composed of types of features, is hardly unique to Taiwan. Most of the cartoon character designers I interviewed had studied art psychology and used typologies of color and shape to construct characters designed to be immediately associated with certain personality types and affects (e.g., warm colors and round shapes for easygoing, affectionate characters and cool colors and sharp angles for intelligent, unemotional characters).

The relationship between form and content in the *ang-a* mode of animation does, however, have several aspects that make it distinct from this globalized discourse on the fit between the look of animated characters and the psychological and moral traits communicated through dialogue, movement styles, and extra-diegetic descriptions (such as the texts of advertisements for tie-in products). One of the ways in which the Taiwanese *ang-a* mode of animation is distinctive is that it follows the Chinese folk portraiture tradition; the intent is to capture an individual essence, seen as transcending time, rather than transitory emotional states. During the late imperial period (the period during which Chinese immigrants began settling in Taiwan) it became standard for ancestor portraits to be completely frontal, still, and lacking in facial expression, while at the same time becoming more detailed and three-dimensional. Several art historians have argued that this change reflected a new emphasis on the eternal nature of the soul (Ebrey 1997; Stuart and Rawski 2001; Kesner 2007:48). Su Shuobin (2012) finds that Taiwanese ancestor portrait painters continued to paint in the modular fashion for decades after photography was introduced for precisely this reason—photographs captured only a fleeting moment, while a physiognomically based portrait captured the unchanging essence. It may be for this reason that *ang-a* that capture a character in motion (for instance, "garage kit" models of Japanese manga/anime characters) are more marginal to the *ang-a* mode of animation than those that are still. The only instances of the frozen-in-motion type of *ang-a* that I have seen that were designed in Taiwan were tie-in toys for online games. Vinyl toys with the same frontal gaze as ancestor portraits, and puppets and ball-joint dolls that are designed to be manipulated into many different poses, are much more common types of locally produced *ang-a*. Among my Taiwanese informants, *ang-a* that capture a single instant in time are the least likely to be thought of as having their own agency, the least likely to be talked to, the most likely to be thought of as simply representations of, rather than vessels for, a character.

The modal construction of character form from taxonomies of features also characterizes Japanese manga/anime and game characters, and it might be useful for me to articulate some of the differences between my description of the *ang-a* mode of animation and how animated character construction has been theorized in Japan studies. Probably the most influential theorization of the modal construction of Japanese manga/anime/ game characters has been Azuma Hiroki's concept of "database consumption." Azuma (2009) argues that the focus of manga/anime fan desire shifted between the 1970s and the early twenty-first century, from narrative to characters to what he calls *moe* elements.

Patrick Galbraith (2009) defines *moe* (pronounced *meng* in Mandarin) as "a neologism used to describe a euphoric response to fantasy characters or representations of them." The term originated among *otaku* (Japanese manga/anime fans) in the 1990s. It is written with a character meaning "to sprout," which is a homophone for a character meaning "to burn," and combines the associations of both words. What Azuma calls *moe* elements are modal elements of a character's appearance (mostly visual, some vocal) that elicit *moe* (causing "burning" passion to "sprout" in the viewer) and are spread, often in waves, across characters and franchises—for instance, cat ears, droopy socks, maid uniforms, and baby-like voices. These *moe* elements are explicitly catalogued into databases by fans, as in the TINAMI search engine, where fans can look up all characters possessing a given *moe* element or combination of *moe* elements or see a list of all the *moe* elements possessed by a given character. For Azuma, "database consumption" is driven by two simultaneous desires: the desire for characters—that is, for particular combinations of *moe* elements—and the desire to take these elements apart, to de- and reconstruct the underlying database itself.

The main difference, as I see it, between database consumption and the *ang-a* mode of animation is that the modal elements of the *ang-a* are organized, not into databases, but into taxonomies. Specifically, they are organized through the process that Eve Kosofsky Sedgwick calls nonce taxonomy: "the making and unmaking and remaking and redissolution of hundreds of old and new categorical imaginings concerning all the kinds it may take to make up a world" (1990:23). The difference between a database and a taxonomy is subtle. I want to focus on two principles governing the relationship between form and content in the *ang-a* mode of animation that are absent from Azuma's formulation of the database: the principle of fit or coherence among elements, and the principle of analogism.

Azuma defines database consumption in opposition to the fan aesthetics he sees as historically preceding it, which focused on grand narrative and then on characters. What interests him about the modal construction of manga/anime characters is the way that focusing on *moe* elements takes characters out of the context of narrative. When fans focus on the affective function of characters—on their arousal of the *moe* response—individualized psychologies (that is, consistent motivations), of either the characters or their creators, become beside the point. What makes *moe* elements interesting for Azuma is that they are substitutable and that they can be combined randomly.

Of course, *moe* elements appear to be "random" and infinitely substitutable only from within the *otaku* subculture. From the outside, the range of *moe* elements in the *otaku* database appears culturally limited. *Moe* elements clearly have meaning, in the sense that they have connotations within various scales of culture (manga/anime subculture, Japanese culture, East Asian culture, global pop culture), just as the elements of the face and *zaoxing* of Taiwanese *ang-a* do. Cat and bunny ears are associated with femininity, sexuality, and playfulness; wire-rimmed eyeglasses with intellectualism; maid costumes with aristocratic settings, domesticity, and subservience; and so on.

The elements of the *zaoxing* and face of the Taiwanese *ang-a* can also potentially become decontextualized *moe* elements. A few Pili fans who are also fans of Japanese manga and anime do, indeed, say that certain character elements (feathers, an evil laugh) are *meng*, and some Japanese *moe* elements (such as cat ears) have been adapted by the Pili *zaoxing* group for puppets.

The difference between Azuma's database consumption and the Taiwanese *ang-a* mode of animation here is mainly one of attention and emphasis. While Japanese *otaku* (or at least, Azuma) focus on the emotional effect of separate, substitutable *moe* elements, Pili fans focus on the relationship between elements, on how the elements of a character's appearance fit together. To put it another way, database aesthetics focus on the vocabulary of character elements (and Azuma focuses on the arbitrary nature of the sign—anything can become a *moe* element), while Pili producers and fans focus more on the grammar of character elements.

One of the value terms that came up over and over in my interviews with Pili workers and fans was *xietiao*. *Xietiao* can be a verb meaning "to negotiate, coordinate, or harmonize" or an adjective meaning "coherent, consistent, and harmonious." Scriptwriters use *xietiao* to describe the process of editing they do to ensure that characters stay "in character" across scenes, episodes, and series, even though a different person is writing their dialogue for each scene. One fan, Ah Lan, explained to me what it means for a puppet's appearance to be "harmonious." She told me she would never buy a puppet if it was "incoherent" (*buxietiao*). "*Buxietiao*," Ah Lan said, "is when there's one part of the puppet that you can't help but keep looking at, it sticks out, so you can't see the whole puppet." I went with Ah Lan and some of her Pili fan "sisters" to a boutique selling Pili *fenshen* puppets, to look at a female character puppet she was thinking of buying. They all thought it was very pretty, but they didn't like the blue eyelashes. One of them said, "We Chinese just can't get used to those blue eyelashes. That's what we mean by '*buxietiao*.'"

The coherence of an *ang-a*'s features is assessed in relation to a nonce taxonomy of role types. Characters in Chinese puppetry, as in Chinese opera, are divided into the role types of *sheng* (the young male role), *dan* (the female role), *mo* (the old man role), *jing* (the military general or painted-face [*hualian*] role), and *chou* (clown).[18]

In 2006, I had the opportunity to interview one of the oldest and most revered puppet carvers in Taiwan, Xu Bingyuan, who had carved icons and traditional puppets, as well as the puppets for Huang Junxiong's 1970s television puppetry series, *Shi Yanwen*, and many of the early Pili characters. He described the process by which he carves a puppet head this way:

They [the scriptwriters] don't need to tell me who the character is; they just say, like for Shi Yanwen, his age, and that he's handsome, and then I carve it for them. . . . As for the form of the face [*lian xing*], I have to think of it myself. Because I've been carving for fifty years already, goodies and baddies, I already know the forms of their faces. They just tell me the age of the character, if it's a man or a woman, and I carve. . . . I think as I carve; I can't make a drawing first! I've carved since I was a kid. . . . I just pick up the knife and make the area over the eyes a bit higher or rounder . . . make the nose a bit smaller. For each body type [*xingti*], each part has to fit with the others.

For Xu, the role types became unconscious templates as he learned his craft, and this deep familiarity allowed him to make the adjustments necessary to create coherent puppets to meet the demands of new media. As he did so, the nonce taxonomy of television puppets evolved from that of stage *po-te-hi*, moving from the world of Chinese history and myth to the original, evolving world of the Shi Yanwen and Pili series.

In exhibits curated by the Pili Company, the displays of puppets are usually organized according to the five traditional role types. But the Pili taxonomy of role types has expanded, and there is a new category for Pili puppets, *za*, which means "miscellaneous" or "mixed." These are puppets that don't fit in the other categories, that combine elements from, for instance, Tibetan Buddhist art and Hollywood monster movies. In the *ang-a* mode of animation, character taxonomies morph through the creation of consciously incoherent or inharmonious character forms. For example, since the late 1990s, the Pili Company has created several characters that we might call transgendered, by combining elements typical of the *sheng* (young male role) with elements typical of the *dan* (female role), such as a *sheng*'s face with a *dan*'s voice.

To sum up, in the *ang-a* mode of animation, emphasis is not on the affective function of individual elements of the character's form but on their relationship. The composition of elements correlates to the composition of character traits. When the relationship between elements is harmonious, characters feel real, in the sense that they fit into known categories, that they stay "in character." When the relationship between elements is inharmonious, though, it may also make the characters feel psychologically realistic in the distinctly modern sense of having conflicting feelings and motivations. It is the composition of elements, not the elements themselves, that producers and fans see as the source of affect.

*Both the assemblages of physical features of the ang-a and the assemblages of psychic features they index signify not only within but also across analogous taxonomies.*

Another way in which the *ang-a* mode of animation differs from the Japanese manga/anime mode of animation, as it has been theorized by Azuma and others, lies in the relationship between the characters and worlds of *ang-a* and real life.

Patrick Galbraith argues that one of the main points on which different influential theorists of Japanese manga/anime subculture agree is that fans make a very strict distinction between what they call 2-D (*er ciyuan* in Mandarin, *nijigen* in Japanese), referring to the two-dimensional world—the diegetic world of manga and anime—and what they call 3-D (*san ciyuan* in Mandarin, *sanjigen* in Japanese), referring to the three-dimensional, or real, experiential world. Galbraith (2009) writes that "the crucible of *moe* is a de-emphasis on the reality of the character and relations with the character." But as Shunsuke Nozawa (2013) points out, there is also a desire for crossover between the separate realms of fantasy and reality, what fans jokingly call 2.5-D. Nozawa gives several examples, including the performances of voice actors. He gives one particularly layered example of an amateur video made by an *otaku*, in which the director takes a mobile device running a dating simulation game out on a date. He holds the device so that the virtual "girlfriend" appears to fit into the real (photographic) environment of Tokyo (although she remains framed by the device). At the end of the video, the virtual girlfriend walks out of the screen, but at the same time, the fan himself enters into the 2-D world, his legs appearing inside the game screen. Galbraith (2009) also describes some other practices that could be considered 2.5-D crossovers: "*Otaku* [male fans] turn cats, war machines, household appliances and even men of historical significance into beautiful little girls to trigger *moe*. . . . [F]*ujoshi* [female fans of male-male homoerotic manga/anime] can rearticulate anything into beautiful boys and sexualized . . . relations." He gives an example from his fieldwork in which two of his *fujōshi* informants create a fantasy scenario in which the road they are walking along becomes a masochistic sub being trained by his dom, one of the cars.

These fan practices fit in quite well with the characterization of Japanese animation culture as being permeated by an animist worldview. Philippe Descola (2013) has outlined four major ontological systems—animism, totemism, naturalism, and analogism—distinguished by the ways that humans conceive of the relationship between interiorities (i.e., psyches, souls) and physicalities (i.e., bodies, the material world). In Descola's scheme, animism is characterized by "the attribution by humans to nonhumans of an interiority identical to their own." He continues: "All the same, this humanization is not complete, since in animist systems these, as it were, humans in disguise (i.e., the plants and animals) are distinct from humans precisely by reason of their outward apparel of feathers, fur, scales, or bark—in other words, their physicality" (129). Since "form is the crucial criterion of differentiation in animist ontologies" (131), the borders between worlds (e.g., human and leopard) are crossed through the transformation of physical form. Thus, in many animist cultures, human shamans are known to send their souls into the bodies of animals or to transform their human bodies into animal bodies, and conversely, animals may take on human form while maintaining their own species-specific interior motivations and habits.

The Japanese manga/anime fan subculture described by Nozawa clearly parallels this animist structure. Where, for example, Amazonian peoples have taxonomies of species worlds, *otaku* and *fujōshi* have a taxonomy of dimensions. Instead of the physical characteristics of skin versus fur or feathers, dimensions are characterized by the physical characteristics of flatness and blank space versus tangibility and detail. Thus manga/anime characters, as Nozawa argues, like plants and animals in animist ontologies, have their own "*sui generis* realness" (Nozawa 2013). The borders between the 3-D and 2-D worlds are crossed in the same ways that the borders between human and animal are crossed—by the projection of human interiority into 2-D forms (as in voice acting), by the transformation of the human body into a two-dimensional body (as in the dating simulation game fan video), by the transformation of a two-dimensional body into a three-dimensional one (as in the practice of cosplay), or more complexly, by the projection of 2-D-human interiorities into nonhuman 3-D physicalities (as in the imagining of a road and a car as beautiful boy manga characters in a sadomasochistic relationship).

The Taiwanese *ang-a* mode of animation, in contrast, is grounded in what Descola calls an analogist worldview, rather than in an animist one. For Descola, analogical ontologies are characterized by "the grouping within every existing entity of a plurality of aspects the right coordination of which is believed to be necessary for the stabilization of that entity's individual identity, for the exercise of its faculties and dispositions, and for the development of a mode of being in conformity with its 'nature'" (2013:212). One of Descola's two main examples of analogist ontologies is ancient China (specifically, Daoist divination manuals).[19] The distinction between (Chinese) analogism and (Japanese) animism plays out in subtle differences between the *ang-a* mode of animation and the database consumption mode of animation.

What makes the taxonomies of *xiangxue* (face reading) distinctive is that each feature maps onto other taxonomies—for instance, geography (the forehead, cheeks, chin, and nose are analogous to the north, east, west, south, and central regions of China), animals, zodiac signs, the four elements (earth, air, water, fire), the seasons. Each face, then, indexes an assemblage of propensities (what François Jullien [1999] calls a *dispositif*, or disposition) that is a microcosm of a particular arrangement of elements in the cosmos and is analogous to an infinite number of other microcosmic assemblages (e.g., battle formations, the organization of dishes in a meal, a musical composition, the weather on a particular day).

Where Japanese (and Taiwanese) fans of Japanese manga/anime tend to see the 2-D and 3-D worlds as completely separate, yet with the possibility of individuals crossing between them, in the *ang-a* mode of animation the virtual worlds of *ang-a* (the afterlife, the diegetic world of the Pili puppetry series) are seen as analogous to the human experiential world. Pili characters are seen as psychologically believable in a way that Japanese *moe* characters are not. Even though the Pili puppetry narratives are in a fantasy genre where most of the characters have magical powers, Pili fans tend to see the characters' personalities—both their particular assemblages of traits and the taxonomies from which those traits are drawn—as having real-world counterparts (see chapter 4).

The drawing of analogies between taxonomies is a common, even obsessive practice among Pili fans. The Pili Company's publication *Pili xingzuo Feng shen bang* (Huang Qianghua 1999)[20] uses one character as an example of each of the twelve Western zodiac signs, listing their cosmological attributions (*shuxing*)—yin or yang, fire, water, wind, or earth—as well as the planets and gems they are associated with, their lucky numbers, days of the week, and so forth and then listing their personality types' good points and bad points. In fan art, characters are often transposed into animals, retaining one or two of the human character's distinguishing features (e.g., skinny or fat, a mole in the same place on the face). Unlike the Japanese *otaku*'s and *fujōshi*'s transformations of everyday objects into beautiful girls or boys that Galbraith describes, this type of transposition is intended, not to enchant or ensoul the material world, but to capture something of the character's essence (for instance, something catlike about a character redrawn as a cat).[21]

The analogistic thinking that characterizes the Taiwanese *ang-a* mode of animation can be applied to Japanese animation by Taiwanese fans. Fran Martin records an interview with two Taiwanese T's (butch lesbians) who are *fujōshi* fans of the Japanese manga/anime franchise *Saint Seiya*, in which they use the characters as ideal types for different types of T personae—for example, "Dragon Shiryu is more like the man-of-culture type, whereas Seiya is more like a kid from the sticks who's come for the fighting, he'll never grow up" (Martin 2008:171). Martin writes,

> Simao and Lucifer's translation of the personality and gender traits of the various male mythical characters in the Saint Seiya manga into the "nonce taxonomies" of Taiwanese lesbian secondary gender (hot-blooded young T; beautiful-youth T; cultured T; martial T; etc.) provides an exemplary illustration of BL's [BL = boys' love, a genre focused on male-male romantic relationships] utility as goods to think with. The fictional characters function as quasi-totemic figures, enabling a symbolic processing of Simao's relationship with available identity categories within a local sex-gender system. (2008:171–172)

It is perhaps significant that the *Saint Seiya* manga/anime franchise fits more closely into the *ang-a* mode of animation than many Japanese franchises. It incorporates "real" (Greek) gods in the narrative and is one of the many "robot suit" genre franchises whose success, Ian Condry (2013, chap. 4) argues, was particularly closely tied to the production of figurines.

I have outlined here a mode of animation that Taiwanese people might recognize as their own, one that brings together various spheres of contemporary social life, including folk religion, entertainment, and commerce. This mode of animation is centered around a particular kind of animatable object, the *ang-a*, which is tangible and basically human in form. The human quality projected into the *ang-a* is personality, which is conceived as an assemblage or disposition of moral qualities and behavioral tendencies. The means by which personality is projected onto the *ang-a* are variable and include design, ritual, puppeteering, and doll play.

The ideal type of the *ang-a* lies in the overlap between Chinese folk religion icons and puppets. Many of the characteristics of the Taiwanese *ang-a* mode of animation are also characteristic of other modes of animation that are not specifically Taiwanese or Chinese, such as Japanese manga and anime or Hindu and Eastern Orthodox practices of icon worship. These include the placement of the *ang-a* as a medium within the context of a media-mix culture, as well as the idea of characters inhabiting intangible, collectively imagined worlds. Other characteristics of the *ang-a* mode of animation overlap with historical traditions within Chinese culture that are not limited to animation per se, such as anthropocentrism and analogism.

In other chapters of this book, I will be looking at some of the implications of framing animation in terms of the *ang-a*. The *ang-a* mode of animation is not the only mode of animation at work in Taiwan and not always the dominant one, and I will also be exploring how the model of the *ang-a* intersects with other practices of projecting human qualities into the material world.

In this chapter, I looked at the *ang-a* mode of animation as extending from the religious image, through puppets that represent divine or later-deified characters, to puppets representing original characters within a fictionalized, magical, and timeless Chinese world, to the imported, mass-produced collectible toy. In the next chapter, I will reverse direction and ask how the rise of the global media-mix animation industry might be influencing religion in Taiwan. Most of my examples in this chapter came from the world of puppetry, because Chinese puppets have traditionally been a type of *ang-a* that mediates between the sacred and the profane. In the next chapter, I will look at another type of mediating *ang-a*, deity figurines (*shenming gongzai*), a new type of *ang-a* in the twenty-first century that rematerializes gods as cute manga characters.

# CHAPTER 3

# The Cutification of the Gods

In July 2007 the FamilyMart convenience store chain in Taiwan began giving away miniature vinyl figurines of Daoist and Buddhist deities, called Hao Shen Gongzai (Good God Figurines), in exchange for proof-of-purchase seals.[1] The company hired the Taiwanese design firm DEM Inc.—owned and managed by Demos Chiang, one of former president Chiang Ching-kuo's sons—to design the toys. The series turned out to be unexpectedly popular; FamilyMart estimated that the toys increased its profits by 20 percent for the quarter (Li Xinyi 2008:8). FamilyMart released a second series in December 2007, which proved to be just as popular, and produced two more series in 2009 and 2010.

These toys were almost universally described as "Q" (cute) or *ke ai*—(loveable or adorable).[2] *Ke ai* is often used to translate the Japanese *kawaii* and the English "cute," although its range extends beyond describing things seen as childish or vulnerable.

Describing or representing spiritual entities as *ke ai* is by no means a new phenomenon in Taiwan. David Jordan reports an informant saying that "immortals struck her as rather 'cute'" in the late 1960s (1972:39).[3] Some gods have also been represented in a cute style for centuries, especially the Earth God (Tudi Gong, the lowest position in the Daoist imperial hierarchy, in charge of a single village or urban neighborhood), the God of Wealth (Cai Shen), and the round-bellied Maitreya Buddha (Milefo). These gods' icons are usually shown smiling. Cute plastic or ceramic figures, as well as cartoon posters, of the God of Wealth are a ubiquitous part of Chinese New Year decorations and also adorn many shop counters year-round.

Nevertheless, the FamilyMart toys were recognized as being adorable in a different way from earlier puppets, statues, and New Year posters of these gods, combining features thought of in Taiwan as Japanese and European. In some ways, they closely resembled Japanese *yuru kyara* ("wobbly" cartoon characters, often used as mascots or brand logos, of which

FamilyMart's first Good God Figurine series. Author's collection; photograph by Ellie Huang.

Hello Kitty is the most famous). In particular, they had two characteristics not found in representations of cute gods before the twenty-first century—neoteny and what I have called in the introduction a stripped-down style.[4] "Neoteny" refers to the figures having oversized heads and tiny bodies—that is, the (exaggerated) physical proportions of an infant rather than an adult. By "stripped-down style," I mean the reduction of features and details. For instance, the faces of all the FamilyMart figurines were entirely smooth surfaces, the eyes and mouths were simple geometric shapes or lines, and none of the figurines were given noses. The choice of vinyl with a matte finish also connected the Good God Figurines to the high-end tie-in toys of Japanese manga and anime characters produced by companies such as Kodama. The "comfortable" tactile quality of vinyl distinguished them from both the mass of other promotional toys, which are usually made from PVC, a shiny, hard plastic, and from more traditional cute figures of Daoist and Buddhist deities, which are usually made of either PVC or brightly painted plaster.

The toys were also given a "European" feel by the use of relatively simple, geometric designs reminiscent of Germany's Playmobil figurines and by the color palette, which eschewed both the traditional palette of Taiwanese temple art (dark reds, blues, and greens) and the bright primary colors of most American, European, and Japanese children's toys in favor of designer colors such as olive, aubergine, and brick red (what we might call Ikea colors).

Following the success of the first FamilyMart series, a number of folk religion temples in Taiwan decided to commission their own cute god figurines to sell as souvenirs. Some temples used designs provided by volunteer worshippers, some hired professional designers, and others held contests to choose the design for their toys. The deity toys produced by temples are quite varied in terms of styles and materials. Among these, many return to the more traditional color palettes and hard, shiny materials, but the characteristics of neoteny and stripped-down-ness are almost universal.[5]

Although the deity toys craze peaked around 2010 and sellers claim that sales are declining, a wide variety of such toys is currently available in Taiwan and they remain a popular type of collectible. Rather than fading away, the cutification of deities seems to have become a ubiquitous part not only of Taiwanese consumer culture but of Taiwanese folk religion as well. Today, cute cartoon images of deities adorn a wide assortment of commercial products. Not only toys but T-shirts, pens and pencils, greeting cards, fans, and so on, decorated with cute cartoon images of gods and goddesses, are common items for sale in temples, souvenir shops, stationery stores, and even designer boutiques. Cute animations of gods appear in advertisements not only for temple activities but also for restaurants, credit cards, and other services. Cartoony images have also come to play an increasingly visible role within religious art, architecture, and ritual performance. Large inflatable cartoon images of gods can often be seen at the entrances to temples on festival days. SpongeBob SquarePants and friends have been painted into the murals adorning temples (Xie Zhongyi 2009). Electronic San Taizi troupes, which incorporate elements of commercial animation and electronic music and dance moves into a traditional genre of festival procession, are now a common features of temple festivals, movies, television programs, and national events such as the 2009 World Games in Kaohsiung. The troupes have been hailed by both the popular press and government agents as embodying a sincerely playful Taiwanese spirit.

What are we to make of this rapid change in the aesthetics of Taiwanese religious visual culture? What are the implications of deities being represented as cute cartoon characters? As I argued in the previous chapter, the *ang-a* has traditionally been a nodal form animating and connecting the worlds of commerce, politics, entertainment, and religion.[6] But the *ang-a* mode of animation is not the only one at work in Taiwan; it is simply the one that most Taiwanese people would identify as the most "traditional" or "local." There are many genres of animation jostling together in contemporary Taiwan, and the *ang-a* mode of animation overlaps in practice with modes of animation that come with Japanese manga and anime and their fandoms. In transnational practices, such as design education and cosplay, where aesthetics and ideas about what makes characters seem to have lives of their own are drawn from both Japanese and Chinese traditions (as well as from North America and sometimes Southeast Asia), different modes of animation transform each other over time.

I began my discussion of the *ang-a* mode of animation by asking what Taiwanese puppetry, manga, and anime fans mean when they say they are "worshipping idols." I will begin my exploration of the implications of the cutification of Taiwanese deities by asking what Taiwanese folk religious worshippers mean when they say they are "fans" (*mi*) of a certain god or goddess. In this chapter, I want to look at the connection between religion and popular culture from the opposite direction, to look at how styles and modes of interacting with intangible characters move from "foreign" modes of animation, particularly those that have emerged in the Japanese manga/anime industries and fandoms, into the heart of the Taiwanese *ang-a* mode of animation, local religious practice.

Chinese art historians have noted that changes in the aesthetics of religious art are often accompanied by textual evidence of changes in religious belief. For example, changes in the style and production process of tomb figurines reflected changes in concepts of the afterlife (Berger 1998; Wu Hung 2006). I will make a similar argument here. The appearance of *shenming gongzai* and other manifestations of the cutification of deities has been accompanied by new ways of talking about gods and religion. I was particularly struck by three trends I noticed within the discourse of my urban informants in their twenties and thirties. First, the forms in which gods are concretized, and the personality traits encoded in those forms, were more important to many of my young informants than they were to older icon carvers and temple officials I had interviewed. Icon carvers and temple officials often told me that the way an icon looks "doesn't really matter," so long as the deity is recognizable; while both the god's soul (including personality traits) and divine power (*ling*) enter the icon when its eyes are ritually opened, it is the *ling* that is most important to worshippers. Cute deity toys elicited comparisons with older styles of representing gods, and my young urban interviewees interacted differently with different types of statues of gods based on aesthetic qualities. Divine power and personality seemed less separable for them than for older religious specialists. This coming together of personality and power is intimately related to the second trend I noticed in the discourse of young Taiwanese—they talked about the manifestation of supernatural efficacy (*lingyan*) more in terms of emotional effects than in terms of material effects. In other words, efficacy is being redefined as affect. Finally, many of my informants were explicit about the role of worshippers' projection in animating icons. They see the gods' presence in the human world, if not their existence per se, as an ongoing project of collective imagination.

These concepts are not particularly new. We find similar ideas about the nature of divinity and efficacy expressed throughout the historical and ethnographic record. But significantly, they are usually expressed by people who are socially marginalized, especially women but also lower-class men.

Thus, the importance of gods' personalities, the conflation of efficacy and affect, and the acknowledgment of worshippers' imaginative labor as necessary to divine presence are not contrasted with the beliefs of the older generations so much as with the beliefs of those people most often cited by anthropologists of Taiwanese religion—Daoist masters, temple committee members, and other folk religion experts, the majority of whom are middle-aged or older men, heads of households with economic, social, and political capital. Among my informants, traditional gender and class divisions in terms of religious belief and practice are evident, but the interpenetration of Japanese manga/anime subculture with the Taiwanese *ang-a* mode of animation has made the beliefs of women and lower-class men less marginal, especially among young urban office workers.

What *is* new about this discourse is that these ideas are being reexpressed in a language that takes new terms from the realm of the media-mix character industries and manga/anime fandom, including cuteness or adorability (*ke ai*), acceptability (*jieshoudu*), intimacy (*qinqiegan*), and imagination (*xiangxiang*), and redefines some traditional terms of Chinese folk religion discourse, including blessings (Holo: *po-pi*; Mandarin: *baoyou*), efficacy (*ling*), and relational destiny (*yuanfen*), filtering their meanings through the lens of contemporary Japanese modes of animation.

Before I move on to discuss the connections between the cutification of deities and the reframing of religious discourse in terms of commercial animation, I want to first present the context into which cute deity toys intervened.

## Taiwanese Folk Religion at the Turn of the Twenty-First Century

A large amount of research has been done by anthropologists and sociologists on how Taiwanese religious practices and beliefs have changed since the end of the Japanese colonial period (in 1945). Here I will outline three trends that many scholars seem to agree on that are particularly relevant here: (1) the spread of the worship of specific deities from subnational communities based on kinship and residence to national and international communities; (2) the commercialization of folk religion; and (3) the mobilization of folk religious practice for ethnic and national identity politics.

First, the trend on which most anthropologists have focused in the past decade and which is a condition of possibility for the other two trends is the deterritorialization of deity cults. Before the Japanese colonial era, Taiwanese folk religious temples served as the centers of towns and urban neighborhoods that had usually been founded by one or two families who migrated from the same area in Fujian. In the 1930s, Japanese anthropologist Okada Yuzuru characterized Taiwanese folk religion as being organized by "worship circles" (*jisiquan*), in which geographical residence, kin relations (lineages), and the worship of specific gods overlapped. But when the Japanese built a railroad system on Taiwan, deity cults began to spread, and pilgrimage became part of folk religious practice (Jones 2003). Randall Nadeau and Hsun Chang summarize how the disentangling of kinship, native place, and worship have continued since the end of the Japanese colonial era:

> Religion on Taiwan today is no longer limited to the ancestral veneration and temple-based deity cults of traditional popular religion. Political liberalization, economic expansion, modernization and urbanization have been accompanied by new forms of religious expression, in two principle directions: 1) the growth and spread of islandwide deity cults and the commercialization and politicization of temple organizations (no longer tied to particular localities and their patrons) and 2) the weakening of ancestral cults and neighborhood associations and the growth of "new religions" and voluntary religious associations, especially in urban areas. (2003:293–294)

In many ways, Taiwan here follows a process of the individualization of religious belief and practice that has been seen as an integral part of modernization in Europe and North America, particularly with the recent rise of New Age spirituality (Wei-Ping Lin 2015:173). The deterritorialization of the worship of specific gods and the proliferation of new religious organizations has meant that for the younger generations in Taiwan, religious beliefs and practices have simultaneously become a matter of personal choice and a way of participating in a national (and sometimes transnational) community.

The second much-remarked-upon trend in Taiwanese folk religion is commercialization. Some aspects of this trend simply reflect phenomena that have seen periodic rises and falls throughout Chinese history, such as the private sale of religious goods and services (e.g., fortune-telling and geomancy). New to the late twentieth century is what we might call the increasing corporatization of temple organizations. Since the 1970s, many large temples in Taiwan, especially those that are central to island-wide deity cults, have applied for legal status as nonprofit foundations (*caituan-faren*; literally, financial-group legal person). This status makes them tax exempt, but it has also, in some ways, redefined the very purpose of temple leadership. Temples have always seen themselves as being in competition for worshippers and for the right to claim primary ancestry and superior efficacy for their main icons. This competition is now manifest in terms of financial and organizational development as well. The temple committee members I spoke with had titles such as "CEO" and "vice president." They see growth as an unquestioned goal of temple organization. Thus, since the 1980s, many temples have undertaken increasingly grand construction projects, including hospitals and schools as well as temple buildings, established new charity foundations, and organized large, expensive, and spectacular ritual and fund-raising activities. Many of these events are now cosponsored by local governments. Another aspect of this trend is the rise of temple tourism, including, but not limited to, organized pilgrimage groups. Again, local governments have been instrumental in encouraging temples to market themselves as attractions to bring income not only to the temple but to surrounding businesses. Animation intersects with this trend of commercialization in the new practice of using cute cartoons of deities as brand logos.

Finally, many scholars have noted how "folk religion" (*minjian zongjiao*) or "popular faith" (*minjian xinyang*) has been mobilized as a synecdoche for ethno-national culture. DJ Hatfield traces this back to the Chinese Cultural Renaissance campaign of the Chinese Nationalist Party (KMT) in the 1960s–1970s, which was both a reaction to the Cultural Revolution in the PRC and an attempt to restore moral order to counter the effects of rapid industrialization and urbanization in Taiwan. Before the start of the Sino-Japanese conflict, the Japanese colonial administration on Taiwan had either left popular religious practices alone under the rubric of "local customs" or occasionally regulated them as "wasteful practices" and "superstition." The KMT's Cultural Renaissance movement (*wenhua fuxing yundong*) reframed these practices as "religion," embodying and transmitting traditional Chinese moral values (in opposition to Western modernity), and mobilized the field of temple organization and ritual as part of "the late martial law project of reconstructing Chinese tradition through Taiwanese popular practices" (Hatfield 2010:64). This reframing of folk religion as a synecdoche for Chinese culture made it available for mobilization by other identity projects, especially the project of defining Taiwanese culture as separate from Chinese culture (Hatfield 2010; Clart and Jones 2003). The phenomenon of the cutification of deities is one way in which Taiwanese folk religion is currently being mobilized for a new subcultural sensibility in which Taiwanese identity is redefined yet again, this time as multicultural.

## Religion and the "Office Worker Tribe"

The design team at DEM Inc., the executives of FamilyMart, and the Taiwanese press all assumed that the majority of buyers of the Good God Figurines would be urban, college-educated, salaried workers in their twenties and thirties, the so-called office worker tribe (*shangbanzu*). When I interviewed members of temple committees, they all told me that the production of cute deity toys was a way to attract "young people" back to the temples. Although the target market for these toys was almost always defined in generational terms, there was clearly a class element as well. Secretaries at temples in southern Taiwan told me that, in fact, plenty of local young men were actively participating in *zhentou/tin-thau* (processional performance troupes) and other temple activities. When temple organizers said they wanted to revitalize religious feeling and participation among "young people," they actually meant college students and office workers, those whose move into the urban middle class meant they had less time for, or interest in, the work of maintaining traditional community ties.

The office worker tribe is usually assumed to be the most secularized group in Taiwan. Taiwanese sociologists have argued that increased education correlates with a decline in "occult" beliefs (Chiu 2012) and that the practice of ancestor worship is declining among the younger generation (Chen Hsinchih 2012). My fieldwork has been done mostly among the office worker tribe of Taipei, and my experience is that while my informants may not participate in temple-organized activities as regularly as people of the same age in small cities and towns, they do not differ all that much in terms of the range of their religious identifications and beliefs.

A 2004 national survey on religion by the Institute of Sociology, Academia Sinica, found that 31.7 percent of the population of Taiwan self-reported as followers of folk religion (*minjian zongjiao*), 24.8 percent as Buddhist, 15.8 percent as Daoist, 4 percent as Christian, and 21.5 percent as having no religion (Lin Pen-Hsuan 2012:164).[7] The young animation fans I have interviewed over the years fall into similar percentages. When I surveyed fans who collected puppets or character toys (from 2009 to 2011), approximately 7 percent identified themselves as Christian, while 20 percent each defined themselves as Buddhist or as having no religion. The rest (over 50 percent) identified themselves as followers of folk religion.

Surveys, however, tell us little about what people think or the intensity of their beliefs.

This chapter is based primarily on interviews I conducted with thirty-six people specifically about deity toys between 2009 and 2011. My interviewees included designers, manufacturers, commissioners (both commercial clients and temple committees), and collectors. Since many of them were selected for interviews specifically because of their involvement with religious organizations, they cannot be considered representative of the population as a whole. Nonetheless, the designers and collectors I interviewed did seem to reflect the same range of practices and beliefs I found among collectors of puppets and character toys more generally.[8]

One thing I found in my interviews was that people who answered a survey question about their religious faith (*zongjiao xinyang*) with "folk religion," "Daoism," or "no religious faith" usually, when questioned in more detail, turned out to have virtually identical practices. These people were the majority of my office worker tribe interviewees. They did not worship at their homes in the city but worshipped both gods and ancestors whenever they went home to visit their parents. Many said that they would not make special trips to temples to worship any particular god, but that if they happened to pass a temple they would stop and *pai-pai* (worship). Some said that they occasionally attended temple festivals to enjoy the "hot and noisy" (Holo: *lau-jiat*; Mandarin: *renao*) atmosphere.[9] In general, folk religion was for them an object of nostalgia.

Another thing that characterized this group was that no one I interviewed who identified themselves as having no religion identified as an atheist (*wushenlun*). Rather, they tended to see themselves more as agnostics. People often used double negatives when talking about their participation in ritual. One shopkeeper told me he had "no religion," but he kept a piggy bank of the God of Wealth, a gift from a relative, on his counter and told me he had had its eyes ritually opened and placed a charm (*fu*) from the temple where it was purchased between the figurine and its stand, in order to make it efficacious. He said, "You ask if I believe or not. Well, just don't not believe! That's not the same as going out of your way to believe."

The range of my informants' beliefs and practices does not actually seem to indicate much change, in terms of intensity of commitment, from the 1960s. For one thing, almost all of my informants in their twenties and thirties were unmarried, and ethnographies from the 1960s and 1970s indicate that folk religious worship was mainly an activity taken on by people with their own families—mothers worshipping at home and, for special requests, in temples, while male heads of household took leading roles in calendrical rituals. Significantly, the one married deity toy collector I interviewed, a professional photographer, said that he had considered himself "not religious at all" until his parents died, after which he started taking his family to temples to worship Mazu and Guan Yin. He collected deity toys as an educational tool for his three-year-old daughter.

Doing fieldwork in a rural town in northern Taiwan in the late 1960s, Stevan Harrell (1977) categorized villagers according to three attitudes toward religion. He found one small group of what he called true believers, who accepted passed-on religious beliefs without question, and another small group of nonbelievers. But the majority of people, he found, were "practical believers," who accepted or rejected discrete tenets of folk belief (such as "geomancy of graves influences fortunes of descendants") based on experiential evidence. My own experience over the past twenty years indicates that this general pattern still seems to hold, that the majority of Taiwanese people I know are practical believers, although, as I shall discuss, what counts as experiential evidence and efficacy these days may be defined more in terms of subjective feelings than miraculous occurrences.

One way in which members of the office worker tribe do seem to differ from older generations is in the fluidity of their religious beliefs and practices. Lin Pen-Hsuan (2012) found an increase in religious mobility (that is, individuals changing their self-reported religious identity) correlating with increased geographical mobility. The majority of my interviewees in their twenties through forties were not living with, or near, their parents. Most had moved to Taipei or Kaohsiung for university or work, and many of them had lived in several different cities. Many of my interviewees, including temple officials, designers, and collectors, told me that Taiwan has "religious freedom," something also emphasized in government publications and tourism literature. Many also stressed their personal commitment to "respect for all religious faiths."

A good example is Ah Xian, a designer who was also a fan of Japanese animation and Pili puppetry. He told me that when he was growing up, his family had worshipped at local temples, mostly Mazu and Qing Shui Zushi. He had been baptized when he attended a Catholic middle school and later became a Buddhist. At the time of the interview, several of his family had joined the Buddhist Compassion Relief Tzu Chi Association, while he worshipped Mazu and Guan Gong. He had several Christian friends and visited their churches with them sometimes, and his clients included Buddhist and folk religious temples as well as Christian church groups. He said:

You need to have tolerance for religions. Each religion has its good points. Of course they also have their bad points, but not many. . . . You need to study their good things. Like Christians tell us we should have love for all humanity, Buddhists tell us we should be compassionate, Daoists teach us . . . a respectful attitude toward nature. I think if we let these religious faiths penetrate our lives, when we have to face problems, it's really helpful.

Another young man, a design student, told me that he liked to "play with" (*wan*) different religions by participating in folk religious festivals and Buddhist retreats and visiting Christian churches.

As I have argued previously (Silvio 2007), in many ways the Age of Animation makes end runs around modernity, in that contemporary technologies of animation and animation fan practices are often seen, explicitly or implicitly, as rediscovering or simply continuing local traditions dating back to before the Industrial Revolution. Ah Xian eschewed the religious studies/sociological definition of "world religions" (universalist, having sacred texts) that became hegemonic in many parts of the world, including China, by the late nineteenth century (Masuzawa 2005). Instead he saw "religions" as they have been seen by most ordinary Chinese people since the Han dynasty, as philosophical and ethical schools of thought. Buddhism and Daoism have always been referred to as teachings (*jiao*) in Chinese. Most of my interviewees did not see the worship of specific deities and identification with specific religions as mutually exclusive, any more than they would see sociology and physics as mutually exclusive. For them, preindustrial Chinese tradition and postindustrial global New Ageism converge.

With this background in mind, let us now return to the deity toys and what the cutification of gods reveals about the intersections of religious and commercial, and local and imported, modes of animation.

## Commercial Strategies: Cuteness and Acceptability

Virtually all of the people I spoke with claimed that the function of cute deity toys was to elicit the feeling of intimacy (*qinqiegan*). But different groups of people defined intimacy in different ways. The commercial clients and manufacturers tended to use the word "intimacy" to mean familiarity and a sense of cultural ownership. In other words, they defined intimacy as something like brand recognition and, interestingly, saw it as something produced by the selection of content rather than style. FamilyMart had given away small plastic toys of Japanese manga/anime characters for previous promotional activities, but when the company went to DEM Inc., it asked the firm to design toys with "Taiwan flavor." At the time, designs based on local culture were popular with the youth market and were being actively encouraged by the government (through, e.g., sponsorship of themed design contests). When I interviewed Penny Lin Shihong, the young man in DEM's graphics department who designed the first FamilyMart series, he told me that the FamilyMart team chose the gods because they would be familiar to most Taiwanese people.[10] In fact, DEM held focus groups to find out which of Lin's god designs were most instantly recognizable and eliminated the more obscure gods from the series, winding up with Mazu, Guan Yin, Guan Gong, Cai Shen, Tudi Gong, San Taizi, Milefo, Wen Chang Jun, Zhong Kui, and Yue Xia Lao Ren.

The owner of a ceramics factory that manufactured figurines for temples in southern Taiwan explained the commercial advantages of Buddhist and Daoist deities' cultural familiarity this way:

> If you make a figurine of a character that no one knows, you can't sell it. You have to spend many years and lots of effort building up character recognition. But if you make a toy of a familiar cartoon character like Doraemon or Mickey Mouse, then you have copyright problems. With toys of gods, you avoid both problems—everyone recognizes Mazu, but there's no copyright.

Choosing gods as the content of their toys provided commercial clients with a legally safe, preexisting emotional connection between the product and customers.

In choosing the style of figurines, the advantage of the *yuru kyara* ("wobbly" cartoon character) style from a business perspective was that it provided acceptability (*jieshoudu*). Making sacred images into commercial products ran the risk of creating controversy, and both FamilyMart and the temples that produced deity toys managed this risk through cuteness. The aesthetic of blankness, a key factor in the *kawaii* style, is strongly associated with Japan, and Japanese designers have theorized that the relatively blank, featureless face allows viewers to project their own emotions onto an object (Yamaguchi 2011:202). When FamilyMart and DEM opted for a relatively blank cute style for their deity toys, their strategy mirrored that of Sanrio. As Christine Yano has argued, Hello Kitty's global appeal is largely the result of Sanrio's deliberate construction of a "play frame" around the character, allowing her to be re-created in a wide variety of styles and contexts: "A play frame raises out-of-the-ordinary possibilities: one may take license beyond expectation, beyond norms, beyond values, even while retreating into the shelter of jest. . . . '[W]ink as play' holds the power to silence or incorporate one's critics" (Yano 2013:265).

The cute style renders the religious meaning of the figurines ambiguous and resonates with the post-1990s localist discourse that claims that Taiwanese culture is especially nimble at absorbing elements from foreign cultures (Silvio 2008). It also mirrors the play between commitment and detachment associated with the "hot and noisy" atmosphere of both the temple festival and the market (Hatfield 2010). Displaying cute deity toys can be interpreted as a sign of piety, as part of a youthful fashion style, as an expression of pride in Taiwanese cultural identity, or any combination thereof. As one collector put it, "You can give them [the FamilyMart deity toys] as gifts to anyone. If you gave your grandmother a toy of Doraemon, she'd think it was weird, but you can give her these."

The idea that cute style renders universally acceptable what might be considered sectarian signs was also reflected in the fact that the style seemed to provide an effective zone of harmony between Christians, Buddhists, Daoists, and nonbelievers. The owner of a Japanese restaurant told me that she had moved the altar with the image of Guan Gong that she worshipped every morning from the dining room to a back room after Christian customers complained.[11] But she kept several of the FamilyMart deity toys on display near the door, saying, "For people who believe, they can be gods; for people who don't, they're just toys."

The idea of religious tolerance as an integral part of Taiwan's multiculturalism was also evident in the production process, in that designing toys of deities worshipped by (familiar) cultural others was common. For example, in 2010 the pastor of a Protestant church commissioned a series of "Good Jesus" figurines for the Easter season. Anyone who spent a certain amount at one of the participating local stores would be given a coupon that could be exchanged at the church for a figurine. The pastor told me the figurines were intended to improve relations between the church and the local community by encouraging members of the congregation to shop in local stores and encouraging patrons of local stores to visit the church. He asked a young secretary who worked for his charitable foundation in Taipei to do the designs; she was not herself Christian but found working for the church "interesting." I also encountered a case in which the sole Christian employee of a handicraft company designed all of its clay figurines of cute Daoist and Buddhist gods.

While this "cute effect"—universal acceptability—makes sense as a marketing strategy, it doesn't really explain why Taiwanese people found deity toys appealing. After all, the fact that the toys were seen as unobjectionable may explain why some people bought them as gifts or displayed them in places of business, but most people collected the toys for their own personal use, and few people choose to buy a specific object just because it is inoffensive. As I've noted, for almost everyone the positive appeal of the toys was phrased as "intimacy." But for those whose main interest in the toys was not in marketing them, intimacy meant something more than mere familiarity or acceptability.

## Intimacy and Modernity

The temple committees who commissioned deity toys, and the few designers who were themselves believers, defined intimacy quite differently from the commercial producers—not as something that already existed between gods and Taiwanese people but as something that needed to be created. For them, the cutification of gods was a strategy to restore intimacy that was perceived as having been lost between the office worker tribe and the gods.

Several scholars have noted that in Japan, cute representations of authority figures are common. Yano, referring to D. W. Winnicott, analyzes how these (often zoomorphic) cute representations work:

> First, kyarakutā[12] can act as surrogates for specific persons or institutions where anxiety may be housed. . . . In this, kyarakutā render potential elements of fear or discomfort kawaii, and thus more approachable. Second, kyarakutā can act as a more generalized comforting presence in daily life. . . . Here, kyarakutā such as Hello Kitty serve as transitional objects bridging the gap between the "wet" uterine warmth of the family to the "dry" detachment of individual life, for adults and children alike. (2013:67)

Several of my informants used "intimacy" to refer to this sense, created by cute objects, of authority as something approachable and comforting.

For temple leaders, intimacy was the main marker of modern social relationships. If traditional folk religion is structured by the "imperial metaphor" (Feuchtwang 1992), in which the hierarchies among the gods and between gods and humans mirror the hierarchies of the human imperial court and between the imperial bureaucracy and the common people, then to modernize folk religion means to update this metaphor and to reframe political relations as emotional ones. One officer of a Mazu temple that sold deity toys put it to me this way:

Each generation is different. The older generation respected and feared the gods. If the god spoke, it was just like an order from the government; you did what they said. People thought like that in the 1940s. But now it's 2008. In Taiwanese society back then, most people were illiterate, so they were dependent on religion . . . they'd do whatever the god said. But now the level of Taiwanese people is higher, everyone can read, they can judge right and wrong for themselves. Of course, these figurines bring the distance between people and gods closer. It's like in the past, [when] the distance between teachers and students was very far. The teacher could beat the students and only had to teach them to read. But now the relationship between teachers and students is more like the relationship between older and younger siblings.

Some deities have always been treated in an intimate, familial way. In particular, the two main goddesses worshipped everywhere in Taiwan, Mazu and the bodhisattva Guan Yin, are often perceived as maternal, although legend portrays them both as having been virgins in their earthly lives before deification. Informants told me that they thought of Mazu as "having a motherly heart [*mu xin*]" or "like an older member of my family." Not surprisingly, both of these goddesses were part of the first FamilyMart series, along with several other benevolent gods such as the God of Wealth. Different avatars of the goddesses (the Black-Faced Mazu and the Child-Sending Guan Yin) were selected for later series.

For other gods, especially those near the top of the Daoist imperial hierarchy and the "dark" (*yin*) gods associated with death, intimacy was something that required more work to create. The City God is both high in the imperium and dark—one of his functions is to judge the souls of the dead. In 2010 the recently formed Federation of City God Temples produced a series of cute keychains of the City God and his generals for sale during the New Year season. The design for the series of toys was done by Xiao Long, a college student majoring in communications at the time. He had an uncle who was on the board of the federation, and Xiao Long was one of the few designers I interviewed who was himself an active worshipper of the god he cutified. He told me that a few years before the interview, his mother became ill, and no doctors could give a definitive diagnosis or cure. He and his father would pray for her recovery at every temple they went to. After they worshipped the City God on an outing, his mother's illness suddenly improved.[13] He saw designing the cute images of the City God and his generals as a way of reciprocating the god's aid. He described his motivation this way:

The Civil Judge records your life, how many good deeds you've done and how many bad deeds. It's the Military Judge who carries out the sentence, so if you've done too many bad things, you'll be punished. So people have a stereotype of the City God. But I think if you haven't done anything bad, if you've done good deeds, then it's a positive thing. People might be afraid, maybe they've done bad things, so I think the City God temple actually serves to keep people vigilant. It's not there to make people feel afraid. I hope I can rectify this impression people have.

Studies of the *kawaii* aesthetic in Japan have argued that the effect of softening distant, powerful, and scary subjects is a result of the *kawaii* style's abjection of the authority figure represented as cute, which places the viewer in a relationship of power over the object, even to the point of eliciting sadistic impulses: "Someone who personifies *kawaii* is not a mature, beautiful person, but feminine, childish, submissive, and pure, which is considered an inferior one to me" (Yomota, translated and quoted in Koma 2013:8; see also Kinsella 1995; Ngai 2005; Yano 2013). Thus, the cute is close to the grotesque (as evidenced by the numerous objects, both fine art and commercial products, in which the two are seamlessly combined) (Ngai 2005; Yomota 2007). Both cuteness and grotesquerie are effects that can be produced by neoteny, by the distortion of the human figure into a sort of wobbly baby shape. Indeed, in several of the deity figurine series I have seen in Taiwan, neoteny is particularly strong when the represented gods are high in the imperium and/or dark. Almost all of the cute figurines of such gods commissioned by temples have oversized, round, wide-open eyes, while the eyes of benevolent gods such as Mazu are far more varied.

But I think that what is going on in the cutification of Taiwanese deities is slightly more complex. None of the sponsors, either temples or commercial enterprises, wanted to make the gods seem powerless or pathetic. For all of the designers I spoke with, what made designing deity toys different from designing other character goods was the fine line they had to walk between making the gods cute and maintaining their dignity. They all aimed for a style that was cute but not too cute, to create intimacy without eliciting feelings of pity or superiority.

To a large extent, the strategy of cute-but-not-too-cute seems to have been effective. Many people I talked to said that looking at deity toys made them feel calm and content, as opposed to eliciting the sort of squealy excitement that is sometimes associated with the more childlike *kawaii* aesthetic. Here, the Taiwanese idea of intimacy seems closest to the healing or comforting effect often associated with cute character goods in Japan. Indeed, many Japanese "healing series" (*iyashi*; Mandarin: *liaoyuxi*) characters, like the Taiwanese deity toys, combine cute form with powerful content—for example, Rilakkuma, a.k.a. Relax Bear. Most collectors reported that they kept deity figurines on their desks or carried them attached to purses or book bags, because looking at the toys made them feel more peaceful and optimistic in a generally hostile environment of competition and economic uncertainty.

Several of my interviewees collected both Japanese manga/anime character toys and Taiwanese deity toys, and they reported interacting with them in very similar ways. Sumei was twenty-nine when I interviewed her. She had grown up in Taipei. Her father was an engineer, and she was working in the personnel office of a large hospital. She identified folk religion as her faith and considered herself more religious than most of her colleagues, who "only worship when they need something." She collected teddy bears, Doraemon toys, and the FamilyMart deity toys. It is significant that Doraemon is a mentor figure within his manga/anime world. Sumei said this was why she liked the anime more than others: "In other cartoons, it's all about competition; the hero has to be strong. But the protagonist of Doraemon is weak; he relies on Doraemon to help him realize his little dreams." She told me:

> I keep Doraemon by my side, so when something happens that's frustrating, I feel he can give me support and help me get through it. . . . Sometimes coworkers will steal credit for your work. . . . You've worked on it all day, it was really difficult, and then your coworker goes to the boss and says they did it. Sometimes I feel like I spent so long working on that and in the end someone else took the credit, and the more I think about it, the more frustrated I get. But then I think, anyway, if you look at it in terms of results, in the end the work got done, and everyone's happy. I don't need to go fight over who did it. Then I feel more relaxed.

It is significant that Sumei turns to her Doraemon toys precisely when she feels overlooked, unseen, or misapprehended by other (real and not cute) authority figures.

For Sumei, deity figurines served the same function as the Doraemon toys, and she placed both around her bed. Of her deity toy collection, she said: "What's important is I display them there, because I feel peaceful with them there. . . . I feel more relaxed, I feel my heart is more at ease. That's what's important."

If the cute effect can make the object seem abject in relation to the viewer, it also has a flip side. The cute object induces a kind of mirroring effect, cutifying (and in some sense making abject) the viewing subject. Sianne Ngai notes this effect in terms of language: "Resulting in a squeal or a cluck, a murmur or a coo, the cute object seems to have the power to infantilize the language of its infantilizer" (2012:87). Sharon Kinsella's work on the *kawaii* aesthetic in Japan in the 1980s alerts us to the fact that consuming cute objects is just one aspect of the *kawaii* trend; another is turning oneself into a cute object, through carefully adopting gestures, speech styles, and clothes aimed at making one appear sweet, pure, childlike, and (ironically) incompetent and spontaneous (Kinsella 1995).

That this mirroring effect, the cutification of the viewing subject, is an important part of the appeal of Taiwanese deity toys becomes evident in the way that some of my interviewees compared deity toys with the icons in temples. Several of the collectors I interviewed reported that they had been frightened of the gods as children, but that they felt "blessed" or "protected" by the deity toys. Ruyi, a thirty-six-year-old elementary school teacher who remembered vividly both daily and annual *pai-pai*s at her grandparents' home in the countryside, tellingly explained the difference between "real" deity images (*shenxiang*) and deity toys in terms of the gaze:

> I don't dare look directly at real *shenxiang*; I feel it's disrespectful . . . but I feel you can look at *shenming gongzai*. They make me feel I can get close to them . . . so the feeling I have in my heart of not liking to look at *shenxiang*, it disappears. That's mostly because they're cute.

In Taiwanese temples, the most powerful icons are usually partially hidden from the gaze of worshippers. The primary icon is placed in the highest central position in the very back of the altar, farthest from the worshipper. Many gods, including Mazu and the Jade Emperor, wear headdresses with beaded veils that cover the forehead and sometimes the entire face. Although the Hindu concept of *darsan* (the vision of a god that bestows blessings on the worshipper, who sees and is seen) has been applied to Buddhist images (Faure 1998), in Taiwanese folk religion the gaze between worshipper and deity is not necessarily meant to be shared equally.[14] The physical hiddenness of the idol, especially its face, as Alfred Gell argues, accentuates the sense that there is something behind the veil, inside the idol (1998:96–154). The rough correlation between an icon's lack of visibility and its power fits with the idea that the gods are "three feet above your head" (Wei-Ping Lin 2008:460)—in other words, you can't see them, but they can see you.

This lack of visibility of the god's face may, however, be a source of comfort as well as fear or awe. Anthropologist DJ Hatfield tells the following story of his interview with an image carver in Taiwan:

> "Why do you suppose," he asked, "that Mazu images wear these crowns, with beads hanging down in front of the face?" I assumed that the pendant beads veiled the noble face of Mazu from unclean human eyes. However, the image carver disagreed with this interpretation. Instead, Kho pointed out, common people designed the crown. . . . "[T]he crown was made so that when officials or superiors would look down at their inferiors or the common folk, they would not see clearly. It is only when they do not see so clearly that their rule is a good one. Among us common people, there are few who are perfect. . . . The beaded crown forces the one in a superior position to lose the power to supervise, causing him/her to be less severe. So that when we come into the temple, one of us may be secretly laughing, the other secretly eating something. But she will not see our faults, and we will hear her say, 'It matters not, child.'" (2010:237–238)

The cute style of many deity toys gives them just this sort of forgivingly fuzzy gaze. All of the gods in the FamilyMart's first, second, and fourth series of Good God Figurines have eyes that are represented as curved lines, like flattened, upside-down U's, rather than round. This gives the appearance of eyes squeezed shut by a wide smile, even though the mouth is very small, making the benevolent gaze appear to be directed at no one in particular.

Cutification, then, transforms the hidden, surveillant gaze of the temple icon into the comforting gaze of the healing character. Deity toys create intimacy by encouraging the viewing subject to get closer to the god through a kind of imaginative mimesis of their cuteness. Looking at the cute deity toy, consumers can see themselves as they wish to be seen by authority. Looking at Doraemon, Sumei can see herself as she wishes her boss would see her, as a productive and harmonious worker who cares more about end results than personal credit. Looking at a FamilyMart Mazu toy, Ruyi may see herself as childlike in Mazu's maternal eyes and worthy of blessing and protection. Looking at a cute cartoon version of the City God, worshippers may be able to see themselves as "vigilant" citizens, innocent enough to be trusted with self-surveillance.

## Blessings: The Deity Toy as Talisman

While all of my informants were in agreement about the feeling of intimacy between deity toys and consumers, they had quite divergent characterizations of the relationship between the toys and the gods they represent. During my interviews, I asked people whether or not the toys could be considered *fenshen* (branch icons)—that is, whether they could function as vessels for divine presence. I got a range of answers to this question. A small minority answered either absolutely yes or no, that *shenming gongzai* were either "just toys" or that they were, indeed, a form of *fenshen* and could be worshipped as such. The majority of people I spoke with, as well as people who wrote in journals, newspapers, and blogs about deity toys, took a position somewhere in between these two; they saw the deity toys as being more than "just toys" but less than "real" *shenxiang*. Most people took the toys to be a form of talisman or charm, an object that was imbued with the god's power (*ling*) but did not "have the god" inside. They said that that toys might be able to influence the real world by providing protection and blessing (*baoyou/po-pi*), but they could not work as a medium for communication with a god. I will address how those who answered that *shenming gongzai* absolutely were not *fenshen* or that *shenming gongzai* were indeed *fenshen* conceptualized the relationship between gods and their various images in the next section. But first I want to focus on ambiguities within the idea of the talisman, which encompasses differing concepts of blessings and efficacy.

Many people described the toys as *jixiangwu* (literally, lucky objects), a term that can be used in describing mascot characters and as a general term for the kinds of small objects that one can get at temples. The term is used especially for small cloth bags filled with incense ash from the censers in front of a famous icon, which can be carried on the person or hung from a car's rearview mirror or the lamp of a study desk to bring the owner protection and good fortune. Such objects are ambiguous because they are tied to what is often criticized as the "utilitarian" and "commercial" aspects of Chinese folk religion by religious and ethno-national purists.

The FamilyMart corporation emphasized this aspect of folk religion in their marketing. All of the series were in similar cartoon styles, but each had a special functional component. For instance, the second series were hollow and filled with tiny fortune sticks that could be shaken partially out of the toy, and each toy in the fourth series played a musical instrument—each one had a battery-operated music recording, and when linked together, the toys played in harmony.

Within the Chinese pantheon, different gods specialize in different areas of life, and people will pray to specific gods for specific purposes. For instance, people pray to Cai Shen (the God of Wealth) for financial success and to Guan Gong for success in work endeavors generally. Many people travel to the Xia-Hai City God Temple in Taipei to make offerings to the icon of Yue Xia Lao Ren (the Old Man in the Moon) there, because that icon is considered particularly effective in helping single people find marriage partners. Wen Chang Jun is considered the god of scholars, and students (and their parents) make offerings to him before taking exams.

In the first series of Good God Figurines, each toy came with a card describing the specific type of good fortune the god would bring. For example, the card that came with the toy of Wen Chang Jun reads: "Do you suspect your brain is disabled? Don't let yourself become useless, with a totally empty brain, while you are still young. Quickly pray to Wen Chang Jun, and he will protect your intelligence. You'll ace your exams, and you will be full of talent."

The designers of *shenming gongzai* series made the functions of the gods even more distinctive than they tend to be in the minds of most worshippers. Many gods, like Mazu, Guan Yin, and one's neighborhood Tudi Gong (Earth God), can be prayed to for almost any need. But in FamilyMart's first series, the range of their efficacy was narrowed. Each toy in the series was also a seal, with a single character embossed on the bottom. Guan Yin's was *fu*, Mazu's *lu*, and Tudi Gong's *shou*—happiness, success, and longevity. These characters are usually associated with the eponymous Three Immortals, but by assigning these characters to the three most worshipped deities in Taiwan, the marketers made them equivalent, in terms of having a specific function, to the others in the series—for example, *cai* (genius or talent) for Wen Chang Jun and *guan* (high office) for Guan Gong.

This brought the gods into the overlapping space between the *ang-a* mode of animation and the mode of database consumption (Azuma 2009) of manga/anime characters. It made the "jobs" of gods into equivalent, substitutable, and combinable elements within a taxonomy. The specificity of each deity's function became a sort of *moe* element, working as both an identifying characteristic and a source of affective potential across different styles and media and potentially eliciting the desire to understand the taxonomic system underlying character construction.

Temples that commissioned their own deity figurines also had the figurines designed specifically to be used as talismans. Some came on strings to be hung over rearview mirrors. One temple commissioned a pen-and-pencil set with cute figurines of Wen Chang Jun on the cap, which students could use to take their exams. Some temples encouraged buyers of their cute figurines to pass them over the incense burners in front of their main icon, as they would with the other traditional talismans on sale.

Many collectors took this advertised talismanic function of the figurines quite seriously. There is a long tradition of icons of Guan Gong being placed on altars in places of business, usually above the cash register. Now deity figurines of Cai Shen adorn the shelves of many counters and window displays in Taipei's small shops and are often glued to the front of the

A temple-commissioned Mazu figurine with a talisman containing ashes from the Mazu icon's burner. Author's collection; photograph by Ellie Huang.

portable stalls in night markets. Sumei (the Doraemon toy collector quoted above) told the following story:

> Most people will pray to Guan Gong for help with their careers, for good luck in their work. Once, I put a *shenming gongzai* [from FamilyMart] of Guan Gong in my office. I don't know if it was Guan Gong's blessing or what, but after I put it in my office, for the next two weeks after that, we were super busy, we had a huge amount of work to do every day, we were just really, really busy. One of my coworkers said it was since I put the Guan Gong figurine in the office that we started to have such a lot of work to do, and she said, "Ha! It was you! It was because you put Guan Gong in our office—take him home! Don't keep him here." So then I took Guan Gong home, and after that, I don't know why, but it seemed like after I took him home, our work got more relaxed, we weren't so tired.

She also noted that while she could put a figurine of Guan Gong in the personnel office, it would be bad to put one near the sick rooms, since "good business" for a hospital meant sickness for more patients. Sumei and several other women collectors told me they had given away toys of the Child-Sending Guan Yin, since they did not want to get pregnant.

The talismanic aspect of the toys is where they become an object of contestation for different ethno-national identity projects. For both the KMT and the Native Soil Consciousness movement of the 1970s–1990s, making folk religion a synecdoche for Chinese or Taiwanese culture involved purification, drawing sharp distinctions between those practices that fit within the model of "religion" and those that did not, which were labeled "superstition." The *taike* sensibility, which emerged in the late 1990s, was a reaction to these purification projects. The term *taike*, originally a derogatory term referring to the island's Holo speakers, was revalorized first within the subculture of electronic dance clubs and quickly extended to styles of dress, theater, and cinema. Where many Native Soil artists and writers had located the authentic Taiwanese spirit in rural traditions and elite intellectual radicalism, the *taike* sensibility celebrated the "vulgar," "mongrel" popular culture of the urban working class (Silvio 2009). The cutification of the gods, including deity toys and the electronic San Taizi (*dianyin San Taizi*) troupes, is part of one trend within this sensibility, in which revered symbols of Taiwanese identity are modernized for a youth market through blending with elements from global popular culture.[15]

A 2008 article in the *China Times*, based on an interview with Buddhist scholar Chiang Tsan-teng, suggests that the problem with the toys is that they are symptoms of a broader trend of commercialization and utilitarianism:

> Figurines [*gongzai*] have a market and rise in value. They are seen by most people as talismans [*jixiangwu*], they are no longer purely religious objets d'art. They correspond with the "self-interest" [*li ji*] psychology of Taiwanese folk religion—"If you believe in the gods, then you can receive benefits." Chiang Tsan-teng says, from cute god figurines to people going to dark [*yin*] temples to pray for winning lottery numbers, we can see that Taiwanese religion still isn't able to escape from the pragmatism of "If you believe, you can receive some benefits." . . . The result of this lack of civilization [*renwen suyang*] is that religious creative works don't start from the aesthetic point of view but start from the market point of view—"are they efficacious or not [*ling bu lingyan*]?" (Lin Shangzuo 2008)

This criticism is grounded in the perspective of organized Buddhism's centuries-old critique of Chinese folk religion's this-worldly orientation, a critique that has been sharpened by the influence of academic religious studies grounded in a Victorian evolutionary model in which the most "civilized" or "advanced" religions are those that draw clear boundaries between the material and the spiritual (Masuzawa 2005). Chiang draws as well on a long tradition of academic and state discourses of modernization denigrating "irrational superstition." He also ties this critique to the more recent concern with the commercialization of folk religion in Taiwan.[16]

But of course it is precisely this emphasis on the pragmatic, this-worldly efficacy of talismans that both the producers and consumers of deity toys find appealing. When Chiang's opinions were re-posted on a blog focused on the creative industries, several readers posted defiant responses that expressed the *taike* sensibility. For example:

> Maybe buying religious tie-in products [*zongjiaoxing zhoubian shangpin*] is like the article says, [that] it carries a utilitarian mind-set. But this isn't a bad thing. Taiwan started as a pirate's nest. (We can go back to the Three Kingdoms period. What East Asian pirates didn't come to this place outside the borders of civilization for fresh water or to trade? When you're trying to survive, how can you not be utilitarian?) In comparison, some Eastern and Western countries take an overly serious view of religion— you can't violate what's sacred, and some religious groups always get called heretics. Taiwanese religion's tolerance, diversity, and liveliness is something worth treasuring.

Nevertheless, most of my informants were influenced by the anti-utilitarian discourse, at least insofar as they were uncomfortable claiming to believe unconditionally in talismans' efficacy. Some of them said that they treated deity toys as representatives of the gods, but only in a self-consciously jokey way. For instance, one graduate student in engineering told me he took a figurine of Cai Shen with him when he went to play mahjong, and kept it by his side at the table. Then he said with a grin, "If I'm losing, I can scold him." Many told me that "the gods help those who help themselves," that the gods would bless you, but only if you worked hard for what you asked for.

One way that my interviewees defended the talismanic function of the deity toys as transcending pragmatic self-interest was by defining blessings (explicitly or implicitly) as spiritual rather than material. Several people told me that the blessing they felt they received from the deity toys was a diffuse feeling of harmony and contentedness. One woman who manufactured handmade deity keychains for sale at temples told me,

> I've heard a theory that Chinese religion is like Western psychotherapy—when you feel anxious or upset about something, then a Westerner might go to a psychologist, but Taiwanese people go to the temple. If you *pai-pai*, it makes you feel better. The *gongzai* do that too. You see this cute, smiling Mazu? It calms you down, makes you feel better. So if someone hangs a *gongzai* from their rearview mirror, maybe it will really keep them safe, because they'll feel more calm and drive better.[17]

Here the efficacy of the deity toy as talisman is exactly the same as the efficacy of the deity toy as a "healing product." Cuteness and divine power work in the same way; efficacy is affect, and vice versa.

## Relational Destiny and Commitment

In general, Taiwanese people don't talk about believing in the existence of gods as a category (until they are approached by a social scientist wielding a questionnaire); rather, they talk about whether or not they are worshippers/followers (*xintu*) of specific gods. The word *xintu* is composed of the character for belief (*xin*) and the character *tu*, meaning an apprentice or disciple (a martial arts master, for instance, has *xuetu*, study-disciples). Participating in worship of a god or goddess, even regularly, does not necessarily make one a *xintu*. Rather, what makes one a *xintu* is having *yuanfen* with that deity.

*Yuanfen* (Holo: *ian-hun, ian*) might be translated as "fate" or "destiny," specifically in regard to relationships. It is a common term in everyday discourse with several overlapping meanings. One either has *yuanfen* (*you yuanfen, you yuan*; Holo: *u ian*) with a person or thing or does not have it (*wu yuanfen, wu yuan*; Holo: *bo ian*). One of the most common referents is a relationship with a lover or spouse, where it means a relationship that was "meant to be." One can also have *yuanfen* (or lack it) with a job or an apartment. Sometimes it simply means serendipity; one has *yuanfen* with people or objects that come into one's life unexpectedly, just when they are needed. The concept of *yuanfen* came up very often in my interviews with puppet and character toy collectors. Many of them told me that *yuanfen* was the most important factor in deciding whether to buy a particular puppet or toy. Sometimes this referred to the serendipity of finding a rare collectible at a time when one could afford to buy it. But more often it referred to a subjective feeling rather than a circumstance. A few people told me that *yuanfen* was "like love at first sight." Pili fans said they felt *yuanfen* when they found a puppet that looked like the image of the character in their mind. Fans also claimed to feel they had *yuanfen* with places and cultures, with media franchises, with puppetry, and with particular fan communities.

In the discourse of my interviewees who were the sponsors, designers, or collectors of deity toys (and others with whom I had discussions about religion), the kind of *yuanfen* that transformed people into *xintu* had several sources. Some of them had *yuanfen* with a particular god for what we might call traditional reasons—that is, the same reasons that anthropologists' informants reported in ethnographies from the 1960s and 1970s. For instance, Xiao Long, the designer of the cute City God keychains, had *yuanfen* with the City God because he had personally experienced the god's *lingyan* (manifestation of efficacy) when his mother's illness was cured.

Xiao Ma had another type of traditional *yuanfen* relationship to Guan Gong through his family. I sought out Xiao Ma because he published a blog dedicated to his toy collection. He had, he was pretty sure, collected every deity toy ever made in Taiwan and some from elsewhere. In his twenties, he was working as a computer technician for a large company. He had grown up in a suburb of Taipei, and his father ran a small, unregistered private temple (*gong miao*) to Guan Gong and performed healing exorcisms (Holo: *siu-kia*<sup>n</sup>). He told me that his family had worshipped Guan Gong for over a hundred years. He had a special collection of Guan Gong figurines, which included figurines of Guan Yu (the historical general who was deified as Guan Gong) from various *Three Kingdoms* series.

For others, the efficacy that resulted in *yuanfen* was manifest, not in the answering of a prayer, but simply in what was perceived as successful communication between god or goddess and worshipper. A temple official told me the story of a young man who had a dream in which he saw the image of a god he did not recognize. He travelled to temples all around the island until he finally found an icon of an obscure local god that looked just like the image in his dream. He then became a *xintu* of the god, even though he lived in a different city. Luxue, a secretary at one of Taiwan's central Mazu temples, told me she started working there because she felt she had *yuanfen* with Mazu. This *yuanfen* came partly from a feeling of familiarity—she grew up near the temple. But she started identifying as a *xintu* after she prayed to Mazu to help her have a child. Luxue told me she had asked for a son and thrown the *poah-poe* (divination blocks), but they came up "laughing." She asked for a daughter, and the divination still indicated that the goddess was laughing. She asked, "How about twins, then?" and got the same answer. Frustrated, she left, but when she went to the doctor a few weeks later, she found out that she was already two months pregnant—Mazu had laughed at her because she asked for something she already had. Soon after, she left her job at a computer company and applied for a position at the temple. She felt that her getting the job was evidence of *yuanfen* too, because most employers are unwilling to hire a woman who is married and pregnant.

But for others, *yuanfen* came from a feeling, a general sense of well-being they experienced after worshipping a particular god. Ah Xian, the designer I quoted earlier on the importance of learning from all religions' teachings, considered himself a *xintu* of Mazu because he had grown up worshipping her; like a few others I talked to, *yuanfen* in this instance came from family tradition and familiarity. But he also was a *xintu* of Guan Gong, because after a friend had taken him to worship Guan Gong, he had the feeling that Guan Gong was "taking care of his business and helping him with cases." He sometimes ran into difficulties, he said, but he was able to get through them because he felt that he was always blessed and protected by Mazu and Guan Gong.

Sumei, the hospital personnel secretary and Doraemon toy collector, told me she felt particularly close to the god San Taizi (Nuozha). When she was around ten years old, she often had nightmares. Her mother told her that San Taizi could expel unclean things, and gave her a small bronze figurine of the god to keep in her bedroom. Sumei still keeps it on her bookshelf. She said she doesn't know if it's efficacious, but she prays to it (although without lighting incense) if she isn't sleeping well. Despite this,

Sumei said that she deliberately left the FamilyMart San Taizi toy behind when she moved to another house:

> Actually, when I got [the FamilyMart] San Taizi, I was kind of dumb-founded, because I felt it wasn't good-looking. Maybe it's because the San Taizi from my childhood was so dashing [*shuai qi de*], . . . and when I got that San Taizi, I felt it just wasn't right. I thought it doesn't really look like the god. . . . Because with a god I like, then the way his *gongzai* looks, it has to match the appearance I have in my mind; otherwise it's not right.

Sumei's words here mirror those of Pili fans who describe having *yuanfen* with a certain *fenshen* puppet as "finding the face that matches the character in my mind." Significantly, the more often young Taiwanese designers and collectors described *yuanfen* with a god in terms of affective experience (sleeping peacefully, feeling confident in the face of problems at work) rather than more tangible experience of *lingyan* (such as the curing of a disease), the more important the appearance of the god's image became.

In the last chapter, I argued that one characteristic of the Taiwanese *ang-a* mode of animation is that the appearance of the *ang-a* is interpreted within a cosmological system of analogism, where a disposition of physical features maps onto a disposition of psychological and moral traits. Philippe Descola has argued that belief in fate is inherent in the analogical ontology: "Each entity, anchored at a particular spot, pursues the ends that destiny has fixed for it in accordance with the dispositions that it has been allotted. . . . In contrast to the freedom of action that animism allows to existing beings endowed with similar interiorities, analogical worlds are burdened by the weight of destiny" (2013:213).

Traditionally, the concept of *yuanfen* has been associated with the concept of fate, and the presence or absence of *yuanfen* (especially *yinyuan*, destiny in relation to marriage) is determined by the match (or not) between the potential partners' dispositions, as analogically revealed in their birth-dates or facial features. But in the discourse of young urban Taiwanese, especially those involved as producers and consumers in the cultural creative industries, *yuanfen* has become more about intersubjective feeling than cosmological alignment. In their discourse, *yuanfen*—and religious belief more generally—seems to have much in common with Japanese manga/anime fans' experience of *moe* (*meng* in Mandarin), which Patrick Galbraith (2009) defines as a "euphoric response to fantasy characters." Galbraith argues that *moe* is an affective response to the virtual possibilities offered by images that are explicitly separated from the real. The agnosticism of many Taiwanese in their twenties to forties ("Just don't not believe!") might be seen as similar to how manga/anime fans approach fantasy characters—not (just) as a state of waiting for experiential evidence of some kind of tangible efficacy, as it was for Stevan Harrell's "practical believer" informants in the 1960s, but as a way of keeping open the potential for intersubjective engagement, having an openness to the affective catalyst of *yuanfen*. Within this discourse, the ontological status of gods is largely irrelevant, as it is for media "idols," in that it doesn't really matter whether the idol is a real person such as a singer or a two-dimensional manga character—they are objects of *moe/meng* and *yuanfen* only as virtual personalities.

## Imagination and Presence

If the question of whether or not gods exist is often left unasked in Taiwan, the question of whether or not deity toys are icons was seen by many, including Chiang Tsan-teng, as critical to analyzing what the trend of cutification meant for Taiwanese religion. As I have discussed, when I asked my interviewees if deity toys were *fenshen* (branch icons), the majority of them answered that the deity toys were something in between, that they were a form of talisman. Here, I want to discuss the minority of my interviewees who answered either that deity toys were "just toys" or that they could indeed be a form of religious icon.

When I began doing interviews about deity toys, I expected that the most important factor in people's answer to this question would be whether or not they identified themselves as *xintu* (worshippers). I also expected that age might be a factor in how people thought about the relationship between deity toys and icons, since acceptance of cutification tended to divide along age lines. I found that this was not the case. Instead, the dividing line was, consistently, gender. All the people I interviewed who said that deity toys were only toys or souvenirs were men (with the exception of one Christian woman); all those who said that the figurines might be considered *fenshen* were women.

For both male temple officials and for male designers and collectors who identified as *xintu*, icons were separated from "mere *ang-a*" through ritual. For instance, when I asked the vice executive director of a major Mazu temple in central Taiwan whether the cute figurines of Mazu that were sold in the temple's gift shop could be considered *fenshen*, he replied, "No, they are just souvenirs, proof that you've been to the temple." I said that some other temples asked a religious specialist to bless their figurines. Did this temple do that? He said, "No. That would be a mistake; it's like ritually opening the eyes [*kai guang dian yan*] of a *shenxiang*. It's good to believe but not to be superstitious." Other male temple officials told me that dotting the eyes was not only superstitious but dangerous—it might invite hungry ghosts or animal spirits into the toy.

Many women who identified as *xintu*, however, believed that what made an *ang-a* into a *fenshen* was not ritual but imagination (*xiangxiang*) and that therefore deity toys could become *fenshen*, regardless of whether any formal ritual had been performed. After my brief interview with the vice executive director quoted above, he assigned a female secretary to give me a tour of the temple. She took me to a basement room where several life-size statues of Mazu were on display. I noticed a group of older women who seemed to be praying to one of the statues. I asked the secretary if the eyes of the statue had been ritually opened. She said, "No. But some people believe that you don't need to do that. If you worship [a statue] for long enough, it will naturally become a real icon." Another female secretary at a different Mazu temple answered my question about whether the cute figurines they sold were *fenshen* affirmatively:

> Some people just need a photograph. If you worship that, then it will have that power, it will be a *shenxiang*. Mazu isn't just carved out of wood. However we imagine her, she will be inside that image. She has no limits. So if we imagine that it [the toy] holds Mazu's power and we worship it, we can do that.

For male temple officials, in other words, the process of animating the *ang-a* (bringing a god into the icon) belongs exclusively to a class of (male) ritual specialists and depends on physical manipulation of material objects. For female worshippers, animating the *ang-a* is more a process of psychic projection onto material objects and can be accomplished by any viewing subject.

Among the men I interviewed, class was also a factor in their beliefs about efficacy and cuteness. The men who claimed that deity toys were "just toys" were all middle-class. While the working-class men I met tended to insist on the division between true religion and superstition, they, like women, also emphasized the important function of worshippers' imagination in calling forth divine presence. For example, in 2011, I attended a lecture by You Zhongbin, the leader of the Beigang electronic San Taizi troupe. Most traditional temple processional troupes (*tin thau*) are composed of young men from rural and working-class backgrounds, many of whom are unemployed high school dropouts often described in the media as loafers and gangsters. One traditional *tin thau* performance involves young men marching in formation wearing large, heavy masks (*toa sian ang-a*) of the god San Taizi, represented as a dimpled child. Since around 2005, more and more troupes have been reinventing this performance tradition, accessorizing the masks with sunglasses, cartoon-style gloves, feather boas, and other props, and dancing energetically to hip-hop or electronic dance music rather than carrying out the traditional march steps to drums, gongs, and *suona* (a reed instrument). The electronic San Taizi troupes are often seen as a manifestation of *taike* sensibility (indeed, You said they took their moves from *taike* club dance) and can be seen as another part of the cutification-of-gods trend. At the end of his lecture, someone in the audience asked You a question about the propriety of representing San Taizi this way. He replied, "We have a saying: In the West, they say that God created people in his image. In Taiwan, people create the gods from our imaginations. Lots of gods aren't really like that, but that's how we imagine them."

Steven Sangren (2000) argues that the concept of *ling*, or efficacy, is a combination of Durkheimian objectification of social power and Marxist alienation of social labor. In particular, he writes that "the value produced in women's domestic activity is transformed in their participation in ritual to forms that constitute a 'surplus' made available for extraction by mainly male community leaders" (Sangren 2000:155). When women worship with the goal of reproducing the patriarchal family, they attribute the effects of their own social reproductive labor to a power outside themselves, the divine power of the gods. The number of worshippers and the amount of incense burned are seen as signs of the efficacy of specific *shenxiang* and temples. Thus, women's participation in ritual is crucial to building the power and reputation of specific *fenshen* and temples, a kind of power that is an important basis for the arena of local politics controlled by male community leaders. One could extend Sangren's argument here to say that given that the community leaders who run most temples are not only male heads of household but also successful businessmen, a similar transfer of lower-class (especially young) men's ritual labor into these men's political assets is also taking place.

Women's attitude toward deity toys challenges the idea that women are unconscious players in this process of alienation and expropriation. Sangren himself notes that Taiwanese worshippers acknowledge that the gods' power is dependent on their own continual practice (see also Wei-Ping Lin 2008; Hatfield 2010). The women I interviewed attributed the agency of deity toys—their ability to protect, comfort, and bring good fortune—to the gods

# CHAPTER 4

# *Ang-a* Globalization

Marketing the Pili International Multimedia Company's
Puppetry Overseas

In the previous chapters, I outlined a Taiwanese/Chinese *ang-a* mode of animation in which figurines are invested with personality and psychosocial agency, and I looked at how the *ang-a* mode of animation interacts with a Japanese manga/anime mode of animation within the sphere of religion. In this chapter, I examine how the *ang-a* mode of animation spreads out from Taiwan and interacts with other culturally specific modes of animation in the sphere of commercial entertainment. Specifically, I look at how globalization is imagined and practiced by the Pili International Multimedia Company and the fans of its puppetry videos. What does globalization look like when viewed through the lens of animation? How do the Pili Company and Pili fans negotiate between the *ang-a* mode of animation and the aesthetic systems and business models that have emerged in North American and Japanese animation industries?

In a now famous 1990 article, Joseph Nye argues that since the 1970s, within the field of international relations, power has become diffuse, due to several factors, including the growth of multinational corporations and the spread of new transportation and communication technologies. Within this new field, the hard power of military force has become more costly, and "soft power" has become more important. Nye writes, "If a state can make its power seem legitimate in the eyes of others, it will encounter less resistance to its wishes. If its culture and ideology are attractive, others will be more willing to follow.... [A] country that stands astride popular channels of communication has more opportunities to get its messages across and to affect the preferences of others" (1990:167, 169). Commercial cultural products, such as cinema and popular music, are an important resource of soft power.

This idea was taken up with great hopes by many national governments, who made policies encouraging the development of national creative industries. The idea of projecting soft power through cultural media has been particularly appealing in Japan, South Korea, and Taiwan (Kong et al. 2009). These are countries that are already relatively prosperous, with strong high-tech industries, but in terms of hard power, they are still dependent on American military protection. The idea of cultural appeal is perhaps particularly important in Taiwan, which is cut off from one of Nye's other resources for soft power, participation in international organizations.

The Pili International Multimedia Company is seen by many in Taiwan as a potential producer of national soft power. The company produces a type of animation that is unique to Taiwan, blending the traditional art of glove puppetry (*po-te-hi*) with cinematic video editing and CGI (computer-generated imagery), which they call "digital *wuxia* (swordsman) *po-te-hi*." The company is considered one of the most successful enterprises within Taiwan's cultural creative industries (*wenhua chuangyi chanye*); it has received many national industry awards, and its directors and staff frequently participate in (and organize) conferences with government bureaucrats, academics, and other industry leaders with themes such as "Developing from Subcontracting to Branding to E-Commerce Platform Design" and "One Source, Many Uses: Border-Crossing Creativity." Within creative industry discourse in Taiwan, the Pili Company serves as a synecdoche for contemporary Taiwanese culture as a whole, with a distinctive way of blending the local and the global, the traditional and the hypermodern. Many in Taiwan see the globalization of the Pili Company's market as a means of increasing the visibility and value of Taiwanese culture, particularly in mainland China, Japan, and North America. Pili puppetry has the potential to create emotional attachment to Taiwan in a way that technology corporations such as ASUS and Acer, which have much larger overseas markets, do not.

In this chapter, I want to look at how Pili is trying to expand its appeal beyond Taiwan from three angles. First, I will look at the practical strategies that the Pili Company has employed in order to develop markets in China, Japan, and North America. Second, I will look at how Pili's sphere of affective influence has grown through the work of fans. Finally, I will look at how the process of globalization is imagined within the Pili videos. Here I will try to answer the question of what the ideological "message" of Pili might be.

As I wrote in chapter 2, Pili puppetry is deeply rooted in what I call the *ang-a* mode of animation, in which the human qualities of personality and charisma are projected into human-made three-dimensional anthropomorphic figures. Here I will focus on the ways that the Pili Company's different globalizing projects have attempted to integrate aesthetic styles, narrative genres, and business models taken from the United States and Japan into the local *ang-a* mode of animation, with varying success. I argue that these projects have been least successful when puppetry is treated as nothing more than a technology that can be decontextualized from its aesthetic traditions and used to convey any narrative content. They have been most successful when *po-te-hi*'s roots in Chinese cultural history are emphasized and when overlaps between the *ang-a* mode of animation and Japanese modes of animation are emphasized.

## Background: The Development of the Pili Company in Taiwan

The Pili International Multimedia Company was founded by two brothers, Huang Qianghua and Huang Wenze (Chris and Vincent Huang).[1] Company publications, as well as academic research on the company, trace the origins of Pili's "tradition of innovation" to the brothers' grandfather Huang Haidai, a master puppeteer who received a National Award for the Arts in 2002 at the age of 102, confirming his status as a national treasure.

Huang Haidai was born in 1901 in rural Yunlin County. As a child he studied classical Chinese literature, and at the age of thirteen he joined his father's *po-te-hi* troupe, which performed in the martial style, accompanied with *bei guan/bak-kuan* music that featured drums and gongs. The plots were taken primarily from well-known Ming-dynasty novels in the military history, *wuxia* (swordsman), and mythological genres, such as *Romance of the Three Kingdoms* (*San guo yan yi*), *The Water Margin* (*Shui hu zhuan*), *The Seven Heroes and Five Gallants* (*Qi xia wu yi*), *Investiture of the Gods* (*Feng shen bang*), and *Journey to the West* (*Xi you ji*, also known in English as *The Monkey King*).

From 1936 to 1945, the Japanese colonial administration banned the performance of traditional Chinese theatrical genres on Taiwan, but some puppetry troupes, including Huang's, were allowed to perform patriotic plays in Japanese, with Western-style orchestral music and puppets in kimono or contemporary dress. The 1950s and 1960s saw a huge boom in the entertainment industry. Media that were introduced during the Japanese era but had been largely limited to urban elite centers, such as commercial theater and cinema, spread throughout the island and became available to the majority of the population. Taiwan's most popular entertainment genres, *koa-a-hi* (Taiwanese Opera) and *po-te-hi*, regained their dominance of commercial theater and were remediated into each new medium, including cinema, radio, and LP recording. Although the growth of the mass media in

Taiwan during this period opened up new possibilities for *po-te-hi*, it also brought new competition, primarily from popular culture genres imported from the United States and Japan. American GIs stationed in Taiwan during the Korean and Vietnam Wars brought with them American popular music, cinema, and comics, and Taiwan's military and economic dependence on the United States during this era opened the Taiwanese market to American distributors. Throughout the 1960s, Hollywood dominated the Taiwanese box office. Japanese popular culture, although officially banned by the ruling Chinese Nationalist Party, was smuggled in and remained popular with the local population who had been educated in Japanese.

To compete with these imports, Taiwanese puppeteers began to create new, hybrid forms of *po-te-hi*. The most popular of these was a style known as *kim-kong-hi*. *Kim-kong-hi* adapted narratives from *wuxia* novels and used a more vernacular form of the Holo language. Puppeteers began to incorporate more popular musical forms, including setting Holo lyrics to popular American and Japanese tunes. The most defining characteristic of *kim-kong-hi* was special stage effects, such as dry ice, flashing lights, and mechanical sets. Huang Haidai and his son Huang Junxiong were influential in developing this style.

The first Taiwanese television station began broadcasting in 1962. Although *po-te-hi* was televised in the 1960s, television *po-te-hi* did not really take off until March 1970, when Huang Junxiong produced his first series for the Taiwan Television Company, *Shi Yanwen, the Confucian Swordsman of Yunzhou* (Holo: *Hunchiu tai lu kiap—Su Iambun*; Mandarin: *Yunzhou da ru xia—Shi Yanwen*). Previously, televised *po-te-hi* had captured ratings around 70 percent, but Huang's serial achieved an unprecedented 97 percent (Pili International Multimedia Company 2000; Georgette Wang 1984:173).[2] Even though the Government Information Office restricted Holo-language programming between 1974 and 1989, the series kept going. Between 1984 and 1990, Huang Junxiong cooperated with his sons Vincent and Chris (Huang Wenze and Huang Qianghua). Under their influence the Shi Yanwen series gradually segued into the Pili series, and it switched to the China Television Service. In 1991 the Huangs left the television station and began producing directly to NTSC videotape. In 1994, Huang Junxiong handed over the troupe to his sons, who built their own studio and offices and established the Pili International Multimedia Company.

As in the 1950s, the arrival of new media technologies in the 1990s signaled both new possibilities and new sources of competition for *po-te-hi*. The 1990s saw the relative decline of the US entertainment industry and the rise of Japanese media globally, as well as the rapid introduction of digital media technology, such as the Internet. The Pili International Multimedia Company established itself in an environment dominated by Japanese television programs, manga, anime, and computer games, as well as Hollywood cinema and, in the twenty-first century, the rise of the Korean Wave of soap operas and cinema.

Chris and Vincent Huang have developed a style that continues and expands on their father's innovations. The Pili serials are known for their use of digital special effects and for the beauty and detail of their puppets, as well as for complex characterization. Carrying on the *kim-kong-hi* tradition, the Pili serials are a bricolage that includes pan-Chinese popular culture genres as well as images, music, and plots adapted from Japanese and American cinema, comics, and animation. Chris Huang often refers to the Pili style as "between traditional *po-te-hi* and anime."

Each series consists of thirty to sixty episodes, each one hour long. Between 1985 and 2018, the company produced more than seventy continuous series, with thousands of characters. The narratives are extremely complex, with several subplots woven into the main plot. Each series continues the story from the previous one, usually with an unresolved subplot taking center stage as the major dramatic conflict is resolved. Continuity is maintained by the presence of recurring characters and themes and by the practice of ending each episode and each series with a cliff-hanger.

The Pili Company has been using computers for all editing and special effects since around 1995. In 2000 the company released a feature film, *Legend of the Sacred Stone (Sheng shi chuan shuo)*, which marked a turning point in the development of the Pili style. The equipment purchased for the film was retained for use in the video serials, including digital video cameras and new CGI and editing software, and many of the technicians hired for its production stayed with the company. After the production of the film, the company switched from using VHS tapes to using DVDs for distributing episodes of its regular serials.

Structurally, the company mediates between industrial and postindustrial models. In some ways, it remains a family enterprise, like those that provided the base for Taiwan's "economic miracle" of the 1970s. The studio is located in the family's rural hometown, Huwei. Chris Huang is the company's CEO (*dongshizhang*) and the head of the script-writing group; Vincent Huang is the managing director (*zongjingli*) and does the voice recording. Chris' wife, Liu Lihui, is the company's marketing director, and both Chris' and Vincent's children have recently joined the company in various roles. The senior puppeteers and directors have been with the Huangs since the 1970s. Many of the junior artists grew up in Huwei and hung around the studio as children. The skills of puppeteering, video editing, costume and prop design, and script writing are passed on through an informal apprenticeship system. Mastering new technologies is also an internal process, outside of any formal education system. The video directors and postproduction crew learned to produce Pili's wide range of CGI effects by experimentation. But the Pili International Multimedia Company is hardly a mom-and-pop operation. It is a parent company with several subsidiaries and has hundreds of employees. Pili stocks have been traded internationally on the OTC (Over-the-Counter) market since 2014. They earned over US$20 million in 2016.[3]

From the 1990s through 2009, VHS tapes and then DVDs were released through video rental stores. Over 95 percent of the nearly two thousand video rental chains and family-run video rental stores in Taiwan had contracts with the Pili Company (Huang Neng-yang 2001; Pili International Multimedia Company 2002), and the Pili tapes and DVDs were the most reliable source of income for these outlets. In the mid-2000s, as more and more people watched films through cable television stations and the Internet, most of the video rental stores in Taiwan folded. The Pili Company negotiated a contract in 2009 to sell its weekly new episodes through the FamilyMart convenience store chain and then the 7–Eleven chain as well. Another channel of distribution is the Pili satellite television station, established in 1995, which rebroadcasts episodes from two or three older serials several times a day, as well as locally produced costume dramas and *Super Pili Club*, a show that previews upcoming episodes, holds contests for fans, and reports on Pili fan club events.

Pili's fan base comes primarily from the first generations to grow up with little or no memory of martial law, surrounded by a heterogeneous and transnational popular culture and immersed in digital technoculture, who are starting careers in the transforming economy. The range of their occupations reflects the shift toward service and information sectors (although, as with many media fandoms, there is a high number of writers, designers, and performers among the most active fans). The relationship between fans and the company is intimate, with the Pili Company workers regularly reading and participating in online fan discussions and the company hiring many of the most active fans to work in its production and marketing departments.

## The Pili Company's Overseas Marketing Projects

The Pili Company began its overseas marketing in the late 1990s, when its Taiwan audience was at its peak. Chris Huang has been quoted many times saying that he wants to make Pili "the Disney of Asia," and he told me in 2006 that its ultimate target was the US market. As he put it, "If you can get Americans to like it, that lets other countries know that this is something acceptable."

The Pili Company's first major attempt to reach audiences outside Taiwan was the film *Legend of the Sacred Stone*, production of which began in 1999. The Pili team knew that if they wanted to start a new fan base from scratch, the extreme complexity and length of Pili's ongoing serials would be a huge obstacle. According to Jill Huang,[4] Pili's overseas marketing director at the time, an agent who had worked for the art cinema director Hou Hsiao-hsien suggested that the best way for Pili to open overseas markets would be to first produce a feature film and show it at international festivals.

While *Legend of the Sacred Stone* was still in production, the company hired an American distribution agency and took clips to the Cannes Film Festival. Several European distributors showed interest, but none of them worked out. The Pili Company's agent for Asian distribution, however, was able to get contracts to dub and screen *Sacred Stone* in mainland China, Japan, and South Korea. The Pili Company also sold dubbing and broadcast rights for some of its older series to television stations in a few mainland Chinese cities and in Japan, although only a few episodes actually aired.

Later, the company hired a new agent for marketing outside Asia, who was based in Hong Kong, and through her also switched to a different distribution agent. The new agency, Distant Horizon, was based in South Africa but had an office in New York that specialized in marketing Asian action-genre films and television shows, primarily to an African American audience. After several years of trying to sell the rights to *Sacred Stone* in the United States, Distant Horizon suggested that Pili start again with a television serial instead. Pili negotiated a new contract, giving Distant Horizon the rights to its 2001 series *Battle for the Throne* (*Zheng wang ji*). Distant Horizon then contracted with the Animation Collective production team, who completely transformed the series, writing an entirely new English script, reediting the footage, and adding a new hip-hop theme song. In this version, called *Wulin Warriors*, the protagonists were a troupe of wisecracking teenagers, along the lines of the *Teenage Mutant Ninja Turtles* franchise.

In the 1970s, this strategy of "glocalization"—recasting an original action genre show to make it more American—had been a great success for the Japanese producers of *Jyu Renja*, which was remade into the extremely popular *Power Rangers* series (Allison 2006). *Wulin Warriors* was finally broadcast on the American Cartoon Network in 2006, but both North American and Taiwanese audiences who saw it were unimpressed.

Taiwanese audiences (who saw it only through tapes sent by relatives and friends in the United States) found the transformation of their complex, mature heroes into pizza-gobbling teens to be a kind of sacrilege. American fans of Japanese anime found the puppetry bizarre, especially since the new voice track did not sync with the characters' movements (the mute swordsman Ye Xiao Chai was transformed into the most talkative of the Wulin Warriors, but his mouth, of course, never moved). The Cartoon Network cancelled the show after only two episodes, due to insufficient ratings.

These early attempts at globalization were disappointing. Jill Huang attributed the lack of success in these first endeavors to several factors. First, the Pili workers were unfamiliar with the conventions of marketing in Europe and North America and thus asked too high a price at first. Second, there were cultural misunderstandings; most of the agents they tried to work with did not understand the plots of the series and automatically associated puppetry with children. But not being familiar with North American or European culture themselves, the Pili Company had to trust its agents' understanding of audience tastes. And finally, there were no lawyers in Taiwan who specialized in international entertainment law; the Pili legal bureau had trouble understanding contracts even though its staff could read English, since some terms mean different things in different countries.

During this period, the Pili Company also tried to market its videos and other products in East Asia, concentrating on mainland China. Chris Huang told me that the Chinese market was "naturally easy," because Taiwan and China share the same culture. The idea of "cultural proximity," as many scholars have noted, has been crucial to the success of Japanese and Korean idol dramas, fashion, and pop music throughout the region. The Japanese and Korean creative industries, through techniques such as using idol drama stars as spokespersons and using Japanese and Korean phrases in advertisements in Taiwan, tie their products to nation-branding projects that present Japan and Korea as sites of a more sophisticated modernity than that in other parts of Asia (Shu-ling Huang 2011). As Koichi Iwabuchi (2002) argues, young Taiwanese consumers find in these products an image of a distinctive East Asian modernity that feels more attractive and accessible than the modernity of the West.

When Chris Huang and the other Pili workers talk about the cultural proximity of Taiwan and China, they talk mostly about a shared history rather than a shared modernity. But they also believe that their blend of puppetry and CGI represents a kind of modernization of this shared history that is unique to Taiwan. Chris Huang put it to me this way in a 2006 interview:

*Po-te-hi* originally came from Zhangzhou and Quanzhou [regions in Fujian Province] and was then developed and enhanced in Taiwan. There are a lot of *po-te-hi* troupes on the mainland, but they are doing things from twenty, thirty years ago. . . . I believe where you came from isn't very important; it's how you continued to push forward after you arrived. If you don't push things forward, then they will quickly disappear. . . . Where you were born doesn't matter; what matters is how you were raised.

By 2010 the Pili Company had good reason to trust in the appeal of Pili to mainland Chinese audiences as both shared heritage and distinctive modernity. Pili had acquired a large fan base there without doing anything; fans throughout China were watching its productions avidly on pirated Internet videos, able to download episodes the same day they went on sale in Taiwan, and by 2010 Taiwanese fans were complaining that Chinese members were outnumbering local fans in the official fan club.

Nonetheless, some differences in business norms and political culture proved to be huge obstacles to the company's ability to open up a market in mainland China. According to Jill Huang, one difficulty was the amount of unchecked video piracy. Another obstacle was that Pili's videos had to pass through strict censors, who tended to reject them on the grounds that they were too violent. Yet another was that business in China was largely conducted through personal relationships (*guanxi*) rather than formal contracts. The Pili Company therefore needed to spend a lot of time and money on personal trips to China and hosting dinners. Finally, even if Pili representatives were able to build up personal relations with agents in the PRC, who in turn had built up personal relations with the necessary government officials, the process had to start all over again whenever there was a change in the dominant political faction at any level of government.

In 2010 the Pili Company sent an exhibit of its puppets and videos, along with Jill Huang and a cosplay troupe, to participate in the Hangzhou International Comics and Animation Expo. There, Jill met with the CEO of Fanfan Inc., a comics publisher and Internet content provider, who had been introduced by a Taiwanese friend. They agreed to collaborate on a project to produce a short video series, an *wuxia* version of the classical romance tale *Liang Shanbo and Zhu Yingtai*. They chose this tale because it is set in Hangzhou, and the city government was offering money for projects promoting the city's cultural heritage.

The Pili Company had primary artistic control for the series, titled *Butterfly Lovers* (*Xi hu die meng*), coming up with the plot outline, shooting the video, and voicing the dialogue in Mandarin. Fanfan provided research materials and some outdoor establishing shots. The script was passed back and forth between the two companies, with each one making adjustments. The original plan was for Fanfan to release the videos for streaming to subscribers of its Internet platform. But after a change in city government leadership, the videos wound up being released in Taiwan rather than China.

Meanwhile, Chris Huang had never abandoned the plan to make another movie after *Legend of the Sacred Stone*. However, after failing to sell the rights at international film festivals, he decided to abandon what he called "the art cinema route." Pili puppetry was an entertainment genre, after all, and what he wanted was a Disney-style hit, one that showcased what was special about Pili. What precisely the unique qualities of Pili puppetry were, however, was not something everyone in the company agreed on. For many, what was special about Pili that would capture the attention of a foreign audience was its style of animation, the combination of puppetry and CGI. For some of the script writers, Pili's complex characterizations and intricate *wuxia* plots were equally important, but these were also seen as barriers to overseas marketing. Chris Huang decided to make a film that combined puppetry and CGI and would have *wuxia* elements in its narrative but would be completely separate from the ongoing Pili serials, with all new characters and settings. Since he was using Disney as his model, he also wanted to target a family audience, which meant including viewers much younger than most Pili fans.

In 2012 the company began production on a new film, *The Arti: The Adventure Begins* (*Qi ren mima: Guluobu zhi mi*). The Pili Company had been experimenting with 3-D cinema technology for a while and had shown some short 3-D films featuring the main Pili series characters since 2011 at the Yilan County Cultural Center, but *The Arti* would be its first 3-D feature film. For this project, Chris Huang directed, Vincent Huang was the executive producer, and Chris Huang's son, Huang Liang-hsun, who had recently joined the company, was assigned to write the script. Under Vincent Huang's direction, a group of young voice actors were recruited to record the dialogue, which was primarily in Mandarin, with some characters speaking Holo. Huang Liang-hsun set up a new company, Bigger Picture Inc., to do the postproduction effects.

*The Arti* was finally released to theaters in Taiwan during the Chinese New Year holiday of 2015, advertised as "the world's first 3-D puppet movie." The film was also shown at international film festivals in Taipei, Seoul, Brussels, and Montreal. A DVD set was released with subtitles in English and Chinese.

Poster for *The Arti: The Adventure Begins*. Reprinted with permission of the Pili International Multimedia Company, Ltd.

Chris Huang had originally planned to make a film based on *Journey to the West*, a story with which he thought Western audiences would be somewhat familiar. But he and the team decided that there were already too many film and animation versions of this story on the market, especially in China. So instead Huang Liang-hsun opted to develop a new story. For inspiration he drew on the story of the Han-dynasty adventurer Zhang Qian, who recorded his travels along the Silk Road. He also drew on recent Hollywood and Hong Kong blockbusters, especially James Cameron's 3-D sci-fi film, *Avatar* (2009). The plot of *The Arti* involves a young brother and sister, Zhang Mo and Zhang Tan, who take a wooden robot named Arti-C designed by their father and go in search of the source of the robot's vitality, the Origin. On the way, they become embroiled in a plot by the prince of the city of Lou Lan to fuel his own robot army by stealing the Origin from the magical Lop tribe who guard it. Eventually Mo, Tan, and Arti-C join forces with the Lop to defeat the prince.

Although many Pili fans and Taiwanese families went to see it, *The Arti: The Adventure Begins* was not a huge success, either at home or abroad. Pili fans at home were disappointed in the disjointed and simplified script and disliked the break from the tradition of having one voice actor recording all the characters' dialogue in Holo. While reviewers overseas were impressed by the combination of skilled puppeteering and digital effects, almost all found the plot derivative. Many English-language reviewers noted the similarities with *Avatar*.

The Pili Company's most recent bid for an international market was a cooperation with a Japanese company. This project came about somewhat serendipitously. The famed Japanese script writer/novelist Urobuchi Gen was a special guest at the 2014 Taiwan International Comics and Animation Festival. While in Taipei, he visited a large exhibit of Pili puppets, "Pili Fantasy World of Puppet Art," and was captivated. He purchased some Pili DVDs and took them back to Japan and began to post on Twitter about them. Some people in the Pili Company saw a news article about Urobuchi's interest in Pili puppetry, and they began to think about proposing an international cooperation with Nitroplus, the game and anime character contents company for which Urobuchi works. Urobuchi was thinking the same thing. The companies contacted each other at almost the same time.

Originally, Pili asked Urobuchi to write the script for a sequel to *The Arti*. But Urobuchi thought it would be better to create his own characters and world with the Japanese audience in mind, and the Pili Company agreed. Together, Pili, Nitroplus, and the Good Smile Company, which models and produces character figurines, created a short video series (thirteen episodes of half an hour each), *Thunderbolt Fantasy—Sword Seekers* (in Mandarin, *Dongli jian youji*; hereafter, *Thunderbolt Fantasy*). Urobuchi wrote the script in Japanese, and the dialogue was then translated into Chinese by a team that included a member of the Bigger Picture postproduction group. Nitroplus character designers created graphic designs for the characters, and the Pili carvers and costume bureau made the puppets and sets based on those drawings, with some consultation from Urobuchi and the Good Smile Company. The puppets had the look of the puppets used in the Pili serials, with elaborate costumes based on ancient Chinese clothing with elements borrowed from Japanese and American fantasy films and video games. The one change made to attract Japanese manga/anime fans was that the eyes of the young female character were made larger and rounder than usual. Wang Jia-Shiang, one of the Pili Company's most experienced directors, then directed the video production, with Bigger Picture doing the postproduction work. Two separate voice tracks were made. The first track was recorded in Holo, with Vincent Huang's son, Huang Huei-fung, voicing all the male characters and a group of local female voice actors performing the various female roles. The second track was in Japanese, voiced by a group of well-known Japanese *seiyu* (voice actors). Since the puppeteers had worked listening to the Holo track, the Japanese script required many small adjustments so that the *seiyu* could make the Japanese dialogue match the puppets' movements, but the general sense of each line remained consistent between the two scripts.

Thunderbolt Fantasy is set in the imaginary country of Dongli, a fantastic version of ancient East Asia, with sets referencing both historical Chinese and Japanese architecture and material culture. The story centers around a gruff swordsman, Shang Bu Huan, who meets with a mysterious stranger, Lin Xue Ya.[5] Together they rescue Dan Fei, a young woman who is the guardian of a magical sword, part of which has been stolen by an evil king. Shang joins Lin, Dan Fei, and a group of strangers with various skills, including a heartless assassin, a master archer and his young, ambitious apprentice, and a spell-casting demoness. The group passes through several trials, finally retrieving the sword.

The series was released simultaneously in Japan and Taiwan in July 2016. In Japan, it was shown weekly on three television stations and was also released on several paid streaming services for a limited time. In Taiwan, the Pili Company released two episodes per week through the 7–Eleven and FamilyMart convenience store chains, along with the regular Pili series episodes. The series was also released on commercial streaming services in mainland China and the United States (bilibili and crunchyroll,

Poster for *Thunderbolt Fantasy—Sword Seekers*. Reproduced with permission of the Pili International Multimedia Company, Ltd., Nitroplus Company, Ltd., and Good Smile Company, Inc.

respectively). Once all thirteen episodes had been released, boxed sets of DVDs went on sale, which in Taiwan included postcards, a booklet of artists' original character sketches, and a cute vinyl figurine of one of the main protagonists.

*Thunderbolt Fantasy* was successful in a way that none of Pili's previous products aimed at overseas markets had been. It was popular with both Pili fans and fans of Japanese anime and games around the world, and it rapidly developed its own international fandom. In the next section, I will compare *The Arti* and *Thunderbolt Fantasy* in terms of the visions of globalization they project and how they represent, explicitly and implicitly, the place of animation within the process of globalization. I will look at the content, in terms of how each work blends regionalized and globalized narrative genres, character types, and technologies. But equally important are the discourses and practices of both producers and consumers. I argue that *The Arti* largely failed to gain an international audience not only because its script was seen as unoriginal and sloppy but also because it drew on a specifically American vision of the place of animation in projecting cultural appeal. *Thunderbolt Fantasy*, on the other hand, succeeded because of its self-placement within an aesthetic system and a fandom structure that was already international. *Thunderbolt Fantasy* worked within the overlap of Chinese and Japanese modes of animation, mobilizing what Ian Condry (2013) calls the "dark energy" of international Japanese anime fandom. At the same time, by working largely within the aesthetic system of the Pili serials, *Thunderbolt Fantasy* was able to expand the appeal of a vision of technological progress as rooted in the Chinese past.

## Wuxia Worlding

The Pili series narratives fall within a fantasy variant of the *wuxia* genre, tales of wandering swordsmen, and both *The Arti* and *Thunderbolt Fantasy* draw on this genre. *Wuxia* is extremely well suited to the construction and projection of fantasies of national culture and national progress because it thematizes Chinese history in a number of ways. First, one of the defining characteristics of the genre is that the stories are always set in the Chinese imperial past, no matter how fantastical that setting may be in practice. Second, *wuxia* is seen as a "traditional" genre. One of the seminal histories of *wuxia*, Chen Pingyuan's *Qiangu wenren xiake meng* (1995), traces the genre back to the Eastern Han dynasty (25–220 CE). Chen's book is required reading for all members of the script group, and this history is familiar not only to academics and professional writers but, in a general way, to most fans as well.

There is also a long tradition of reading *wuxia* narratives as national allegories, in which authors project their utopian or dystopian visions of the contemporary state of China (or Taiwan or Hong Kong) onto *wulin* (literally, martial forest), the marginal world outside the imperium in which swordsmen wander. Several Taiwanese scholars (who are also self-professed fans) argue that the difference between Huang Junxiong's *Shi Yanwen* series of the 1970s and the Pili series as it developed in the 1990s reflects Taiwan's changing political situation. They note that the moral world of the *Shi Yanwen* series was starkly black and white: heroes always acted heroically, and villains were always purely evil. In the Pili serials, however, the distinction between heroes and villains is blurred. *Wulin* has become an arena of stratagems, and heroes and villains are no longer distinguished by their modus operandi.

The political structure of the Pili world has also transformed. As Chen Longting (1991:179) notes, as the Pili series took over from the *Shi Yanwen* series in the 1990s, the focus moved from individual heroes and villains to organizations. The central power of the Ming court completely disappeared. *Wulin* became the entire world of the Pili serials, and *wulin*'s interlinked networks of alliances became increasingly complex. Some interpret these changes in the fictional world in terms of Taiwan's move from the "order" of a Cold War single-party state to the "chaos" of democratization (e.g., Chen Longting 1991; Lai 2001).

Pili's *wulin* is also, obviously, allegorical of more than just the state of domestic politics; it is also a metaphor for the state of geopolitics, a vision of how international relations work in the age of diffuse power. Every few seasons within the ongoing Pili series, a new world with its own set of characters is added to the Pili universe. These worlds have varying forms of government—some are hereditary kingdoms, some are ruled by councils of elders, some are military meritocracies. And the leaders and factions within these worlds are also engaged in networks of shifting alliances, struggling for magical power both internally and across geographical (or dimensional) borders.

Within the *wuxia* genre, characters are dispositions of traits and represent different moral stances toward power. As I mentioned in chapter 2, these characters are read within an analogical worldview, meaning that these dispositions are seen as having real-world analogues. Thus, fans can look directly to Pili characters as role models for how individuals, corporations, and nations may succeed within the contemporary world. One fan, in a submission to an essay contest on the topic "My Favorite Puppet Character," made the connection between the change in heroes and the changing ~~~~~~~~al political economy explicit, constructing a fantasy of Taiwanese pow~~~~~ precarious global (dis)order:

> Huang Qianghua [Chris Huang], who created the character Su Huanzhen,[6] said this about him: "Su Huanzhen's most special characteristic is that he really understands that he must adapt to the changing world. That is to say, he's very smart, very diplomatic, clever to the point of being a bit cunning." . . . Right! It's just that "cunning" that drives me wild! From him I've learned that in this modern world, where the fashions change a thousand times in the blink of an eye, if you maintain the "Shi Yanwen spirit"—perpetually forbearing and forgiving—then on the road of life you will always just stagger along in despair. But when I observed Su Huanzhen's management philosophy, his conciliatory and adaptable lead-ership style, it gave me a new way of thinking about things. It seems that sometimes, if you want to adapt to changing situations, you have to be a bit "clever" and "ingenious." Being conciliatory in managing things is more suitable for modern life. . . . For several thousand years, Chinese people have been influenced by Confucianism. . . . "The inarticulate and silent man" is the real gentleman; this stereotype that "a man with a flu-ent tongue has a bad heart" has prevented our country from having good foreign relations. Each time I see our country besieged in the dangerous world of international politics, I can't help but imagine what would hap-pen if a Su Huanzhen appeared—then who'd be afraid of crossing the border? (He 1997:33–35)

As this quote suggests, Pili fans are captivated by the fantasy that a Chinese hero in the classical mode, "master of both the martial and literary arts," can adapt to become a master of the art of networking as well. Because of his ability to always outthink his enemies, Su Huanzhen is often com-pared to both Zhuge Liang and Cao Cao, the opposing military strategists of *Romance of the Three Kingdoms.* Thus, the Pili worldview dispenses with the Cold War tradition of moral Manichaeism, digging further back in Chinese history for a different, equally Chinese ethics that resonates with the con-temporary global field of dispersed power.

The *wuxia* genre is seen by Pili producers and fans as uniquely Chinese, although they see parallels within the popular Japanese samurai genre. A subculture of Hong Kong kung fu and *wuxia* cinema fans exists in North America, Europe, and the Antipodes, and Ang Lee's 2000 film,

*Crouching Tiger, Hidden Dragon* and the increasing availability of Japanese manga and anime have made *wuxia* better known in these regions than in the twentieth century. Though it was aware of this, the Pili Company still claimed that for a general Western audience, the genre would need to be modified to make it more acceptable. Huang Liang-hsun (2018) said that in writing the script for *The Arti*, he was trying to create a new genre for Taiwan, not traditional *wuxia* but an "Oriental fantasy adventure movie."

Both *The Arti* and *Thunderbolt Fantasy* appear at first to follow the George Lucas strategy of basing their narratives on a supposedly universal myth structure. Both are quest narratives, in which a hero gathers a group of companions and travels to a distant place in order to obtain a magical object. But both of these narratives transform into something else as they progress.

In *The Arti* the quest ends in the magical village of the Lop tribe. The *wuxia* tradition contains many tales of rebellions by minority peoples on the frontiers of China, and the romanticization of indigenous peoples is certainly evident in Taiwan's cinema, literature, and tourism publicity. But the Lop are clearly taken from a Western (post)colonialist imaginary. Like the Na'vi in *Avatar* or the natives in countless stories by settlers, hippies, and sometimes indigenous activists themselves, they are "noble savages" who live in harmony with nature and are forced to defend themselves against a militarized state intent on stealing their natural resources. While the cute CGI bugs that the Lop ride cite Miyazaki Hayao's *Nausicaä* and the overall ecological message here may be seen as just as Japanese as it is American, the magical power of the Origin represents a New Age cosmology very different from the Shinto animist world of nature spirits underlying Miyazaki's oeuvre.

The plot of *Thunderbolt Fantasy* also transforms from a setup as a quest narrative, but unlike *The Arti*, here the quest transforms into a classic *wuxia* tale of political intrigue, as Lin Xue Ya manipulates both the sword-stealing villain and the members of his gathered troupe of heroes, and old enmities are revealed. When Urobuchi began the plot outline for *Thunderbolt Fantasy*, he was already quite familiar with the *wuxia* genre. He had previously designed a *wuxia* online game and had watched several episodes in the Pili serial. Perhaps more importantly, he is known for a dark aesthetic that is quite compatible with Pili. Both Urobuchi and Pili are famous for killing off beloved protagonists, and one of Urobuchi's best-known anime series, *Puella Magi Madoka Magica*, inserts themes of mortality and the high price of wielding power into the usually light magical-girl genre. When Urobuchi designed the plot for *Thunderbolt Fantasy*, he actually accomplished what some scriptwriters in the Pili Company had been suggesting for years as a strategy for reaching a broader overseas market—to construct a typical Pili *wuxia* plot, but simplified by leaving out all the side plots.

A Jie, a Taiwanese YouTuber who produces popular video reviews of anime, manga, and games, says in his review of *Thunderbolt Fantasy*:

> If you've seen Urobuchi Gen's works, you'll really feel that *Thunderbolt Fantasy* is different. In general, Urobuchi's works are heavy on plot and light on characters. The characters he creates usually aren't very charming, but the plotting is really refined. But this time, in order to make the product more popular, he chose to go light on the plot and heavy on the characters . . . to make the characters the selling point. (A Jie 2016)

Azuma Hiroki (2009) has argued that the focus of Japanese manga/anime/game fandom has evolved over the past decades from plots to characters. What A Jie notices is that Urobuchi is honing in on an area of overlap between Japanese manga/anime fandom and Chinese *wuxia* fandom. As I argued in chapter 2, Azuma's theory of characters as amalgamations of *moe* elements and the Chinese analogical conception of characters differ, and in *Thunderbolt Fantasy* it is the analogical mode of character construction that seems to prevail.

Unlike *The Arti*, in which all the characters are either moral heroes or villains, *Thunderbolt Fantasy* is aimed at a more mature audience, and the characters have complex motivations and embody different stances toward power and the relationship between means and ends. Lin Xue Ya, for instance, has a long conversation with Shang Bu Huan in which he outlines his philosophy of life and claims that his main goal and pleasure lie in humiliating the powerful and arrogant, while Shang Bu Huan reveals at the end his goal of ending the arms race. Thus, while *The Arti* feels more contemporary in its technology, with its more intensive use of CGI, *Thunderbolt Fantasy* feels more contemporary in its themes and character construction.

Although the more Manichaean world of *The Arti* (like *Shi Yanwen*) may encourage identification with the leading characters, the diverse moral stances of the characters in the Pili series and *Thunderbolt Fantasy* encourage a more Brechtian position in which viewers stand outside of the world—that is, in the external position of a potential animator. This does not mean that fans do not identify with specific characters in the Pili series or *Thunderbolt Fantasy*—they most certainly do, as the quote from the contest winner above shows. Rather, it means that this identification necessarily comes *after* occupying a comparative point of view vis-à-vis the characters' ideologies.

In terms of their broader settings, both works create diverse geographies, with the protagonists travelling between clearly distinct sites and realms. But the world of *Thunderbolt Fantasy* is in some ways more open than that of *The Arti*. The sites in *The Arti* are more realistic, in that the sets are far more elaborate and detailed and in that both the Han-dynasty capital Chang An, where the story begins, and the Silk Road kingdom of Lou Lan, in today's Xinjiang Province, where it ends, are described in historical and archeological records. Only the underground country of the Lop is imaginary.[7] The relationships among the three realms is quite straightforward—Lou Lan and the Lop are enemies; the Han and Lou Lan are friends.[8]

The geography of *Thunderbolt Fantasy*, in contrast, while still "Chinese" in some sense, is entirely imaginary. The settings are more generic (an abandoned temple, a mountain fortress, a river, etc.) and less elaborately designed than those of *The Arti*. More importantly, the relationships among the realms within the universe of *Thunderbolt Fantasy* are more complicated and mysterious than those in *The Arti*. The country of Dongli, where the action takes place, and Xiyou, where Shang Bu Huan comes from, are now divided by an impassable desert. But they apparently were once a single country and were divided two centuries earlier by civil war. This is all we hear, leaving unanswered such questions as what caused the war and what created the desert. There are equally oblique hints of past conflicts between the demons and the humans, and between several of the characters and Lin Xue Ya, as well as the promise of new sites to be explored by Shang Bu Huan and Lin Xue Ya as they set off together at the end of the series. Thus, Urobuchi deliberately leaves spaces for future worlding, not only in possible future sequel and prequel series produced by Pili and Nitroplus but also by fans.

## Expanding Markets versus Expanding Fandoms

The expansion of a fan base and the expansion of a market, while often overlapping, are not necessarily the same thing, as the Pili Company found out to its dismay in mainland China. The goal of expanding a market is profit; the goal of expanding a fandom is to increase what we might call the affective influence of characters and worlds. Different production models construct different relationships between markets and fandoms.

When the Pili Company produced *The Arti*, it drew on an older Disney marketing model. This model of blockbuster movies targeting the widest audience possible often works well to increase consumption. The Pili Company, like Disney and other American studios, licensed the main *Arti* character images, and tie-in products included toys, T-shirts, and stationery featuring these images. These products allow for a kind of limited interaction between fans and characters, bringing the characters into the everyday life of fans (Steinberg 2012).

This model, however, tends to discourage what Henry Jenkins (1992) calls participatory fandom. This is not only because the Disney Corporation is notorious for its zealous prosecution of what it sees as violations of its intellectual property but also because, as I've noted, the Manichaean moral worlds created in Disney-style films targeting children tend not to encourage an animatorly point of view.

On the other hand, the media-mix business model of Japanese manga/anime franchises, in which *Thunderbolt Fantasy* is situated, constructs a symbiosis between studios and fandoms. The Japanese media-mix franchise is based, not simply on the proliferation of character images across multiple communications and material media, but on what Jenkins (2006) calls transmedia storytelling, with variations on the story and alternative or tangential stories being told in different platforms. Thus, aside from the videos, Nitroplus released two Japanese manga versions of the story—one serialized in the *Weekly Morning* magazine starting July 21, 2016, and another told from the perspective of Dan Fei, serialized in *Champion Cross* magazine starting September 7, 2016—and a light novel has also been published.[9] A transitional feature film was produced between the first and second video series and shown in cinemas in Taiwan and Japan in December 2017, which provides backstory for two minor characters and introduces a character from the Pili series into the *Thunderbolt Fantasy* world.

Japanese animation studios and fandoms are interdependent. As Ian Condry argues, the "feedback loops" between fans and official producers are critical to the process of globalizing Japanese manga/anime markets (Condry 2013, chap. 6). Japanese studios tend to turn a blind eye to the production of original stories and art featuring their characters, even when a large percentage of the *dōjinshi* (amateur original manga/novels/art featuring commercial animated characters) on sale at Tokyo's annual Comiket market are pornographic. The Pili Company has likewise refrained from taking any legal actions against fan-produced art, only moving to stop carvers and vendors from selling unlicensed copies of the puppets. Japanese studios rely on fandoms to train their future employees, and, like many manga and anime production companies, the Pili Company hires many of its scriptwriters based on fan fiction they have written. Many of its other workers also started as fans.

Since both the Pili serials and Urobuchi Gen's anime are popular among Taiwanese *tongren* (creators of fan art and fiction), it is not surprising that fans started contributing to the arena of transmedia storytelling with original stories and art about the main *Thunderbolt Fantasy* characters even before the last episodes were released. In retaining Pili's style of *wuxia* narrative, *Thunderbolt Fantasy* incited fan imagination by providing plenty of *mengdian* (*moe* points or *moe* sparks), especially for *fujōshi/funü*—women who create fan fiction and art in which the male characters are placed in romantic and/or sexual relations with each other. As with the Pili series, the cast of *Thunderbolt Fantasy* is mostly male, and the plot focuses largely on the relationships—friends, enemies, teachers, students—between these male characters. *Thunderbolt Fantasy* even provides what *funü* call a *guan pei*, or official pairing, in Shang Bu Huan and Lin Xue Ya, whose relationship is particularly multilayered and evolving. The amateur fiction and manga produced by Taiwanese *funü* fans include crossover stories in which protagonists from *Thunderbolt Fantasy* enter the Pili series' *wulin*.

*Thunderbolt Fantasy* thus operates in the folk cultural overlap between the *ang-a* mode of animation and the Japanese manga/anime mode, an overlap in which, as I noted in chapter 2, both characters and their worlds are always transforming, and the evolution of characters and worlds is a collective process.

## Representing Magical Power and the Message of Taiwanese Soft Power

Now let us turn to the question of how *The Arti* and *Thunderbolt Fantasy* attempt to project Taiwanese soft power. That is, what are the cultural values and ideologies they project, and how do they do that? Popular culture and consumer products do not project these values and ideologies directly; their soft power effect is emotional rather than intellectual. As Richard Dyer has noted, "[Entertainment] presents, head-on, as it were, what utopia would feel like rather than how it would be organized. It thus works at the level of sensibility, by which I mean an affective code that is characteristic of, and largely specific to, a given mode of cultural production" (1992:18). And as Dyer (1986) also shows in his work on the "star image," the feel of popular culture comes as much, if not more, from discourses surrounding entertainment products as from the products themselves. There is nothing (or not much) in the material qualities of denim trousers that makes them embody, for people around the world, an American ideal of "freedom." That association comes largely from advertising and other pop culture images of cowboys, rock stars, and hipsters wearing jeans and engaging in adventurous, self-expressive, pleasurable activities. Thus, in examining the utopian visions expressed in *The Arti* and *Thunderbolt Fantasy*, we need to look at the video texts but also beyond them to the discourse surrounding them, such as publicity materials, behind-the-scenes documentaries, and fan gossip.

I will argue here that, with Pili, the message is the magic, and the magic is the medium. Soft power is (potentially) projected by Pili through the representation of hard power within its fantasy world—in the specific ways that, within the complex of video texts and surrounding discourses, magical power is tied to puppetry on the one hand and to digital technology on the other.

## Techno-Historiographies: Magical Power in *The Arti* and *Thunderbolt Fantasy*

The connection between magic and technology has a long history within the *wuxia* genre that dates back to the early Chinese cinema. After the technology of cinema was introduced to China in 1896, the genre of fantasy *wuxia* (*shen guai*, or "gods and curiosities" *wuxia*) was crucial to the development of the new industry. Zhang Zhen (2001:44) has noted that the *shen guai wuxia* genre constituted about 60 percent of all films produced in Shanghai between 1928 and 1932.

In a cogent analysis of why this genre was so dominant at this time of political and social upheaval in industrializing Shanghai, Zhang writes, "It is through the innovative play between science and magic, film technology and folklore, avant-garde aesthetics and popular tastes, that the martial arts film came to embody the multiple 'faces' of modernity" (2001:51). Zhang argues, for instance, that the jump cuts from galloping horses to airplanes or motorcycles in the early martial arts films may be read as a "particular procedure of *réfonte* or recasting" that gives the sensation of a "'natural' and delightful crossing of contiguous realms of experience," for "the airplane and the horse are not necessarily antithetical icons for different temporalities and consciousness" (2001:49). To put this another way, the sudden cut from horse to airplane is a multileveled metaphor. It not only represents a historically experienced "leap" from traditional to industrial technologies but visually produces the ecstatic sensation of speed and flight that makes both the knight-errant and the pilot objects of fantasy identification, highlighting a continuity in the desires driving technological change.

The *shen guai wuxia* films of the early Shanghai cinema are part of a tradition on which Pili draws, and the Pili style exhibits many of the same fantasies and techniques. Yet the magic of the Pili world is also quite specific to the digital age, and the play between genres, techniques, and media here condense sensual experiences that include and exceed those of the Shanghai modern. All of Pili's productions are permeated not only with fantasies of flight and strength but also with fantasies of artificial life and intelligence, of travel between real and virtual spaces, and of mastery of databases.

This historiography is explicit in the discourse of the Pili production staff and of Taiwanese historians of *po-te-hi*. Many argue that Pili's use of special effects, including CGI, is just a continuation of a supernatural fantasy genre tradition that can be traced back to the classical Ming-dynasty novel *Journey to the West* and was developed within Taiwanese *po-te-hi* by Huang Haidai (e.g., Chen Longting 2007). When I asked members of the Pili script group, directors, and postproduction staff in the early 2000s how digital technology affected the Pili style, all of them insisted that digital animation was simply a continuation of the *kim-kong-hi* style, that they used digital animation primarily to enhance effects that had been done mechanically in stage *po-te-hi*. One scriptwriter gave me an example: In stage *kim-kong-hi*, mysterious new characters might first appear merely as voiceovers and flashing lights, before revealing their "true" (puppet) form; now, suspense about new characters may be created by having them represented for the first episodes by a computer-generated floating medallion or a wave of colored bubbles.

Members of the production team also insisted that digital animation must remain in the service of puppetry—they eschewed techniques that make the puppets seem "too real," thus erasing the special "feel" of *po-te-hi*, although they disagreed on which specific techniques do so. *The Arti* and *Thunderbolt Fantasy* represent different choices in terms of how puppetry and digital technology are blended.

The publicity around *The Arti* claimed that it was "the first 3-D puppetry movie" and referred to it as *ou dongman*, or "puppet anime/manga." The behind-the-scenes videos that were produced (only in Chinese) emphasized how the use of the latest digital technology was modernizing *po-te-hi*. But many Pili fans saw the 3-D cinematography and the extensive use of CGI in the film as overwhelming the essence of Pili, the artistry of the puppetry.

Urobuchi Gen convinced Pili to go in the opposite direction with *Thunderbolt Fantasy*, since it was the puppetry that attracted him in the first place, and his goal was to introduce *po-te-hi* to Japan. In an interview with Taiwanese video blogger A Jie, Urobuchi says that Pili's puppetry seemed like "a kind of magic" to him, adding, "Because of the capabilities of CG[I], different types of entertainment video products have opened up many different possibilities. But I think that without even realizing it, we've forgotten about 'impossibility.'" What I think Urobuchi means here is that puppetry represents a historical trajectory different from the mainstream trend in animation, one that leans toward alienation as much as immersion, that encourages a more animatorly point of view.

*The Arti* seems to make the connection between magic and puppetry very directly, in that the source of power, the Origin, has the effect of literally bringing wooden figures to life. We might expect this self-reflexive highlighting of the magic of animation to appeal broadly, in a way similar to Pixar's *Toy Story* movies. There are a couple of reasons I think the film fails to project this vision of power as animation.

The first is that the animating power of the Origin is natural—that is, it is not human-made, and its effects are biological. The Origin can bring anything to life—not just Arti-C and the prince of Lou Lan's robot army but also dead bodies and plants. The Origin enlivens material things, but it does not give them souls or personalities, the critical aspects of humanity that are projected in the *ang-a* mode of animation. Arti-C does seem to have some things in common with the ideal-typical *ang-a* (see chapter 2). He has a personality, expressed primarily through eyebrow movements since he is mute, and he is incorporated into the Zhang family. Arti-C is human-made, and Zhang Mo has a wristband that can control Arti-C's movements. But his artifact-ness is ambiguous. Mo's wristband is used only during some fight scenes; most of the time, Arti-C acts completely autonomously. Aside from logical inconsistency, this renders Arti-C incoherent in terms of his mode of animation; he is simultaneously a little bit like a Taiwanese deity statue, a little bit like a robot, and mostly something like a pet.

The second reason I think *The Arti* fails to project Taiwanese soft power in its representation of magic as animation is that this magical animating power is explicitly disassociated from Chinese culture. One could, potentially, read the Origin as a displaced representation of the Chinese concept of *qi*, the energy/life force that flows through the natural world. However, the Origin is the cultural property of the Lop, who are exotic to the Han Chinese. The goddess of the Lop, Fair, who controls the Origin, is blonde, and the ritual she performs is nothing like any folk Daoist, Buddhist, or even Shinto ritual but very much like the fake-indigenous ritual of the Na'vi in Cameron's *Avatar*.[10] It is also perhaps significant that Arti-C's name in Mandarin is Ah Xi, or "Westie."

By contrast, in *Thunderbolt Fantasy*, a wide variety of types of magical power are represented. Some of these are quite common in Pili's regular series; characters shoot beams of light from their hands and swords, and they make symbols appear in the air with gestures. What is interesting here is that some of the most important magical skills are not only represented through the technologies of puppetry and digital technology but also represented as having effects that replicate the affordances of puppetry and digital technology. And unlike in *The Arti*, this reflexivity highlights technologies related to the Taiwanese *ang-a* mode of animation. Let me give a few examples.

There are two instances in which magical power endows objects with life in the sense of autonomous motion. More accurately, they are instances of de-animation or reverse animation, where life/motion is taken away. The first is when the demoness Xing Hai stops an army of zombies. She does this by transforming them into the ordinary dead, by singing to them. The voice, as I will discuss more in the next chapter, plays a central role in both the art of *po-te-hi* and in fandom. What is also interesting here is that Xing Hai needs to adjust the pitch of her song according to when the zombies originally died, because the spell works by reaching their memories. In other words, in order to control the zombies' biological lives, she must control their souls. In the Valley of the Doll (*ang-a kou* in the Holo soundtrack), the company is attacked by a stone giant. Shang Bu Huan deactivates it by stabbing a paper charm (*fu*) located inside it. Remember that in Taiwanese folk religion such charms are one of the objects placed inside deity statues to bring the god inside them.[11]

The magical powers of the two main protagonists are more parallel to the powers of new media than to those of folk animation. Lin Xue Ya is an illusionist; he blows smoke from his pipe to make people confuse friends for enemies. He also has a magic hood that transforms Shang Bu Huan's face into his own. While disguise is a common plot feature in Chinese opera and puppetry, masking and anonymity are also salient and much-discussed features of online sociality, particularly in Japan (Nozawa 2012). Shang Bu Huan's magic is revealed in the final episode, when he faces the demon god Yao Tu Li. The puppet of Yao Tu Li draws clearly on the monster design style of Guillermo del Toro, the director of the *Hellboy* movies (based on an American comic book series) and *Pacific Rim*, which draws on the Japanese *mecha* (human-piloted robot) manga/anime genre. The dialogue is worth quoting here:

YAO TU LI: Bow down, pitiful rodent! The only hope of your kind, the Tian Xing Jian sword, is lost!

SHANG BU HUAN: . . . Swords are nothing more than tools. . . . Whether [a sword] cuts something or protects someone just depends on who uses it.

YAO TU LI: You creatures, with lives shorter than an insect's! What could you hope to accomplish with your feeble limbs?

SHANG BU HUAN: Well, let's see. With two arms and ten fingers, we can make use of tools. And the good thing about tools is that you can always get a replacement.

Shang Bu Huan then makes gestures that create a small whirlwind around him, and a computer-generated Chinese scroll appears, on which are ink brush drawings of thirty-six magical swords that he has collected. He selects one, which becomes three-dimensional in his hand, and uses it to slay Yao Tu Li.

Shang Bu Huan is talking about swords here, but we could read this scene as an allegory about animation itself. We might see the del Toro–esque Yao Tu Li as a citation of the best of what the "possibilities" of the mainstream trend of immersive animation opens up. Shang Bu Huan responds with the magic of the archive, a very different affordance of digital technology. Lev Manovich (2001) argues that one of the main things that makes digital media different from older media is the "principle of transposition," digital technology's ability to render analog media into mathematical code and, from there, into other media forms—for instance, to render audio recordings as visual images (e.g., radar and sonogram), to turn text into 3-D animation, and so forth. Shang Bu Huan's magic thus operates at a level that is meta to all the other characters, for he controls not just one medium but the archive of animation tools and could potentially store, manipulate, and transpose all of them.

The rapid and startling transformation of puppets into digital images, of two-dimensional images into three-dimensional ones, and the juxtaposition of old and new media in the same frame is a hallmark of the ongoing Pili series, as is the representation of magic through and as the animating power of digital technology (Silvio 2007). A similar type of reflexivity and the representation of magical power in terms of the archival function of animation media is also characteristic of Urobuchi Gen's work. For example, in *Puella Magi Madoka Magica*, the magical illusions of the witches take the form of undulating cinema reels and floating puppets. Thus, another overlap between the signature styles of Pili and Nitroplus is that both create self-reflexive fantasy spaces in which digital technology's capacity to absorb the functions of previous technologies becomes world-making power, and identification with this power is a major attraction for fans.

*Thunderbolt Fantasy* succeeded where *The Arti* did not primarily because of the higher quality of the script and the use of a more established regional marketing model. But I think it also succeeded because in keeping the style of media reflexivity shared by Pili and Urobuchi, it captured the message of Pili in a more compelling way. Representing the magic of animation as a natural force does not imply any history; it cannot be traced backward or forward in time. Representing magical power as a set of tools, as an archive of technologies, opens up possibilities for a multitude of both cultural historiographies and narratives of future transformation.

## Getting the Message: International Reactions to *Thunderbolt Fantasy*

*Thunderbolt Fantasy* appealed to Taiwanese who were already fans of digital *wuxia po-te-hi*. Pili fans tended to see it as a Pili product and to compare it with the ongoing Pili series. Some fans felt that the quality of the regular Pili scripts had declined over the past few years, since a number of core members of the script group from the early 2000s had left. They appreciated *Thunderbolt Fantasy* for the quality of Urobuchi's writing, and some said it reminded them of their favorite Pili scripts, although some also felt that the quality of the puppeteering and voicing by relatively new artists was not as good as that of the Pili series.

*Thunderbolt Fantasy* also succeeded to a remarkable degree in globalizing the fandom of digital *wuxia po-te-hi*. The series proved popular among fans of Japanese anime around the world who had never seen *po-te-hi* before, and some of these went on to look for other Pili videos. Aside from the available Chinese- and English-subtitled versions, fansubs (subtitled versions made by fans) have been made in many languages, including Vietnamese, Bahasa Indonesia, Spanish, Portuguese, Italian, French, German, Polish, and Czech.

Anime fans tended to view *Thunderbolt Fantasy* from the opposite angle to that of Pili fans, seeing it not as a Pili work with a new scriptwriter but as an Urobuchi Gen work in a new medium. Reviews in both English and Chinese by anime fans often started with an admission that the reviewer was not used to, or was even antipathetic toward, the use of puppets or "dolls" and questioned why such a series would be presented on forums dedicated to anime and manga. However, while many anime fans simply declined to watch a puppetry program, those who did tended to change their minds. The average rating for reviews on the American crunchyroll website was 4.6 out of 5.

A Jie, the Taiwanese YouTube reviewer cited earlier, began his review in a way typical of those anime fans who were won over in both Taiwan and North America:

> I really like Urobuchi Gen's work, but *po-te-hi*, mmm . . . I don't really understand it. I feel like it's just this old, out-of-date thing and never had much interest in it. But since I watched *My Little Pony*, I no longer have prejudices against any kind of artwork. Still, with *Thunderbolt Fantasy* I still felt a little bit like, *po-te-hi*? But it turns out . . . Wow! WOW! (A Jie 2016)

What I find interesting in these fan reviews is that the presence of *po-te-hi* puppets calls up a cascade of associations with other nostalgic genres or works of animation. For A Jie and other Taiwanese fans of Japanese anime, *po-te-hi* is a culturally overfamiliar genre, but it can also call up associations with American children's cartoons. For most of the English-language fan reviewers, *po-te-hi* is culturally unfamiliar, but it brings to mind culturally intimate puppetry genres, from Jim Henson's Muppets to Gerry Anderson's Thunderbirds to Punch and Judy.

I think that one of the main appeals of Pili's soft power message lies in the way that its reflexivity creates a direct link between the hyper-contemporary or futuristic and the folkloric past. By positing a set of historically grounded Chinese aesthetics as the driving engine behind digital animation, Pili's implicit historiography makes an end run around the modern and its realisms, both psychological and material. *Thunderbolt Fantasy* thus has more in common with the work of auteur Japanese animators such as Oshii Mamoru and Miyazaki Hayao than at first appears. It works because it can be read by global audiences simultaneously as a singular exotic fantasy and as an adaptable model for constructing new aesthetic and technological histories through the idea of animation.

# CHAPTER 5

# Cosplay

## Embodying Animation, Animating Bodies

In this chapter and the next, I will return to the possible relationships between animation and performance. In chapter 1, I distinguished animation from performance based on the idea that animation is the construction of social others through materialization, while performance is the construction of social identities, or selves, through embodiment. In these chapters I want to explore what happens when different aspects of performance and animation are intertwined in practice. In chapter 6, I will look at the construction of national identities through animated stereotypes. In this chapter, I focus on the practice of cosplay, in which fans re-create animated characters through embodied performance.

The word "cosplay" originally referred to the practice of dressing up as manga/anime characters, and that is still its core meaning; it is also sometimes extended to refer to dressing up as fictional characters from any media franchise, either animated or live action, as well as members of pop music bands. The term is originally Japanese, pronounced as "*kosupure*," and is short for the English "costume play." There are many different stories regarding when and by whom cosplay was started in Japan, but most trace its origins in some way to the interactions between Japanese and American science fiction fans in the 1980s. Japanese anime/manga cosplay is often seen as having been inspired by fans dressing as characters from live-action television series such as *Star Trek* at science fiction conventions in the United States, which began in the 1960s (Winge 2006; see also Kotani 2018). After it became popular at amateur comics and science fiction conventions in Japan, cosplaying Japanese manga and anime characters, along with American comic book characters, was then taken up by American fans as more and more Japanese manga and anime were imported. By the late 1990s, cosplay was a standard part of the comics/animation/games conventions that sprang up in cities throughout East Asia and North America, and now there are cosplay events and cosplayers posting to online forums

The Pili Company's introduction of digital technology in the mid-1990s saw a further increase in the young, urban, and female audience. In 2005, I conducted surveys at video rental stores in Taipei and Kaohsiung and found that renters of Pili DVDs ranged in age from sixteen to sixty-six, with over half between the ages of twenty-five and thirty-five and fewer than 15 percent over forty-five. More than 60 percent were men.

But while men are in the majority of the passive audience for Pili—that is, the group who merely watch the videos—women make up the majority of active fans, those who organize and join fan clubs, attend events such as puppeteering demonstrations and fan club outings, and participate in activities such as writing fan fiction and cosplay. During my fieldwork, I found that on average women made up 80 percent or more of fan club memberships and attendees at fan events.

The development of Pili's fan subculture has relied on the spread of digital media. Pili fandom began to grow rapidly at the same time that the Pili Company began to incorporate digital technology into its production process, starting in the late 1990s. The development of Taiwan's high-tech manufacturing sector in the 1990s was accompanied by the rapid adoption of computer technology in many areas of daily life. By the early twenty-first century, all offices and schools and most homes had personal computers. By 2006, over 65 percent of households had Internet connections, and 87 percent of people aged twelve to thirty-five were regularly online (*Taipei Times* 2006).

Fans of the Pili series began to contact each other and organize soon after the Pili cable station began broadcasting in 1995. Fan club officers told me that the development of Pili fan organizations relied heavily on college BBSs (bulletin board systems) in the early stage and later the World Wide Web as well. In 1996 the company, at the urging of fans, founded the official Pili Fan Club. Aside from producing a glossy monthly magazine, the company also maintains a website and an electronic newsletter for its members. According to the Pili Company's statistics in 2000, 65 percent of its official fan club members were between the ages of eighteen and twenty-five (Pili International Multimedia Company 2000), and in 2015 more than 80 percent of the fan club membership was between the ages of twenty-one and forty (Pili International Multimedia Company 2015:35). Once the club was established, fans began to organize booster clubs for individual puppet characters, and again the company helped them set up formal organizations with elected officers. Today there are hundreds of Pili fan clubs, including the official ones, school organizations, and smaller private clubs organized via BBS, the Internet, Facebook, or friendship networks. The Internet has also been indispensable to the growth of fan communities in mainland China, where pirated videos of the Pili serials were passed around for years while the Pili Company tried unsuccessfully to establish legitimate channels for online distribution.

Cosplay is only one of a wide range of activities that Pili fans engage in. These activities tend to be gender specific. Female fans prefer creating *tongrenzhi* and cosplay, while male fans are more interested in amateur puppetry, vocal imitations, and making videos, although there are many exceptions. Collecting and photographing puppets seems to be a shared passion.

According to cosplayers and convention organizers I have interviewed, the practice of holding large conventions where manga and anime fans can sell and buy *tongrenzhi* and the practice of cosplay were imported from Japan to Taiwan together in the 1990s. The first *tongrenzhi* convention in Taiwan, Comic World, jointly organized by the Japan Systems Engineering Corporation and a Taiwanese manga store, was held in Taipei in 1997. In 2002 the convention was renamed Comic World Taiwan (CWT) and organized by its own company (Wang Pei-ti 2015:162). Since then, the number of CWT conventions held per year has increased, and in 2018 there were five conventions in the cities of Taipei, Taichung, and Kaohsiung, as well as one in Hong Kong. *Tongrenzhi* are also sold at numerous smaller events organized by specific fandoms. One can now usually find at least one or two of these events going on every weekend in Taipei. Cosplayers have been part of *tongrenzhi* sales events since the beginning.

Cosplay now occurs in a wide variety of venues and forms. At *tongrenzhi* events, the majority of cosplayers simply dress up, walk around, and pose for photographs. CWT also organizes cosplay contests as part of its conventions, and cosplay contests are held by other media and fan organizations as well. Cosplay contestants may merely pose, or they may perform dances or dramatic skits. Photography is an integral part of cosplay. Many cosplayers have friends or professional studio photographers take pictures that they post online in their own blogs or in local and international cosplay photography forums. Groups of cosplayers frequently organize trips to scenic spots to take photographs. Anime and game companies also often hire cosplayers to be emcees and visual attractions at promotional events.

According to my interviewees, Pili fans were selling their *tongrenzhi* at the first Taiwanese conventions. They started doing cosplay soon after, some say first at the request of the Pili Company for a promotional event. Pili cosplayers currently participate in both multi-fandom events and events organized by the Pili Company, official and unofficial Pili fan clubs, and small groups of their own.

## Taiwanese Traditions of Performance and Animation

Taiwan is one of many Asian countries where puppetry and drama are paired as the two main traditional media for the transmission of local mythology, folklore, and history. *Po-te-hi* and *koa-a-hi* (Taiwanese Opera) hold a similar status in the Taiwanese national imaginary that *wayang kulit* and *wayang orang* do in Indonesia and kabuki and bunraku do in Japan.

Both *koa-a-hi* and *po-te-hi*, like opera and puppetry genres throughout China, construct characters through a taxonomic system that, as I argued in chapter 2, is characteristic of the *ang-a* mode of animation. In this system, all individual characters are constructed from a taxonomy of role types, moving from the general to the specific. The primary division is between the male (*sheng*) and female (*dan*) roles. The characters are then classified through further binary choices between young or old and literary or military.[2] From there, the choices expand—for example, aristocrat or commoner; clown, hero, or villain; and so on. In the Pili serials, some further distinctions are made between human or nonhuman; Confucian, Buddhist, or Daoist; Chinese, Japanese, or Western; and so on.

Another aspect that *po-te-hi* and *koa-a-hi* share (along with other traditional Chinese opera and puppetry genres) is the stylization of voices and movements.[3] Male and female roles have different repertoires of standard steps and gestures and different vocal registers. As the role types are further refined, these repertoires are narrowed. One important part of this system is the still pose, which in Mandarin is called the *liangxiang*. The *liangxiang* is usually performed at the end of a sequence of movements and encapsulates the essence of a character's qualities and state of mind.

Despite their intertwined histories and their similar modes of constructing characters, *koa-a-hi* and *po-te-hi* differ, of course, along the lines I outlined in chapter 1 for the differences between performance and animation generally. Most significant here is the way that *po-te-hi* characters are created through striated media, while *koa-a-hi* characters are embodied organically (this will be discussed in the next section).

Another significant difference between traditional *koa-a-hi* and *po-te-hi* is in the gender compositions of performance troupes and audiences. Since the early postwar years, the majority of *koa-a-hi* performers in both male and female roles have been women, with the women who play the male roles being the stars, and the audience has also been mostly women. *Po-te-hi*, in contrast, is traditionally a masculine genre, with almost all voicers and puppeteers being men (in its entire history, the Pili Company has had only one female puppeteer and has used female voice artists only in its side projects, never in the main series); the audience is traditionally mostly male as well.

Pili cosplay draws on both *po-te-hi* and *koa-a-hi* traditions in different ways. Keeping in mind this context of how Taiwan's acting and animation traditions are related and how they diverge, I want to turn now to the Pili Company's innovations in terms of its striation of media in character construction before I discuss the specific styles of cosplay that Pili fans have developed. Significantly, women became the most active Pili fans and developed a form of cosplay modeled on the striations of puppetry during the same period when the Pili Company's process of character construction became marked by an increasingly complex division of labor and media and its style became increasingly visually and psychologically realist.

## The Pili Company's Character Construction Process

Each choice among taxonomic categories in the creation of a Pili character necessitates the selection of specific sets of codes in different modalities—language, voice, movement, costume, facial features, music—each of which is the responsibility of a different unit within the Pili production team. The Pili production process starts with the script-writing team, who usually begin creating characters by coming up with role types and names. The script supervisor outlines a plot, which is discussed by the team. The supervisor then makes scene outlines and assigns members of the group to write the dialogue for each scene. At the same time, sculptors contracted by the Pili Company carve several heads for each character, based on brief descriptions provided by the script group. One head is chosen for each character, usually by the CEO, Chris Huang, in consultation with the script group. Once the script is completed, it is sent to the managing director/ voice artist, Vincent Huang, who starts creating voices for the new characters and recording the dialogue. It is also sent to the "appearance bureau" (*zaoxing zu*), which starts to construct the puppets' costumes and hair, sometimes using sketches provided by the script group, and to the props department, which begins to make each character's swords, fans, and other accessories and also to construct the elaborate sets. Character designs and the plot outline are sent to the music group, who compose signature tunes for each character as well as theme music for the credits and background music for various types of scenes. Once the dialogue and music have been recorded and the construction of the puppets is completed, filming begins. Puppeteers manipulate the puppets while listening to the voice track, and the director (*daobo*) instructs them and the camera operators from a booth

above the set. The *daobo* edit each scene as the video feeds from each camera come into their monitors, and they have a limited set of digital special
effects that can be inserted during this preliminary editing. Once a full
episode is shot and edited, it is sent to the postproduction bureau, where
background music, subtitles, and more elaborate special effects, such as 3-D
animation, are added.

As I noted in chapter 2, in the *ang-a* mode of animation, the sense of
the character's coherence is dependent on several media fitting together,
each with its particular code. In other words, a character who spoke in the
deep voice characteristic of the military male role but who used the fluid,
continuous gestures of the female role would be considered "mismatched"
or "incoherent" (*buxietiao*). The Pili artists often use such mismatches to
create more complex or unusual characters, but the mismatches must be
motivated (e.g., the character is gay or transgender). Let me now turn to
some of the Pili Company's innovations in four of these media/codes: the
material puppet, puppeteering, the voice, and cinematography.

## Puppets and Puppeteering

Changes in the Pili style have had the effect of endowing the characters with
an increasing sense of corporeality, if not organicity. This is most obvious
in changes to the puppets. One of the primary changes reflects the direction of developments in digital animation—the puppets have become more
three-dimensional. The carved faces, since the making of the film *Legend
of the Sacred Stone* in 2000, have more planes and more wrinkles than the
earlier puppet faces did. Japanese animation has been very influential with
the Pili artists, and spiky hair, long noses, cleft chins, and pointy elf ears
are features of many Pili puppet heads. The demon or cyborg characters
have even more protrusions—tentacles, mandibles, and spikes of all sorts.
Fans now refer to the older puppets, with their comparatively flat features,
as having "cookie faces." Main characters who have been part of the series
since the 1980s, such as Su Huanzhen and Ye Xiao Chai, change their look
regularly (e.g., old puppets are replaced with new ones), but they retain their
most distinctive features as they become more realistic.

The puppet bodies have also become more visible and more three-
dimensional. Traditional puppet costumes are robes that hang from a line
across the shoulders; large, stiff epaulets are distinctive of the puppets of
the 1970s and 1980s. Since the mid-1990s, Pili costumes soften or remove
these epaulets. In the late 1990s, characters were introduced who wore trousers rather than the traditional robe, and now most male and some female

characters have visible legs. Pili has also introduced characters with three-dimensional breastplates (both male and female). Pili *po-te-hi* heightens the corporeal effect of the puppets by indexing the existence of internal organs beneath the wooden skin. The puppets can weep, bleed, and spit, and indeed, tears, blood, and poison flow in profusion.

Another trend in the development of Pili style is the increased articulation and mobility of the puppets. One of Huang Junxiong's major changes in adapting *po-te-hi* to television was in making the puppets twice the traditional size and giving them moveable elbows, wrists, knees, eyelids, and lips. The Pili Company has continued to enhance the articulation of the puppets' body parts. They now have hands made of rubber over wire (rather than of wood), and the fingers can be bent individually. Characters can now realistically imitate martial artist Wong Fei-hung's "no-shadow kick," make distinct hand gestures (slow, angry closings of the fist; Buddhist "lotus fingers"; writing magical Daoist characters in the air), and wink.

The greater size and number of articulated parts in the puppets have also necessitated the development of a new style of puppeteering that brings the puppeteer's entire body into play. Pili puppets are around two feet tall and very heavy. Puppeteers use their right hand to control the puppet's head and right arm, and their left hand to control the puppet's left hand with a rod. When seen in live performance or working in the studio, Pili puppeteers often seem to be dancing. Ironically perhaps, the more invisible the body of the puppeteer becomes, the more organically the puppet moves.

### Puppet Voices

Video *po-te-hi*'s tension between organic unity and the distance created by striation is most vivid in the voice track. In the main series, Pili follows the traditional practice in which all the voices, young and old, male and female, human and other, are recorded by one voice artist. This may be the only aspect of the Pili videos that emphasizes, rather than occludes, the modality-striation of traditional *po-te-hi*. Every attempt by the company to vary this—for instance, having a group of actors record different characters' voices—has been rejected by the fans. As one member of the production staff put it, "It's like a superstition. If it isn't Vincent Huang's voice, the fans won't accept it."

One of the effects of Vincent Huang's recording, I believe, is that it makes the corporeal voice the center from which a sense of organic unity extends into all the other codes. Another effect is that it ties organic unity to the nation. The association of Vincent Huang's voice with national identity is partly related to the fact that contemporary Taiwanese ethno-nationalism posits the Holo language as the sign of authentic national belonging. But there is more to it than that. The melding of the voice, the organic body, and the nation was made clear to me during a dinner with a group of young women fans. They told me that the Pili Company was trying to train the youngest Huang brother to do voice recording. But, they told me, he was raised in the United States. As one woman parodied his "American" voice—saying typical Pili lines in a rap rhythm, adding the occasional "Yo!"—she brought her whole body into the performance, punctuating lines with the diagonal, downward-pointing hand thrust and the nodding head that rappers often use. When I have seen fans imitating Vincent Huang's voice, on the other hand, their gestures are those of the opera or of the circular head motion of Confucian recitation. Vocalization leads naturally to gesture, and gesture expresses a distinctly and consciously local habitus.

### Cinematography

Pili workers and fans often say that Pili has become increasingly "cine-matized" (*dianyinghua*) since the introduction of digital cameras and editing. In Pili, cinematography contributes to the illusion of life in two distinct ways. First, the camera movement is combined with that of the puppets to create the illusion that the puppets have biological life. Second, the use of close-ups creates the illusion that the puppets have internal lives, that they have thoughts and emotions.

The fight scenes, for which Pili is famous, combine the stylized movements and flight of traditional puppeteering with the cinematic editing style of Hong Kong action films. Over the years, the shots in the Pili fight sequences have gotten shorter and more varied in terms of angle, increasing the effect of a sense of speed, mobility, and a fragmented point of view.[4] The simultaneous, constant motion of both puppets and camera creates an impression of pure kinesis. This hyperkinesis often gets in the way of following the narrative and identifying with the characters, and this is one reason that the Pili serials retain the stage *po-te-hi* convention of all fight scenes being accompanied by a narratorial voice-over describing the action and the protagonists' feelings.

If the speed of Pili's cinematic editing invests the characters and their world with life, it is relative stillness and the close-up that invest them with feeling. The striation of codes in Pili denaturalizes the relationship between the body's coherence and that of the character, but this is only one side of a tension that is crucial to both puppetry and the digital media generally—the tension between intellectual distance and emotional identification. As one Pili fan succinctly put it to me: "It's obviously completely fake, but when your favorite character dies, you still feel really sad." Fans know perfectly well that the puppets are mere constructions of wood, cloth, and audiotape; nevertheless, the Pili characters are very real to them. Pili fans are famous for their extreme emotional attachment to their favorite characters.[5] Where does this emotional investment come from?

In the Pili videos, intense emotion is indicated by the close-up of the puppet face, and all of the micro-gestures that indicate emotion—the eyes closing, the fist curling up, the placement of a hand on a sword hilt—are shot in close-up. The illusion of life and the illusion that the puppet has a psychology, created via movement and the close-up, are brought together in scenes where the puppet character makes a dramatic entrance (e.g., arriving at the scene of a showdown) or the first appearance of a legendary character we have only heard about in the dialogue. At such moments, the puppet often performs a still pose (*liangxiang*), with the camera moving toward it from behind, above, or below in a way that keeps the face hidden. The camera then circles around the puppet, presenting moving but fragmented shots of different parts of the character's body from a variety of angles and ending, finally, with a close-up of the face.

Gilles Deleuze (1986) notes that the cinematic close-up has the ability to turn the human face into a pure object and, likewise, to "facify" objects. The puppet face is both a human face and a piece of wood, and there is something redundant and, for many, disconcerting about the close-up of the puppet face—an object objectified, a face facified. The close-up of the puppet allows for the viewers' projection of emotion but at the same time makes them aware that they are projecting into a thing, a nonorganic palimpsest of codes, and that affect comes always simultaneously from the inside and the outside of the self. The puppet close-up embodies the idea that affect is cultural, that the codes by which we communicate emotion are always exterior to us, even when we are experiencing affect most intensely and personally.

So what happens to the tension between puppets as objects and puppets as characters with lives and emotions of their own, when the characters are reenacted by cosplayers?

## Pili Cosplay Practices

I divide the current practices of cosplay into two main types, posing for photographs and performance. Fans dress as the Pili characters and pose for photographs in two venues. They attend large *tongrenzhi* conventions with thousands of others, and they also organize their own, smaller cosplay photography sessions. Cosplay performances are done at fan club events and take the form of skits and dances. The skits are almost always comic, and they thematize display and gender reversal. Many narratives involve the

Pili cosplayers from the Limitless Cosplay Theater Troupe. Photograph by the author.

male characters competing in some sort of fashion show (*zou xiu*), which is judged or commented on by female characters. In dance performances, female characters tend to dance in the national dance (*guo wu*) style similar to Chinese opera choreography, while male characters do either choreographed sword-fighting routines to Pili theme music or line dances to popular music.

Although their content varies, Pili cosplay skits often replicate the structure of gendered spectatorship in *koa-a-hi*. Since the majority of characters in the Pili series are male, much Pili cosplay takes the form of cross-gender performance. Thus, like *koa-a-hi*, many cosplay skits present women dressed as men as spectacular objects for female enjoyment.

Pili cosplay often looks like *koa-a-hi* and is motivated by similar structures of desire, but the two are quite different in terms of how the character is constructed and what it is that gives the character their sense of coherence, vitality, presence, and realness. In *koa-a-hi*, it is the disciplined body of the actor that makes the character seem to have both life and personality. The character is seen as an extension of the actress' persona, which develops over time through the mutual penetration of what actresses see as their innate characteristics and the habitus acquired through physical training. *Koa-a-hi* actresses specialize in either male or female roles, based partly on their physical characteristics (e.g., height, vocal range) and partly on their personalities. Most feel that after they are assigned to play either the male or female role type exclusively, over time the stylized movements and speech registers become unconscious and influence their comportment offstage as well as onstage (Silvio 1999).

In Pili cosplay, in contrast, the embodied performance is modeled on the construction of the character in the Pili serials. The cosplayed character is striated by the separation of the media/codes of costume and makeup (*zaoxing*), gesture, voice, and photography. While in the Pili videos the puppets have become increasingly humanized (i.e., organicized), in cosplay the humans become puppetized. Affect is created by the combination of the *liangxiang* and the codes of glamor photography.

## Cosplay Bodies

When asked how important a person's face and figure are for cosplay, most fans agreed that what was most important was the fit between the cosplayer's physical form and the character being cosplayed. Fans frequently criticized cosplayers they thought were "too fat" to be playing hardened swordsmen, or, as one cosplayer told me, "There are some characters that are very cute and round. If someone who's too skinny coses [cosplays] them, it doesn't look right." They also said that skin color was important—a dark-skinned fan should not try to cosplay one of the pale elfin characters. This sense of fit is brought up most frequently in decisions about whether to cosplay male or female characters. Many of the women who cosplayed female characters told me they did so because they were too short to play the male roles. Here the discussion sometimes extends to questions of habitus, and athleticism or a vague sense of being "unable to catch the flavor" of a gendered role type may influence decisions on which character to cosplay. This discourse of fit resembles very closely that of *koa-a-hi* actresses when they discuss why they specialize in the male or female role type. Yet, unlike *koa-a-hi* actresses, cosplayers never speak of their cosplaying as influencing their offstage habitus or sense of their own personality. I believe this strict separation of onstage and offstage is partly due to cosplay's status as play, but it is also an effect of cosplay's puppetry-like striation of the body, particularly its restriction of the body to a mostly still surface.

At conventions, the majority of fans do not make any special effort to hold their bodies "in character" except when they are in front of a camera. As one fan put it, "The most important thing's the *pose*."[6] Most cosplayers say that they have not studied any movement discipline; they learn the appropriate poses by watching the Pili videos and ancient costume serial dramas, practicing in the mirror, and looking at photos of themselves and others posing in costume.[7] When cosplayers do say they want to move in character, they speak of it in terms of an absence of incoherent movement rather than the construction of a coherent movement style. Thus, some fans say that if they are in costume, particularly that of a swordsman, they will try to avoid "horsing around" as a matter of "respect for the character." The privileging of the pose is evident even in cosplay skits, in which, in the early 2000s (before even amateur cosplayers began to professionalize their stage skills), the performers tended to pantomime their lines in a jerky series of poses and subside into a sort of affectless "waiting" stance whenever their character was not the focus of the action. The other main forms of physical movement in cosplay performance are the line dance and the sword routine. These performances are characterized by repetition—the movement sequences loop.

The implicit guiding principle that I can deduce from all the cosplay performances I have seen in Taiwan is that the cosplayer's body should move smoothly from pose to pose. This principal becomes apparent if we look at the styles of movement that cosplayers avoid. First, they generally avoid imitating the movements of puppets. I have only seen one instance

of cosplayers moving as though they were wooden puppets being manipulated by a puppeteer, in a humorous video performed by a group of young
men. Second, cosplayers generally avoid moving too organically—that is,
moving in a way in which the flow of motion seems "naturally" propelled
by momentum. This is how a pair of modern dancers who were hired to
perform at a large fan event in the early 2000s moved. The dancers enacted
a story of developing passion between two characters, frequently changing
speed and mood. Their style was clearly influenced by the American school
of modern dance, which, as Hillel Schwartz (1992) points out, emphasizes
the graceful flow of energy from a center of gravity outward through the
whole body. Some fans I spoke to afterwards found this dance boring or
meaningless (*wuliao*) and claimed not to understand it. I think this was
because the modern dancers were clearly *performing* the characters—psychologically introjecting the roles and expressing them through organic
movement—rather than reanimating them. Schwartz argues that modern
dance's organicity was a reaction against industrialization and its fantasies
of mechanization. Cosplayers, in contrast to interpretive dancers, replicate
the frame-to-frame techne of manga or cinema animation when they move
from pose to pose.

## The Voice in Cosplay

One of the most striking aspects of cosplay performances is the disconnec-
tion between voice and body, even the virtual disappearance of the voice as
a feature of most cosplay. It is rare for cosplayers at conventions or photo
outings to speak in character. They say they try to maintain the character's
dignity through an absence of incoherent speech or laughter rather than
through any positive vocal performance style.

In most cosplay skits at fan club events, the script is prerecorded,
either by a group of fans or by one male fan, and the cosplayers lip-synch
to the tape. According to a former fan club officer who has been cosplaying Pili characters since 2000, in her first Pili cosplay skit the performers
did recite their own lines. "But," she told me, "when the cosplayers picked
up the microphone, well, they felt very happy, but the people in the audience didn't understand anything they were saying. Most of the players were
women and they didn't have any voice training and couldn't speak clearly."
For the next cosplay performance, she found a male high school student
who was particularly good at imitating Vincent Huang and had him do the
dialogue recording in a studio. Vocalizing the Pili characters is an activity
popular among male fans. As one male fan put it, "Most boys will do the

voices a little. Women's voices always sound like women's voices, but since the female characters' voices are done by men in *po-te-hi* anyway, it's easier for men." It may seem that the preference for male voice actors silences women. But it only does so in the most literal sense. The scripts for cosplay skits are almost always written by women.

Like the close-up of the wooden face of the puppet, the male voicing of the female cosplayer is thus simultaneously what makes the character seem most like the character the viewer knows and thinks of as having their own life, and what makes the viewer most aware of the inorganic, constructed nature of Pili characters. When the puppet body is replaced with a woman's body, while the voice acting is still done by a man, the construction of gender from the disposition of elements in a database or taxonomy in animation is further highlighted.

## Cosplay Photography

Virtually every cosplayer I interviewed claimed that cosplay would be meaningless without photography and that their greatest sense of achievement came from having many people photographing them. Significantly, although there are thousands of cameras at *tongrenzhi* conventions, I have rarely seen a video camera there.

Cosplay photographs use the lighting and framing codes of glamour photography. They can function like film stills, capturing momentary emotions through the frozen-in-motion pose. But they also function like late imperial/early modern Chinese ancestor portraits, aiming to capture the unchanging essence of the character's personality, their analogic disposition of traits. Cosplayers evaluate cosplay photographs using very similar criteria for how they evaluate *ang-a*. The focus is on the gaze (*yanshen*), which must not seem "empty." The harshest criticism of cosplay photos is that they reveal that the cosplayer "doesn't understand" the character, even if the cosplayer's costume and makeup are meticulously accurate.

Cosplay photography aesthetics are one aspect of the impact that the transition from the Age of Performance to the Age of Animation is having on the experience of the body and self in Taiwanese culture at large, and perhaps globally. Pili's addition of a qualitatively new code, that of cinematography, to the striated codes of appearance, movement, and voice of live puppetry makes the characters and their world feel more present and real. The purpose of cosplay photography is the same. Pili fans use nearly the same techniques of posing, lighting, and composition to photograph cosplayers that they use when photographing puppets. They are trying to create a compelling image of a character, not a puppet. Cosplay photography reveals just how much the presentation of self has moved from the performance paradigm to the animation paradigm in the age of digital media. Like the selfie and the emoji, cosplay photography makes the expression of affect dependent on codes exterior to the material body, rather than absorbed into and emerging from it.[8]

## The Relationship between the Cosplayer and the Character

Cosplay is variable not just in terms of styles of costume and embodiment. There is also local variation in terms of whether cosplayers see cosplay as a kind of performance or a kind of animation. Cosplay is one of those actions, like manipulating an avatar in an online game, that can be either performance or animation, or some combination of the two, depending only on how the person doing it is thinking about it. Different styles or practices of cosplay negotiate animation and performance in different ways. A continuum of attitudes exists regarding the relationship between the character and the cosplayer. At one end of the spectrum are those who approach cosplay like Method actors—that is, who see cosplay as an expression of identity and who attempt to psychologically introject and physically express the character's personality. At the other end of the spectrum are those who approach cosplay as animators, who treat their bodies as a 3-D (in both the literal sense and the fan sense of being part of the real world) medium through which the fictional character is (re)materialized. In most communities of cosplayers, there are individuals who fall everywhere on this continuum. But there are also differences between communities in terms of which end of the continuum dominates, as well as in specific practices, how they are combined, and how they are talked about.

Cosplay is sometimes translated into Mandarin by journalists and academics as *banyan jiaose* or *jiaose banyan*—playing a role or role-playing. It appears to many outsiders, in the Chinese-speaking world as well as in North America, quite obviously to be a kind of performance. But Chinese-speaking cosplayers themselves are far more likely to use the loanword *cosplay*, shortened to *cos*, to emphasize its difference from other types of role performance. When they do use Mandarin, they say they *ban*, meaning "to dress as or fulfill the function of a character," rather than *yan*, the verb used by actors.

Most Pili cosplayers I met did not necessarily, as is commonly thought, choose to dress as the characters they most identified with or liked. In fact, many avoided cosplaying those characters for fear of not doing a good enough job. Instead, they chose characters that had the most visual appeal (that were "gorgeous"), that best suited their body type, or that fit in with a group. As I mentioned in the introduction, when I asked Taiwanese cosplayers, "How do you get into character?" I was often greeted with puzzled looks. When I rephrased the question as "How do you prepare to cosplay?" I was usually answered with details of how costumes and makeup designs were made. Their discourse, as well as their practice, revealed that most of the Pili cosplayers I interviewed saw cosplay more as reanimating the character using the body as a kind of puppet rather than as an embodied performance of some aspect of self-identity.

This stands in stark contrast to most North American cosplayers, who see cosplay through the lens of the performance paradigm. Some American cosplayers actually use Actors Studio techniques, such as creating backstories for characters that don't exist in the manga/anime canon, to get into character (Napier 2006). Cosplayers themselves seem quite well aware of a regional East-West contrast in approaches to the relationship between the cosplayer and the character. For instance, an American cosplayer whom I heard speak at a comics and animation convention in Singapore said she was struck by the way that Japanese cosplayers restricted self-expressive behavior when in costume, while Taiwanese cosplayers I interviewed who had seen the American reality show *Heroes of Cosplay* found the American cosplayers on the show claiming that their goal was to "become the character" very odd.[9]

Now let us return to the question of what this particular form of cosplay does for Taiwanese women. Pili cosplay blends *koa-a-hi*'s spectatorial structure (women watching women playing men) and its pleasures with the treatment of the (usually female) body as a puppet to be animated or en-charactered. Why is this particular mixture of ways of constructing and experiencing gendered personhood so attractive to this particular group of women at this particular time? To answer this question, we must first get a more detailed picture of who Pili cosplayers are when they are not cosplaying, and then analyze the relationship between the practices and discourses of Pili cosplayers and the circumstances of their lives.

## Pili Cosplayers

The research that led to my analysis of Pili cosplayers' practices and discourse, aside from participation at different types of fan events, included semi-structured interviews with thirty-one Taiwanese Pili cosplayers. I met them either at events such as a CWT convention or a fan club activity, through online discussion groups, or through introduction by other interviewees. Interviews were sometimes conducted one-on-one, sometimes in groups of three or four, and usually lasted two to four hours. In order to get a sense of the broader Pili cosplay community, I also conducted short interviews (usually fifteen minutes to half an hour) with twenty-two more Pili cosplayers at CWT conventions and large fan events, and, with the help of my research assistant Huang Lingyi, I facilitated an online discussion forum on Pili cosplay and collected basic biographical information from the participants. Forty-eight of the fifty-three people I interviewed were women and five were men, which reflected the gender ratio I found among fans in the online forum and those engaged in other activities such as writing fan fiction and attending fan club meetings. The Pili cosplayers I met ranged in age from seventeen to thirty-three. The average age of those with whom I conducted semi-structured interviews, who were selected mostly because of their deeper involvement in the fan culture, was twenty-four. The average age of the people who were simply willing to talk to me for a short time at events was twenty.[10] Pili cosplayers are thus mostly in the stage of life that is referred to in Taiwan as "entering society"—between school and settling down in a stable job and marriage. However, marriage and a stable job are no longer certain, or necessarily desired, goals for this generation.

My interviewees were quite varied in terms of their work experience. Thirteen were still students. Among the women who had already graduated, the most common professions were clerical (bookkeepers and secretaries) and creative (fashion design, creative writing, editing, music, theater). An only slightly smaller number of the graduates were working low-paying service industry jobs, such as food service and sales, and most of the students were also working such jobs part-time. My female interviewees also included a security guard, a nurse, a professional athlete, a factory worker, a coffee shop owner/manager, and three teachers.[11] Many were working two or more jobs, and most of them had already worked at least part-time at several different jobs. The two men I conducted longer interviews with were both earning their livings in the gig economy, doing jobs that included hair styling, event organizing, teaching music, and hosting a weekly television program.[12] It is hard to characterize such a diverse group, but I can say that this group of Pili cosplayers was fairly typical of fandoms in both East Asia and North America in which women are the most active participants, in that the majority were either in or training for work in the traditional pink-collar sector or in the creative industries.

Among the women I asked, sexual identities reflected the general population. That is, about 90 percent of them identified as heterosexual, and the rest as bisexual, lesbian, or undecided. None of my interviewees were married when I first interviewed them or when they started cosplaying, although many were in relationships. Two women I met with several times over the course of my fieldwork did get married. One of them stopped cosplaying but kept up with other fan activities until after her first child was born; the other did not have children and kept cosplaying after marriage. Both of these women married men who were also active Pili fans, and both worked for the Pili Company before and after marriage. Most of the male cosplayers I talked to identified as straight. However, one out gay Pili fan I interviewed told me that if a man's sexual orientation was unknown, cosplaying at a public event would be read by the fan community as coming out.

## Cosplay as a Play Form of Mediated Affective Labor

To answer the question of what cosplay does for Taiwanese women, we must ask, What is new for this generation? What makes these women's lives different from those of their mothers? In most ways, the answers to these questions are true for women throughout the industrializing world. First, they are more likely to work outside the home, both before and after marriage, and to spend more years in the workforce (Yu 2015). They are marrying later than their mothers did, or not at all (Chen and Chung 2017). Their lives are also penetrated by digital technology in ways their mothers could not have imagined at their age. Thus, to understand how cosplay fits into these women's lives, we need to focus on the areas of work and of interactions with peers (friends, boyfriends and girlfriends, classmates, and coworkers) and on how digital technology is affecting both of these areas.

In terms of transformations in the labor market, Taiwan follows the general trends in North America, Europe, and Japan. Taiwan has seen a shrinking of the agricultural and manufacturing sectors, accompanied by a rise in the service and high-tech/information sectors over the past thirty years (Huang Minming 2001; Tseng, You, and Ho 2002), and new industries such as software and game design have been promoted by the government in the twenty-first century.

Perhaps the writers who have focused most closely on what these general trends mean for workers are the Italian autonomists, especially Maurizio Lazzarato, Franco "Bifo" Berardi, Michael Hardt, and Antonio Negri. Their argument is complex and has changed over time. Keeping in mind that I am simplifying quite a lot here and conflating subtly different ideas from different authors, let me summarize it as follows: As industry has fled from first-world countries, what has taken its place has been what Lazzarato calls immaterial labor—"the labor that produces the informational and cultural content of the commodity" (1996:133). Immaterial labor—aesthetic, communicative, and analytical work—not only is obviously key to jobs in the new creative and computer software industries but also is becoming a larger part of work in other sectors, including the traditional manufacturing sector. All workers are increasingly being forced to put their "passion" into their work, and at the same time, consumers' aesthetic and communicational labor has been recognized an inextricable part of the creation of brand value and actively recruited into that process. Thus, one of the key markers of the post-Fordist age is the interpenetration of production and consumption, work and life.

When they look at immaterial labor in terms of the nature of the work itself rather than the type of product, the autonomists see a division between what Robert Reich calls symbolic-analytical services, or "tasks that involve 'problem-solving, problem-identifying, and strategic brokering activities,'" and affective labor, which produces "a feeling of ease, well-being, satisfaction, excitement, passion—even a sense of connectedness or community . . . the creation and manipulation of affects" (Hardt 1999:95–96).

These two types of immaterial labor are clearly gendered. Symbolic-analytical work such as software design is dominated by men, while jobs that require the creation and manipulation of affect (what Arlie Hochschild [2003] called the "emotional work" of monitoring one's own and others' moods, the Goffmanian presentation of self) are (still) dominated by women.

These two modes of immaterial labor are bleeding into each other, at the levels of both ideology and practice. Hardt and Negri (2000) note that the ideology of information is spreading out from the high-tech sector proper, as factories, schools, government bureaus, and business offices are all being computerized. At the same time, areas of work formerly distinct from the service sector, including manufacturing, are being redefined as providing service.

What I intend to argue here is that although their description of the post-Fordist economy is not inaccurate, the autonomists have missed an important point: that changes in the nature of post-Fordist work are not experienced in the same way by workers in white-collar and pink-collar sectors.[13] The increasing degree of emotional labor required for jobs in fields like computer programming is experienced by workers in those fields as qualitatively new. I have met Taiwanese computer programmers and game designers who found that nothing in their formal or informal education prepared them for the service parts of their jobs, and they were scrambling to learn how to do audience research in order to design user-friendly interfaces or how to deal with clients who keep changing their minds. Given that it is mostly men in these professions, it is significant that the twentieth century has seen more panic in postindustrial countries over the supposed feminization of men, especially after the financial crises of 1997 and 2008 (e.g., metrosexuals and hipsters in the United States, *otaku* and "herbivore men" in Japan) than over the masculinization of women.[14]

What, then, is new about pink-collar work in the twenty-first century? It is not that problem solving and "strategic brokering activities" are only now becoming a large part of their jobs—they always have been. The autonomists have failed to adequately address this question because they see digital technology primarily in terms of its logistical functions (organizing networks and flows) rather than as a set of media platforms. Assertions like Hardt's that "affective production, exchange, and communication is generally associated with human contact, with the actual presence of another, but that contact can be either actual or virtual" (1999:96) get in the way here. They elide the crucial difference between embodied and mediated affective labor—in other words, the difference between performance and animation. I would argue that the change in the medium of affective labor from the body to the screen is the key factor in women's sense that the nature of their work (both paid and unpaid) is changing.

Pili cosplay is evidence of this; we can deduce what is new in the nature of women's work via what is new in the nature of women's play. In order to explain my argument here, I need to first give a very schematic history of the gendered division of labor in ethnically Chinese Taiwanese society.

Among the merchant class of the Fujianese immigrants who settled in Taiwan during the late imperial period, gendered labor was marked, not by a division between affective and analytical labor or between embodied and intellectual labor, but by a division between public and domestic (or outside and inside, *nei* and *wai*; until fairly recently, *nei ren*, or "inside person," was a common way of saying "wife" in Taiwan). Men established and maintained business networks largely through the exchange of *renqing* (literally, human feeling), expressed through hosting, toasting, and reciprocal favors. Women's work was conducted mostly inside the home and included keeping records of and distributing family finances as well as housekeeping and child-rearing.

What changed during the Japanese colonial period was not women's blend of analytical and affective labor but its movement from the domestic sphere to the public sphere. With more education available for middle-class women and the development of a new urban consumer culture in Taiwan in the 1920s, including new professions for women such as teacher, nurse, and department store sales and elevator girls, their embodied immaterial labor became simultaneously publicly visible and commodified. Modernization of gender roles also included the expectation for women to perform emotional labor in the marriage market as well as the labor market. The practice of *xiang qin*, in which potential marriage partners meet in person, usually accompanied by their parents and a matchmaker, became popular during the Japanese colonial era and was supplemented with dating culture in the 1960s.

These expectations for women's public performances of emotional labor have not gone away in the twenty-first century. The most common profession among the female Pili fans I interviewed, *kuaiji*, is a job typical of pink-collar labor in Taiwan since the 1950s. A *kuaiji* is, technically speaking, a bookkeeper. But in many small businesses, especially the family businesses in which many of my interviewees worked, the job may also include such tasks as contacting clients and suppliers, greeting and serving guests, and handling employee complaints.

But since the 1990s, when BBSs, email systems, and then the World Wide Web were rapidly adopted in Taiwan, a great deal of the affective labor that Taiwanese women do has been mediated through digital technology, far more than was ever mediated through older media such as letter writing or the telephone. With smartphone penetration in Taiwan the highest in the world in 2016 (Sodano 2016), most of my informants are communicating through digital platforms such as email, Facebook, Instagram, and Line all day long, for both work and nonwork purposes.

I have argued that from the 1920s to the 1970s, *koa-a-hi* was the most popular entertainment for Taiwanese women because *koa-a-hi* actresses, especially the stars who played the male roles, modeled ways of controlling the new pressures on women to negotiate and perform femininity through the visible body (Silvio 2017). In the twenty-first century, I think that the Pili Company is serving a similar function, providing a model for how to create personae and affect through media other than the body.

Because interaction with the technologies of everyday life is one of the ways in which bodies become gendered, feminist scholars have argued that the introduction of new technologies always holds possibilities, both utopian and dystopian, for the transformation of cultural concepts of masculinity and femininity. Western feminist scholarship on the body in the information age has tended to focus on two fantasies that permeate cyberpunk fiction, academic cybernetic theory, and other speculative discourses around digital technology and that are (sometimes) made manifest in the way that people actually interact with computers. The first fantasy is of disembodiment, of the transcendence of mind over flesh by downloading human consciousness into a computer network, or simply of living one's life primarily in an online virtual world (see Morse 1998; Hayles 1999; Turkle 1995). The second is the fantasy of transcending illness, weakness, and mortality itself through the merging of the human body with machine parts—what Allucquère Rosanne Stone (1995) calls cyborg envy. In the Western context of Christian ideology and Descartian scientism, these fantasies of transcendence have misogynist undertones, when the female body is denigrated as excessive, dumb, weak, and more resistantly thinglike than the male body.[15] Yet these fantasies of transcendence also have their feminist utopian side, holding the possibilities for the creation of ungendered or serially gendered creatures and personae and for the breakdown of Christian and Cartesian dichotomies.[16]

The fantasies of what the body could become that are emerging in Pili culture are more about making the body a medium for animation than making it disappear or making it invulnerable. Perhaps the interface, a material surface facilitating affective communication, provides a more appropriate metaphor for the relationship between the body and technology in Taiwan than the cyborg. In Pili cosplay, the body functions not as an organic totality but as a set of media (gesture, voice) that transmit their specific codes, that remain striated, and that must combine with other non-corporeal media to create a coherent character. There is something quite restful in treating the body as a screen onto which personality can be projected, rather than as a visible manifestation of interior emotional and intellectual dispositions, which must be constantly disciplined into gendered habitus. Pili cosplay is pleasurable because it places the self in the background, in the role of animator rather than performer. I do not mean to say that Taiwanese cosplayers do not actively display themselves or show off their skills. But most of them do see themselves primarily as bringing characters to life, adding to their presence, rather than expressing aspects of their own subjectivities.

Autonomist theorist Franco "Bifo" Berardi writes that in the post-Fordist economy, "capital was able to renew its psychic, ideological, and economic energy, specifically thanks to the absorption of creativity, desire, and individualistic libertarian drives for self-realization" (2009:96). In this system, depression becomes almost inevitable. He quotes Alain Ehrenberg: "Depression begins to develop . . . with the new norms pushing each and everyone to individual action, forcing individuals to become themselves. . . .

The depressed individuals are not up to the task, they are tired of having to become themselves" (Ehrenberg cited in Berardi 2009:99).

I think that Pili cosplay provides a space where the depressive effects of the new economy of affective labor can be held at bay. This is not because cosplay takes place in some protected play-space outside of contemporary capitalism—it does not. Cosplayers' energies and desires are certainly recruited, often willingly, into creating surplus value for media corporations. Rather, it is because Pili cosplay provides a space where Taiwanese women are free from the pressure to become—either the characters or themselves.

# CHAPTER 6

# *Ang-a* Identity Politics

## The Personification of Imagined Communities

In the last chapter I looked at how individual identities, or characters, are constructed through one technology of animation, puppetry, and how treating embodiment as another technique of animation rather than as performance leads to a different way of thinking about the relationship between bodies and identities. In this chapter, I want to explore one way of looking at communal identities through the lens of animation. Specifically, I'll be looking at how the "imagined communities" (Anderson 1983) of nations transform when they are animated through a collective process of personification.

Let me begin with an overview of some of the consequences that anthropologists and others have noted for seeing humanity as a collection of identity categories (nations, ethnicities, genders, etc.). Lauren Leve summarizes these critiques very well. Leve, drawing on a number of contemporary anthropologists and philosophers, argues that national and subnational identities are produced by an "identity machine": "a particular global sociopolitical imaginary, concretized in a constellation of institutions, ideologies, frameworks, structures, technologies, forms of knowledge, ethics, and norms . . . , producing not only the categories of ethnological identity ('ethnicities,' 'tribes,' 'nations,' 'cultures') but also the very ontology of identity that underlies liberal and neoliberal democracy" (2011:517). This identity machine formulates identity according to two related logics, that of the bureaucratic state and that of the capitalist market. In both cases, identity is a kind of misrecognition or deceit.

Leve cites philosopher Jonathan Rée on how the global system of liberal bureaucratic governments, which he calls internationality, "conspires to make us give our consent to state power by disguising it as an expression of our own feelings" (Rée 1992:9). According to Rée, there are several conceptual conflations and misrecognitions involved in how individuals identify with "their" nations. First, he asserts that the idea of "national character" mistakes the product of a Saussurean system—in which signs are actually defined by their differences from other signs—for a natural category with positive content. Thus, the characteristics of national cultures are mistaken as the cause, rather than the effect, of a bureaucratic system, internationality, which works to make boundaries between political entities legible to the elites who govern them. Second, individual identity and group identity are conflated; groups are personified as if they were individuals, and both are mistakenly seen as homogenous, across membership (the British are British because they share the same culture) and across time (the British are British because they share the same memories). Finally, identity (both individual and group) is conflated with consciousness. That is, people are who they believe they are. Thus, not only are all internal divisions within identities ignored, but so is every way that structural power works (on both individuals and groups), from physical violence to the suppression of memory to all kinds of false consciousness.

In terms of identity's imbrication in capitalism, Leve draws on C. B. Macpherson's history of the idea of possessive individualism, the "conception of the individual as essentially the proprietor of his own person or capacities, owing nothing to society for them" (Macpherson 1962:3, quoted in Leve 2011:520). As with internationality, society comes to be seen as the aggregate product of individuals exchanging parts of themselves-as-things, rather than individuals being the products of social relations. When liberal identity politics are based on the idea of identity as property, then ethnic minority cultures can claim recognition as protection from destruction or appropriation (theft) by the powerful.

What interests me here is that while Leve and the scholars she cites write about identity and the identification of individuals with collectivities, none of them mentions performance as part of that process of identification. Instead, almost all of them write in terms of personification, of treating things as if they were people, with powers and intentions of their own. This is not surprising, given that most of them are analyzing identity under global neoliberalism, writing both in and about the Age of Animation.

One of the key characteristics of global neoliberalism is that these two systems that work to fix identity—the system of military-bureaucratic nation-states and capitalism—are more deeply intertwined than ever. Nations are increasingly seen primarily as economic actors and metaphorically compared to businesses—"Nationality, Inc.," as John and Jean Comaroff (2009) put it. Under neoliberalism, the deceit of identity politics takes on a new twist. The self-as-property becomes the self-as-business, self as "a bundle of skills, qualities, assets, experiences, and relationships that must be consciously managed and continually enhanced" (Gershon 2011). And as selves come to be seen as businesses, the process of managing them is most often accomplished, not through embodied performance, but through a kind of self-animation: branding. Branding is taking place at all levels, from the individual to the tribe, the town, and the nation.

In an era when selves are redefined as bundles of assets, and individuals and communities feel compelled to brand their identities, what constitutes resistance? Some anthropologists look directly to alternative conceptions of the ontology of the self. Leve uses the example of the Nepalese Theravada Buddhists with whom she did fieldwork to illustrate the paradox of identity today. On the one hand, Nepali Buddhist teachers are deeply involved in identity politics and have mastered its discourse, working publicly to gain rights for themselves as a religious minority (possessing an enduring culture) within Nepal. Yet at the same time, their beliefs and their practice of meditation are anti-identitarian:

> The Buddhist doctrine of *anatta-vada* insists that "we"—that which people everywhere in the world instinctively think of as "our selves"—are merely the composite products of an unceasing flow of physical and mental sensations and events that arise, take form, and eventually dissolve away again. . . . In other words, Buddhism teaches, the experience of a unified self and hence of personal identity is ultimately false. (Leve 2011:516)

Leve notes that in some ways Nepali Theravada Buddhism echoes the argument of the philosopher John Holloway, who, as she puts it, "takes the ontological argument about the relation of identity and property about as far, perhaps, as it can possibly be taken," by asserting that "it is only by seeing objects as discrete, self-identical objects [as "done" things, as opposed to ephemeral moments of continuous, collective "doing"] that anyone can claim to own them" (Leve 2011:523). For Holloway, any anticapitalist movement must therefore also be anti-identity, and teaching people to realize that identity itself is an illusion is therefore potentially revolutionary. Stuart Kirsch (2014) makes a similar move in a thought exercise in which he argues that the idea of the business as person might work very differently if a Melanesian concept of personhood, emphasizing the dependence of the self on interpersonal relationships and mutual obligations to nurture, were applied to corporations.

Here, rather than looking directly to beliefs about the ontology of the self, I want to see what happens when identity becomes the product of conscious animation rather than of self-performance. Within the Marxist tradition, fetishism—the person-ification of things—is seen as a deceptive and oppressive process in itself, largely because it is seen as caused by, or inseparable from, a process of the thing-ification of persons. But I would argue that this is not necessarily the case—fetishism and personification are modes of animation, and animators do not necessarily lose the humanity that they project into the material world. As with performance, the power dynamics of animation are many and various, and the process is just as capable of exposing ideology as it is of hiding it.

The assumption that fetishism, personification, and animation in general are inherently deceitful follows a long tradition of social evolutionary colonial discourse, in which these practices are associated with children, women, and, most especially, "primitive" peoples (Masuzawa 2007). But recently there has been a move among anthropologists to recontextualize and reevaluate those actual practices called fetishism (by Europeans) (Pietz 1985, 1987; Graeber 2007). It is always a good idea to take a closer look at practices that are abjected and trivialized by association with marginalized groups, for that is often where the seeds of revolutionary strategies are hidden.

In the next section, I want to look at some practices that are framed explicitly in terms of animation and that, like the practices of Nepali Buddhists, work to simultaneously reproduce and denaturalize the neoliberal identity machine. Specifically, I'll look at how "national character" is conceptualized and constructed by the fans of a Japanese animation franchise called *Axis Powers Hetalia*, in which the characters are humorous anthropomorphizations of various nations, both historical and modern.

Anthropomorphism may well be the most abjected way of granting abstract entities agency. Personification, and especially anthropomorphism, is widely considered to be "stupid"—childish, primitive, and trivial at best (as in cute logo characters), emotionally manipulative and jingoistic at worst (as in racial stereotypes or Uncle Sam). Scholars and activists generally agree that representing communities as individuals is always oversimplification, ignoring the diversity within communities, historical transformations, and the complex relations among political, economic, and social structures.

At the same time, personification is acknowledged to be powerful. It is often used as a propaganda tool because its simplification is seen as linked to a capacity for arousing emotion, either positive or negative, and tying it to an object. The Communist Party of China has made notable use of personification since 1989, urging citizens to "never forget national humiliation" and responding to international incidents by claiming that "China's feelings were hurt" (Osnos 2014:140–141). As we enter ever deeper into the age of what we might call the global branding machine, I think it might be time to take a closer look at how marginalized animators—in this case, fans who are mostly women and young and whose sexuality is often seen as queer—personify imagined communities.

The relationship between manga/anime fandom and politics has been analyzed in contradictory ways. Manga/anime fandom is often seen, by both fans and scholars, as most subversive in its creation of a fantasy space for imagining nonnormative gender roles and sexual desires. Several scholars have also seen manga/anime fandom as what Michael Warner calls a counterpublic, establishing modes of stranger interaction that are consciously alternative to those of state and commercial media (Martin 2008; Leavitt and Horbinski 2012). There have been many instances of fan activism, all with the goal of maintaining the fandom as a counterpublic—for instance, campaigns for keeping favorite shows from being cancelled and campaigns against censorship and intellectual property laws that punish fans for creating and distributing their versions of media characters (Leavitt and Horbinski 2012; Jenkins 2006).

On the other hand, manga/anime fans draw very strict boundaries between the 2-D (the diegetic world of manga/anime) and the 3-D (real life). While insisting on an essential difference between fantasy and reality protects them, in some ways, from marginalization as deviants, it is also often seen as leading to a disengagement with practical politics, to a view of the real world as not being open to the kinds of transformations that individuals and networks can easily make in two dimensions. What I want to explore here is what happens when the boundary between 2-D and 3-D is deliberately blurred.

## Background: *Axis Powers Hetalia* and Its Fandom

*Axis Powers Hetalia* (hereafter APH) began in 2006 as a series of four-cell cartoons on the personal blog of Hidekaz Himaruya, when he was studying at the Parsons School of Design in New York.[1] The cartoons gained a large following online, and Gentosha Comics contracted with Himaruya to release printed volumes of APH in 2008. From there, the franchise quickly grew to include more comic books and a series of short online animations that were later released as DVDs with both Japanese and English dubs and subtitles. These were followed by a full-length animated film in 2010, as well as the production of a wide variety of tie-in products, including CDs of the songs from the short anime and the film, a video game, figurines, and products decorated with licensed character images (Annett 2011; Miyake 2013). APH as a franchise thus fits squarely in the model of media-mix marketing that characterizes most commercial animation in Japan (Steinberg 2012).

The vast majority of APH fans are female, and most of these also identify as *funü* (in Mandarin; *fujōshi* in Japanese; "shippers" or "slashers" in English)—that is, women who produce and consume BL (boys' love) fiction, manga, and art, a genre focused on romantic and/or sexual relationships among male characters. *Funü/fujōshi* literally means "rotten/corrupt women," a pun on a word for women in general. In Taiwan, as in Japan, the majority of BL works are *tongrenzhi* (*dōjinshi* in Japanese)—that is, amateur fiction and art using characters from mass media franchises, especially manga and anime. Conversely, the majority of *tongrenzhi* are in the BL genre. Thus, an alternative term for *funü* in Taiwan is *tongrennü*. Although their real-life sexual partner choices and practices mirror those

*Axis Powers Hetalia* products from a fan's collection. Photograph by Ellie Huang.

of the general population (Silvio 2011), *funü* are often identified as "queer" in their sexual desires, by both others and by themselves.

APH was frequently rated the most popular franchise among women manga/anime fans from 2009 to 2011 in Taiwan, Japan, and North America. Although the peak of the "Hetalia boom" has passed, it is still a very popular franchise; in Taiwan, only the domestically produced Pili video puppetry serials have had a longer-lasting popularity or a larger fan base. In terms of structure and activities, APH fandom is typical of other *funü* fandoms. Aside from discussing characters and narratives and re-creating them in *tongrenzhi* and cosplay (see chapter 5), APH fans also make scanlations and fansubs (amateur translations of the comics and animations) in many languages and post them online.

The core characters in APH are personifications of the Axis and Allied powers of World War II—Italy, Germany, Japan, England, America, France, Russia, and China. Himaruya has continued to add new characters, including several micro-nations and a number of ancient empires and kingdoms. He claims that his original inspiration came from reading online military history discussions in which the performance of the Italian army in World War II was often mocked as cowardly and inept (Miyake 2013). The word "Hetalia" combines the word "Italia" with the Japanese word *hetare*, meaning "sad sack" or "loser." The Chinese translation used in Taiwan is "Yidaili," a pun on the name for Italy (Yidali), with the middle character replaced by a character meaning "stupid."

One reason for APH's popularity with *funü* is that the canon already incorporates many of the aesthetics and practices of *tongrenzhi*. In fact, even though Hidekaz Himaruya is referred to as a man in most sources, some of the fans I interviewed were convinced that the animator of APH must be a woman and a *funü*. One obvious thing that unites APH with BL is that the characters are mostly male and are drawn to look young and attractive. The narratives focus on the friendships and rivalries between these cute boys, and at least two of these relationships, Germany-Italy and America-England, are considered by fans to be *guan pei* (official matches)—that is, intimate relationships established within the canon. The intense friendship between the temperamental opposites Germany and Italy is often remarked on by other characters, and we see Italy fretting over whether Germany really cares for him or whether he might like Russia better. Germany and Italy frequently reiterate promises to each other to be best friends forever, and Germany's diary reveals that despite the constant trouble Italy causes him, Italy remains his only friend. England is America's older brother, and in one of the most popular episodes among fans, America tries to clean out his attic and can't, because each item he finds—a toy soldier, a suit—was a gift from England that brings back happy memories. He finally finds a gun from the American War of Independence, which gives rise to a flashback in which America—saying, "I'm grown up now, I just want to be independent!"—trains the gun on England but does not have the heart to shoot as England kneels in tears of rage and disappointment.

One of the main things that makes APH different from most manga/anime franchises is that there is no main narrative line. Both the manga and the anime versions are structured into short vignettes, which are arranged in no particular order, so that an allegorical representation of France and England's competition to colonize the New World might be followed by a scene in which the characters, dressed in modern clothes, discuss how Christmas is celebrated in their countries, followed by a scene in which Germany, during World War II, has a dream about ancient Rome. Fan fiction is often categorized by whether it is set in the canon world or in an alternate universe. For APH, it would be impossible to make this distinction—the diegetic worlds of the canon are as varied as those of the fanon (fans' own circulating narratives and images).

APH's visual style is as disjointed and heterogeneous as its narrative settings. The Allies and Axis nations are represented most often as cute young men, but there are also the "Chibitalia" (*chibi*, or "mini," Italy) episodes, in which Italy and the Holy Roman Empire are represented as cute children, with the neotenic proportions of "wobbly" logo characters. Main characters are also occasionally represented as cats. Himaruya has drawn female character sketches for many of the nations usually represented as young men, and in fan fiction, art, and cosplay, "gender switch" (*zhuan xing*) is common. Fan productions exponentially increase the diversity of styles through which the characters are represented.

Finally, APH is self-reflexive about all of these aspects that it shares with *funü* fandom. In one short vignette in the anime—"Who's Drawing These Pictures?"—America arrives early to a world meeting, to discover England drawing the *chibi* versions of the characters on the chalkboard. France remarks, "They're even worse than our original animation!" and America says, "It's unforgivable, really! How dare that mysterious person flexibly express all of our individual characteristics with skilled sketches using boldly deformed and innovative pop-art styles he probably learned in New York City?!" At the end of the episode, China says he'll take over the drawing from now on. He draws his own face in the style of Mao-era calendar art, with bangs and a braid, and the others gasp in unison, "China, you're a girl?!"[2]

Himaruya is constantly reminding his audience that these are cartoon characters and stereotypical exaggerations, that they are created through a synthetic process that blends and juxtaposes incompatible modes of personification from different art worlds, including high culture (e.g., Modernist pop art) and low culture (e.g., Japanese commercial manga and *dōjinshi* subculture), and that their gender identities exist to be played with.

This type of reflexivity is also very common in *tongrenzhi*, and it would be impossible to trace whether it started with professional animators or fans. One of the most common settings for alternate-universe *tongrenzhi* is the school, especially the manga club, where the characters are portrayed as middle or high school students drawing cartoons of themselves. Another example is a Taiwanese APH *tongrenzhi* manga called "Pocket Police." The setting is a police station. America is the newest officer, and like the other officers, he is drawn in the attractive-young-man form. But his supervisor and partner, England, is drawn in *chibi* style and is only a few inches tall. While tucked into the front of America's bomber jacket, England directs America on how to catch bad guys. England is the mascot of the police station, and Japan has a side business designing and selling posters and figurines of *chibi* England to fans.

So how do the animated national identities of APH differ from collective identities that we perform, that are naturalized as something we simply "have" or "are"? Nationalists, corporate branders, and *funü* all want the personifications they create to have presence, to have a sense of vitality, so that people can establish relationships with them. They are all deeply concerned with affect, with the personified figure as an inciter and repository of emotional attachment. But these groups differ a great deal both in how they see the relationship between the concept being personified and its personification and in how they trace the sources and flow of affect.

In order to elucidate how identity is implicitly theorized in APH, we need to first unpack how characterization works in the APH canon and fanon—what kinds of qualities are projected onto the anthropomorphic characters, what gives these characters their emotional appeal, and what fans see as the source of their vitality.

## APH Characterization: Allegory, Moe Elements, and Ethnic Stereotypes

The characters in APH combine three different modes of personification—first, allegory; second, what I will call the Japanese manga/anime character system; and third, the ethnic stereotype. In this section, I will illustrate how these three modes of personification work, separately and in combination, with examples of some ways Taiwanese fans use APH's Taiwan character. Taiwan is one of the rare female characters in APH, all of whom are relatively minor characters. She is called Wan Niang by fans (the *wan* character is the *wan* in Taiwan, meaning "bay," and *niang* can mean "maiden," "wife," or "mother").

Almost every possible pairing exists in Taiwanese APH *tongrenzhi*. In Taiwan, as in Japan (Miyake 2013), Canada (Annett 2011), and many other countries, the most popular pairing by far is that between America and England. The fans I interviewed attributed this in part to the fact that America-England is a *guan pei*, an official pairing whose friendship and tensions are elaborated in the canon, and also to the fact that these countries are more familiar than other non-Asian countries are to Taiwanese youth, to whom a wide variety of American popular culture is available and who are taught English starting in elementary school.[3] But in Taiwan, as in Japan, the second most popular pairings are those involving the "home" or "self" character. In Japan the second most popular pairing is England-Japan; in Taiwan it is probably Japan-Taiwan, followed closely by China-Taiwan.

The combination of the three systems of personification is clear in the character sketch for Taiwan from the canon comic *Axis Powers Hetalia 6* (in the Chinese translation published in 2013). All the Asian characters wear some sort of costumes based on nineteenth-century dress styles in the canon, with the exception of Japan and China, who are shown in their World War II uniforms and contemporary dress, as well as the occasional kimono or *tangzhuang* (Manchu-style shirt or jacket). On a page featuring character sketches of several countries, Taiwan is shown in a Qing-dynasty-style tunic over a flowing skirt. Her most recognizable feature is her long hair, with a single zigzag strand flying out and a plum blossom (a symbol of the Republic of China) pinned on the left side. The character description reads: "An island maiden who steadfastly persists in her ways. She puts up posters of *moe* characters on the street! Sometimes, she also mischievously goes out of her way just to annoy China." In this character, official nationalist symbolism (the plum blossom) is combined with typical Japanese *moe* elements (the "hair antenna") and personality characteristics (stubborn persistence, mischievousness).

More of Wan Niang's personality traits emerge in the canon story "Ilha Formosa," in which she first appears (*Axis Powers Hetalia 4*). The Japan character (sometimes interpreted by fans as Himaruya himself) visits Taiwan, and Wan Niang takes him to a temple where they perform a divination ritual. Japan receives a bad fortune, but Wan Niang tells him to just throw it away and pretend it never happened. Later, she cajoles another female character, the shy Vietnam, into taking a photo with her, which she then photoshops to give them both huge eyes.

APH characters are allegorical in that they "stand in" for nations. As E. H. Gombrich (1963) points out in his study of European newspaper cartoons, this kind of symbolic personification is closely linked to figures of speech. What political cartoons do, often through anthropomorphism, is to give linguistic figuration (e.g., "justice reigns") a visible form (e.g., a woman in ancient Greek robes holding a scale and seated on a throne) and thus a greater emotional impact. Gombrich argues that the allegorical cartoon works through the same kind of condensation that Freud found at work in dreams and wit: "The fusion of disparate elements results in an unfamiliar and weird configuration which may still hide a lot of sense . . . [but] the neatness of the formulation may even effectively block our reflection whether or not it contains the truth and nothing but the truth" (1963:130–131).

The linguistic figuration of "the nation" can, of course, refer to many things. In APH, what the characters stand for varies from vignette to vignette and different aspects of the nation are condensed within vignettes. Visually, the character's allegorical relationship to the nation is represented through symbolic elements such as a flag or a uniform, and in the vignettes based on historical events, it is clear that the characters' motivations are those of governments, armed forces, or diplomatic missions. When characters in such vignettes are simultaneously represented as having stereotypical personality traits, the wills of the rulers and ruled are conflated.

It is in this allegorical mode that APH has been most controversial. For example, in a well-known case in 2009, the South Korean government censored an episode in which Korea was shown trying to grab Japan's "breast." This vignette was taken by members of South Korea's National Assembly as an allegory for Korea's claim to the disputed Liancourt Rocks. A more general, and frequent, criticism of APH is that in portraying war, especially World War II, as a children's game, it elides such serious issues as fascism, genocide, and the use of chemical and nuclear weapons.

The characters are also often used allegorically by fans. In Taiwan, many APH-inspired one-frame cartoons (the classic format for the political cartoon) are posted online, usually featuring Wan Niang. One example is an image posted on a fan's blog in 2008, when the Legislative Yuan was debating banning imports of American beef that did not meet Taiwanese health standards. Here, Wan Niang is shown beset by America on one side, saying, "Hey, mad cow disease won't kill you anyway—look how healthy I am!" and China on the other, saying, "America's just jealous of how close we've gotten recently; don't listen to him!" Wan Niang faces the viewer and grumps, "Go to hell, the both of you!" During recent election campaigns, some DPP (Democratic Progressive Party) candidates even used the Wan Niang character on their posters.

Another example is a long fanfic (fan fiction) novella titled "Precious Thing," posted on an online Taiwan APH forum. In "Precious Thing," Wan Niang lives with her older brother, China, until he is forced to give her to Japan. Japan is arrogant and cruel, treating Wan Niang as his servant (later household manager) and demanding that she submit to his sexual advances. But he gradually reveals his love for Wan Niang, referring to her as his treasure and his only shelter from the storm of war. Wan Niang, for her part, hates him at first, trying to kill him and escape, then gives up and submits to him, and finally comes to care for him. She comforts him when he returns bloody and defeated from the war, says good-bye to him as he lies passively in his sickbed, and then leaves to return to her brother's house, bravely facing an unknown future (crasnowy 2018a). This story parallels a common trope in Taiwanese Native Soil literature of the 1970s–1990s, in which Taiwan is portrayed (usually by male writers) as a woman whose sexuality represents Taiwan's vulnerability to, or desire for, domination by colonial power.

When APH personifications are in the Japanese manga/anime mode of characterization, the nation is simply a name on which to hang a set of popular *moe* elements. I noted in chapter 2 that, according to Azuma Hiroki (2009), the Japanese manga/anime character is first and foremost a conglomeration of conventionalized visual or aural features selected from an ever-shifting database in order to elicit and intensify *moe* (*meng* in Mandarin), a feeling of excitement that may be erotic, sentimental, or both. For *fujōshi*, Patrick Galbraith (2009) argues, *moe* is generated by the "*fujōshi* formula," in which all types of relationships between male characters are eroticized. Fans do this by pairing up canon characters and assigning them the sexual roles of *seme* and *uke* (*gong* and *shou* in Mandarin)—basically, top and bottom. Some characters in the APH canon, particularly those less familiar to Himaruya and most East Asians (such as Belarus and Ukraine), are based purely on common combinations of *moe* elements rather than ethnic stereotypes.

I should note that these are modes of interpretation as well as creation; the same story may be read as allegorical by one reader and strictly within the manga/anime character system by another. For instance, while most responses to the allegorical story "Precious Thing" talked about how sad it made the reader to think about Taiwan's history of colonization, one fan, reading in manga/anime mode, wrote, "Yes! I like evil Japan! Make him even darker!" A few of the fans I interviewed in Taiwan claimed that they read APH characters only as *moe* characters, consciously ignoring their connection to actual nations.

Although fans are all well aware of the allegorical and *moe*-arousing functions of the APH personifications, when I asked the question "What do the characters represent?" they nearly universally answered that the characters represented ethnic stereotypes. Some common answers I got were "*minzu xing*" (ethnic nature), "*minzu yishi*" (ethnic consciousness), and, most often, "*keban yinxiang*" (stereotype)—literally, "impression carved into a board," a fairly direct translation of the etymological meaning of "stereotype" as a fixed plate for a printing press. As the term "ethnic consciousness" indicates, Taiwanese fans see ethnic stereotypes primarily as conglomerations of psychological traits or tendencies, although these may overlap with Japanese manga/anime categories such as *tsundere* (someone who acts cold but is actually passionate) and *yandere* (someone who acts calm and friendly but is actually psychotic).

As I've noted, the main characteristics of the Taiwan character are her stubborn persistence, mischievousness, optimism, and love of the Japanese manga/anime aesthetic. All of the Taiwanese fans I interviewed were positive about the character. As one of them said, "What's not to like?" Nevertheless, when I asked the question "If you had not seen the Taiwan character in APH and I asked you to design a character that was the personification of Taiwan, what would that character be like?" not one of my interviewees answered by describing a character at all like Wan Niang. For one thing, since they were all *funü*, they all said they would have designed a male character. Indeed, a "gender switch" version of the Taiwan character, called Wan Lang (*lang* is the masculine counterpart to *niang*), appears frequently in Taiwanese *tongrenzhi*. Several said they would create a character who was a typical *taike*—a lower-class young man who wears garish clothes in clashing patterns and speaks in Holo or heavily accented Mandarin. Some said their character would be a *xiao hunhun*, a category often synonymous with *taike*—a young man who spends his days hanging out with his gang, possibly a petty criminal. Others said they would make the Taiwan character a workaholic office worker. Some of the personality traits they associated with Taiwan were loyalty to friends and family, materialism, and being quick to anger but equally quick to forget and forgive.

A 2010 *tongrenzhi* titled "Super Happy Taiwan" might be seen as a rewriting of the canon episode "Ilha Formosa," in which the ethnic stereotype of Taiwan is corrected to reflect characteristics with which Taiwanese people themselves identify. In this short manga, Wan Lang appears dressed in typical *taike* fashion—shorts, a T-shirt, and the ubiquitous blue-and-white flip-flops—but keeping Wan Niang's plum blossom and hair antenna. He takes the Japan character to a night market, where he tries to get Japan to eat stinky tofu and pig's-blood cakes and is generally too loud, playful, and physically intimate for the reserved Japan. Japan wanders off on his own but quickly realizes how much he misses Wan Lang's company, and the two reconcile with a kiss.

What ethnic stereotypes are and how they function within APH personifications are strongly influenced by the overlap of the taxonomy of ethnic stereotypes with the database of the Japanese manga/anime character system. In Taiwan there is also a simultaneous overlap with the *ang-a* mode of animation, in which characters exist in an analogical relation to reality. This has some important consequences for how APH fans approach the idea of national character and its relation to experience.

Current discourse around identity politics often conflates two quite different definitions of the stereotype. So I think we first need to make a distinction between these two different kinds of stereotype, which I'll call dyadic and taxonomic, before we move on to looking at how they interact with each other. Postcolonial critiques of the stereotype (for instance, by Frantz Fanon, Edward Said, and Homi Bhabha) are based on a dyadic model, inspired by Hegel's master-slave dialectic. In this model, the stereotype is a means of negatively Othering one group of people in order to bolster a positive sense of self in the stereotyping group. Neither pole in the dyad (black/white, native/colonizer, savage/civilized, etc.) can exist without the other; they define each other. These types of stereotypes can be wildly self-contradictory. "Orientals," for example, can be both fiendishly cunning and ploddingly stupid, both lazy and trying to steal your job, both kinky Lotharios and effete eunuchs.

The stereotypes personified in APH, at least in the mode that is identified by fans when they say personifications represent ethnic consciousness, are not dyadic but taxonomic. While dyadic stereotypes emerge from situations of extreme power imbalance, such as colonialism, taxonomic stereotypes emerge from situations of relatively equal power. Taxonomic stereotypes arise from situations in which people from different cultural groups are forced to live in intimate, everyday familiarity with each other, on a relatively egalitarian footing—situations such as the city or factory town where multiple immigrant communities are squeezed together or national armies into which men from every community are conscripted as soldiers. Himaruya developed the APH characters when he was studying in New York and claims he was inspired by the discourse of New Yorkers, including members of ethnic communities established many generations ago as well as recent immigrants.

A good example of how taxonomic stereotypes work is this song, sung in the APH anime version in Italian opera style by Italy's grandfather, the Roman Empire, as he sails absurdly across the sky in a barge:

> On Earth, Heaven can be like this—
> The cooks are French
> The police are British
> The mechanics are German
> The bankers are Swiss
> And the lovers are Italian
>
> On Earth, Hell can be like this—
> The cooks are British
> The police are German
> The mechanics are French
> The lovers are Swiss
> And the bankers are Italian

This is quite an old joke—I think I first heard it from my grandmother, the daughter of Russian Jewish immigrants, at her home on Long Island sometime in the early 1970s. It might be seen as a pop culture version of the Boasian Culture and Personality school of anthropology associated primarily with Ruth Benedict and Margaret Mead. The key work in this school, Benedict's *Patterns of Culture*, focuses on the way that sociocultural institutions encourage different styles of behavior. In taxonomic stereotype systems, the question of cause and effect is usually set aside, but the fit between institutions or customs and personality traits is noted (as in the song).

Taxonomic stereotypes are also not completely dependent on each other for their meaning. That is to say, while identity categories are defined in terms of their differences from each other, overlap is possible. We could switch the names "Italian" and "French" in the joke, and it would still make sense. We could also add and subtract nations in the joke without changing the source of its humor.

The difference between dyadic and taxonomic stereotypes is often seen as quantitative—that is, taxonomic stereotypes are seen as dyadic stereotypes "lite," a milder version of the same operation of Othering. I would argue that they are, in fact, fundamentally different. Taxonomic stereotype systems may be encompassed tout court within dyadic systems (e.g., all of the identities in the joke are encompassed by the category "white"), but they do not replicate the structure of the dyad. Taxonomic stereotype systems must include the category of Self, and the relationship between the Self and Others is both horizontal and nonexclusive.

I am not arguing here that taxonomic stereotypes are necessarily "harmless"; rather, I am arguing that the kind of harm they may do is qualitatively different from that of dyadic stereotypes. The main difference is that dyadic stereotyping involves abjection—the Self projects onto the Other those qualities the Self wants to disavow, and the Othered person must then take on these qualities. In taxonomic stereotypes, qualities are projected from Self to Other, but the Self does not necessarily gain the illusion of having lost these qualities. We can phrase this as a difference in the relationship between animator and animatee.

The ethnic stereotype mode of constructing APH characters tends to be the least controversial among fans in Taiwan, and I never heard any *funü* object to APH's ethnic stereotypes simply because they are stereotypes. I think this is because in Taiwan, ethnic stereotypes such as those in APH exist within the analogical ontology of the *ang-a* mode of animation, as well as within nonce taxonomies. That is, the relationship between the anthropomorphized national character and the personalities of real people from a given national community is seen as a relationship not of representation but of analogy. The disposition of traits within the character may be seen as similar to or mapping onto other dispositions of the nation as a whole, such as geography or social structure. This also means that the taxonomy of all the national stereotypes may also map onto the types of individuals within any particular nation. In other words, it would be easy to see Taiwan as filled with German-type people, Italian-type people, Japanese type-people, and so on. And indeed, Taiwanese APH fans do this. For APH fans, the personification of imagined communities is a fractal process. New works are continually being written that personify smaller and smaller communities (e.g., specific regions and cities in Taiwan and specific neighborhoods in those cities) or, more rarely, larger communities (such as continents).

Specific identity categories may be transferred from one system to the other, from taxonomic to dyadic or from dyadic to taxonomic. Such transfers index a significant transformation in power relations. For example, the recognition of taxonomic national stereotypes among Latinos in the United States (Chicanos, Cubans, Dominicans, etc.) within the national mass media may be a sign of the deracialization of the category Latino. For a more frightening example, we can look to the former Yugoslavia. Slavoj Zizek notes that in the Yugoslav army in the 1960s, ethnic stereotypes of Bosnians, Slovenians, Montenegrins, and so on, expressed in obscene jokes, were common. Zizek argues that the existence of such jokes was an index of solidarity among male soldiers (with, as even he acknowledges, women remaining a dyadic Other outside the taxonomy). In the 1990s, as politicians began to openly speak of "ethnic cleansing," such jokes disappeared.[4] These ethnic stereotypes transformed from a taxonomy to a Serb/non-Serb dyad in the lead-up to war.

Both dyadic and taxonomic forms of the stereotype are at play in APH. One thing that APH fandom can provide insight into is how the process of transformation of stereotypes from dyadic to taxonomic or vice versa works. In APH discourse, the ethnic stereotypes tend toward dyadic Othering most when they are used allegorically—that is, when "national character" conflates "the people" with the ruling elite. Ethnic stereotypes tend toward the taxonomic most when they are blended with the manga/anime database—that is, when they mesh two sets of categories that are both filled with elements that may overlap. APH fan fiction is most interesting, and in some cases seems to actually change people's attitudes, when the characters' ethnic-ness is backgrounded, and the allegorical and manga/anime modes are mixed.

Toshio Miyake has argued that while both APH canon and fanon perform complex parodies of national character stereotypes, they both also reflect an unconscious Occidentalism, naturalizing the hierarchies of colonialism and postcolonialism. The European countries are the main characters in the series, in terms of the number of vignettes they appear in and the complexities of their characterizations. Very few non-Western postcolonial nations appear in the series. As Miyake (2013) notes, in most APH *dōjinshi*, "the stronger, aggressive, more experienced, taller, masculine *seme* character is performed by the more powerful nation, while the more passive, younger, effeminate *uke* character is played by the weaker nation." In other words, the Othering structure of geopolitical (state-to-state) power relations is mapped directly onto the dyadic categorization that frames the *fujōshi* formula. While it should be noted that among fans the *uke* role does not necessarily correlate with the qualities of passivity or weakness, there is indeed something disturbing about the reframing of colonial relations as heteronormative "pure love." But some more interesting things may be going on around the edges of the fandom, and I'd like to place the romanticization of geopolitical relations in the context of how *funü/fujōshi* identify with animated characters more generally, and with personifications of their own nations in particular.

In the Chinese-speaking world, it is allegorical representations/readings of the Taiwan and China characters that cause the most friction, both between mainland Chinese, Taiwanese, and Hong Kong fans and, within Taiwan, between fans who identify as Blue (pro-unification) or Green (pro-independence). At the height of APH's popularity, flame wars on Chinese-language fan sites were common. Most fans dealt with *"hei*-ers" (a pun on the Mandarin for "black" and the English "haters") by simply closing off dialogue; several of my interviewees reported having left discussion groups for a while or permanently. The managers of some BBS chat groups and Facebook pages, aside from simply calling for civility and respect, established elaborate rules aiming to direct readings away from the allegorical. For instance, some APH fan sites on both sides of the straits stipulated that personifications must be referred to by their character names (e.g., "Arthur Kirkland" for England, "Wang Yao" for China) and that the names of countries must never be referred to directly. Such methods of dealing with conflict indicate a general sense that minds will not change.

While the mainstream of APH fandom does reflect a trend toward an overlap of dyadic, allegorical views of national identity and the assumption that identification with structural power positions is almost inevitable, in this chapter I am looking for more hopeful potentials. To me, the most interesting Wan Niang stories are those that combine the allegorical and the manga/anime modes of personification. A good example is the story "If They Were Butlers," by the same fan who wrote "Precious Thing." In this story, Wan Niang is a princess and Japan is her butler. This premise is taken from a genre of BL manga/anime in which a group of beautiful young men work as butlers, pampering aristocratic young women. The mistress-butler relationship is usually platonic; the butlers engage in romantic and sexual relationships with each other, displayed for, and occasionally directed by, their mistresses. In recent years, butler cafés for *funü* have emerged in Japan and Taiwan as counterparts to the maid cafés visited by male *otaku* (*yuzhaizu* or *zhainan* in Mandarin). "If They Were Butlers" begins when Japan steps into Wan Niang's bed to wake her with a morning kiss, and she attacks him with a sword. He parries her attacks while cajoling her into eating breakfast. As she is eating, Wan Niang's older brother, China, rushes through the front door, furious that Taiwan has run away from home and is living with Japan. He demands that she return home or he'll destroy her house. She just smiles sweetly at him and then tells him harshly to go home, ordering Japan to send him out (crasnowy 2018b).

Here, Wan Niang becomes a stand-in for the *funü* author herself or, perhaps more accurately, a personification of *funü*-dom. This is a long-established pattern for female characters within *funü* writing worldwide (Silvio 2011; Blair 2010). Thus, in many Taiwanese fan productions, Wan Niang is a minor character who voyeuristically observes the romantic fumblings of England and America (or some other male-male couple), sometimes actively encouraging them to get together. Wan Niang is often portrayed as a sort of mother or older sister figure, the character who understands all the other characters better than they understand themselves and watches them with a resigned good humor.

In its characterizations, "If They Were Butlers" condenses a series of relationships with which many *funü* in Taiwan identify. While they may not all identify with the apparent Green slant of the story, they may still enjoy reading Wan Niang as representing a fierce defender of *funü* subculture against the gender norms of the older generation or as representing Taiwan's Japanophile youths (*harizu*) as active and empowered, rather than passive and brainwashed, in their relationship to Japanese culture.

The uses of "self" characters both as allegorical figures that allow for the representation of historical experiences of violence and oppression that are left out of the canon, and as embodiments of *funü* and *funü* subculture, are not unique to Taiwan. I made a brief search of English-language APH fan fiction sites on the Internet and found that when fans decide to create original characters to represent postcolonial nations not personified within the canon (such as the Philippines and Mexico), they usually gender them female and write them as stand-ins for the *funü*, sympathetically observing and guiding the male couples.

Let me end this section with an example of a *tongrenzhi* that several Taiwanese fans reported actually changed their attitudes toward the China character, a comic written and drawn by a fan whose pen name is Seraph. When I interviewed her, Seraph claimed to be apolitical, but many see her as clearly pro-China. Nonetheless, many of her fans identified as pro-independence. A couple of them told me they had been deeply involved in the 2014 Sunflower movement. The Sunflower movement was a broad protest movement, mostly by students and young people, that included many divergent opinions and discourses but was generally seen as opposing the ruling KMT party. Many of the loudest voices during the protests were virulently anti-China. These fans told me that they really disliked representations of

China by mainland *tongrennü*, which they said always portrayed China as heroic and wise. Yet their sentiments toward the China character had taken a positive turn when they read Seraph's *tongrenzhi* titled *A Good Day for Asia* (*Yaxiya rihe*), a 2009 collection of very short manga. They particularly directed me to a four-panel comic in the collection. The first frame begins with the caption: "Talking with friends one day on MSN . . ." Two fans (who are identified as the characters of Lithuania and Poland and called by their character names, Toris and Feliks)[5] have the following dialogue:

FELIKS: Although China has been very nice to us recently, he's really being a bully in international relations.

TORIS: Yeah, he keeps seducing our allies over to his side.

FELIKS: If you look at them as personified characters, China is like an older brother who overprotects his little sister and won't let any other men date her.

TORIS: But most guys who wanted to protect their little sister would just chase away the men who approach her.

In the background, we see Wang Yao (the China character) standing in front of Wan Niang, threatening some suitor whose face is not shown. Wang Yao scolds Wan Niang while she cries, "Brother, you're an idiot! I hate you!" In the next panel, we see Wang Yao and the suitor walking away, arm in arm. Wang Yao says, "What's the attraction of going out with an immature girl?" and the suitor replies, "Ha ha, yes, you are much more charming than she is . . ." as a stunned Wan Niang looks on in the foreground. In the final panel, Toris and Feliks laugh and agree, "If that's how it is, OK!" The theme of China seducing all the male characters (often while cross-dressed as a girl) while his little sister looks on jealously is repeated in other cartoons in the collection.

I think Seraph's comics are effective in changing Taiwan-identified fans' attitudes toward the China character because they reflexively transform allegorical readings into BL readings and, thus, dyadic figures into taxonomic ones. In this cartoon, we start with a very typical allegorical scene of conflict between elder brother China and little sister Taiwan (in which neither one is set up as the more obvious figure for identification), which switches across the gutter between frames 2 and 3 into a typical BL manga scene. In Seraph's narrative framing, fandom itself is shown as the agent of this transformation.

A comic about China and Taiwan from Seraph's *tongrenzhi*. Reproduced with permission of the artist.

Thus far, I have been talking about how APH's combination of modes of personification holds the potential to change interpretations of stereotypes. But even the power of Seraph's popular manga is limited to transforming attitudes toward anthropomorphized national characters. Whether this has any potential implications for real-world politics is another question. In order to explore this question, we need to turn to the relationship between the 2-D world (the fantasy world within manga/anime) and the 3-D world ("real life"). What, exactly, is the relationship between Wan Niang and Wang Yao on the one hand, and between Taiwanese and Chinese identities as they are lived and experienced by young women on the other?

## The Ontology of the Character and the Ontology of the Nation: Negotiating 2-D and 3-D

Toshio Miyake (2013) notes that among his Japanese female fan informants, there is little interest in attaching APH to the real—either to real gay men, to the artist Himaruya, or to real foreign countries. Although fans may spend a lot of time researching the history and culture of the nations whose characters they want to re-create in *dōjinshi*, they are not necessarily interested in going there. This was true for the women I interviewed in Taiwan as well, and when I asked them if APH had changed their perceptions of foreign countries, they said no.

But when I asked why they thought APH was able to sustain its popularity for so long, what made it different from other manga/anime franchises, the fact that nations are in some sense already "real" objects became important. As one Taiwanese fan put it:

> When you're in 2-D—that is, when you're reading most manga/anime—you're looking for the *moe* power. In APH, you can look in *real life*, in history, the news, and you'll "*moe* up" [*mengqilai*]. . . .
>
> They're countries! Countries actually exist—or at least there's a point of view that maybe they really exist, right? Most manga/anime franchises, even if you like them you won't take them as something that could really appear in the world. You take them as fictional stories; in your mind you're very clear that this is fictional. But this work anthropomorphizes nations. Some characters in it, some events, they really happened. . . . You wouldn't look for elements in the 3-D world [in order to read or write] most franchises. If you want to understand a character better, you would read more *tongrenzhi* or watch the original works again. You can only look in the 2-D world. But with APH, you can take new things from the 3-D world. . . .

With other works, they end one day; then you've gotten out of it all you can get. When that happens, everyone usually loses interest; they go look for the next work that will excite them. But with this franchise, you can get find new elements in the 3-D, so it will never come to an end, right?

To a certain extent, this fan's discourse appears to exemplify Rée's folk theory of the nation—that national identities exist because people believe in them ("there's a point of view that maybe they really exist"). But I think something slightly more complicated is going on here, as the nation's 3-D-ness is seen primarily as the source of APH fandom's openness, its *lack* of fixity and self-identity.

As with the nation, fans have different ideas about the reality of ethnic stereotypes. If fans meet people from other countries who seem to fit the characterizations in APH, it strengthens the reality effect, making the characters feel more as if they could cross the line between the fictional and real worlds. On the other hand, if the fans meet someone, or read about an event, that challenges the stereotypes in APH, they take it as new material, as something that can be assimilated from the 3-D world back into the 2-D to make it grow.

Events in 3-D can challenge the 2-D taxonomies to expand, but at the same time, events in 2-D (new imaginings) can challenge fans to rethink the 3-D. The result is most often that difficult aspects of reality (war, genocide, colonialism) are simply banished from the fantasy space. But it may also be that difficult historical realities force fans to expand their taxonomies and to think of new ways of relating 2-D and 3-D.

This is where an important overlap between the Japanese manga/anime system and the *ang-a* mode of animation comes in. To think about both 2-D characters and the 3-D world in terms of animation shifts the emphasis away from identity and toward vitality. APH characters, like Chinese gods, are endowed with their sense of presence not only through visual media but also through narrative, through the interplay of "world" and "variation" (Otsuka 2010). Thus, their presence is acquired through superscription (Duara 1988), through the layered density of different versions of characters and events, through the simultaneous existence of diverse interwoven and contradictory stories and images (see chapter 2).

The traits displayed by APH personifications in all three of their modes—allegorical figure, ethnic stereotype, and *moe* element configuration—can be extremely contradictory, not to mention the variation from individual fan work to individual fan work. Then why do APH fans see no contradiction between the source of vitality of the APH world, its diversity, and the coherence of its characters? To understand the non-identitarian ontology of the nation here, we have to understand the ontology of the manga/anime character. Shunsuke Nozawa writes that manga/anime characters have a "*sui generis* realness" and that characters in the 2-D world are self-identical across media platforms, narratives, and visual styles only to the extent that they can maintain "(non-in)consistency." That is, characters are not so much "in character" as just "not out of character" (Nozawa 2013).

In APH it is the "point of view that maybe nations really exist" that maintains character (non-in)consistency across variations. Let me illustrate with a comparison. In the world of live-action cinema, Richard Dyer has argued that we need to distinguish between the "real person" of the actor and the "star persona." The star persona is the impression that audiences have of the actor, an impression composed of many elements:

> A film star's image is not just his or her films, but the promotion of those films and of the star through pin-ups, public appearances, studio hand-outs and so on, as well as interviews, biographies and coverage in the press of the star's doings and "private" life. Further, a star's image is also what people say or write about him or her, as critics or commentators, the way the image is used in other contexts such as advertisements, novels, pop songs, and finally the way the star can become part of the coinage of everyday speech. (Dyer 1986:2–3).

In English-language shipper (i.e., *funü*) fandoms based on live-action TV or film series (those that have received the most academic attention in the US and Europe), fan fiction often focuses on the actors rather than the characters. Not only is there a genre called RP (real people) fanfic, but characters in fan fiction who bear the names of the fictional characters may blend in personality quirks, dress and gestural habitus, or narrative situations taken from other performances by the same actor. For instance, fan fiction based on the BBC series *Sherlock* often makes implicit or explicit reference to other roles that have been played by Benedict Cumberbatch, the actor who plays Sherlock Holmes. Thus, there are stories in which Sherlock Holmes delivers lines originally spoken by the villain Khan in *Star Trek: Into Darkness* and fan art that features the dragon Smaug from *The Hobbit* movies wearing Sherlock Holmes' blue scarf. In some popular fanfics, the only thing keeping "Sherlock Holmes" in character is that it is easy to imagine "Benedict Cumberbatch" performing the actions depicted because of his larger star persona.

In APH fan fiction and art, the idea of the nation serves the same function as the star persona of the Hollywood actor in live-action fandom. The sense of organic holism provided to Sherlock fanfic by Benedict Cumberbatch's high cheekbones and sultry voice is here provided by the material existence of the nation—its geography, architecture, and social institutions and the people who identify with it. There's a point of view that nations really exist in the same way that there's a point of view that Benedict Cumberbatch is a real person. That is, the nation, like the star persona, can create overlapping spaces (which will vary in the eyes of different fans) of (non-in)consistency. The physical existence of the film star is not necessary to the vitality of the star image—in fact, the actor's death may itself contribute to the star image, transforming and revitalizing it (see Dyer [1986] on Judy Garland). So too with the nation.

We are talking, then, about an ontology of the nation quite similar to Benedict Anderson's "imagined community"—something that exists, not "objectively" and also not simply because people believe in it, but because its sense of reality comes through the experience of participating in a shared information network.

To sum up, when APH fans speak of the 3-D-ness of the nation, I think it might be something like the way that Nepali Theravada Buddhists speak of the realness of their community when they fight for their rights as citizens. In this animatorly worldview, nations, societies, and individuals do not exist in the sense of having fixed identities—but they do *live* (and die). That is, they exist in the sense that they change. What is important about the nation for APH fans is not whether it exists objectively or subjectively but that it is generative.

## Personification versus Branding

How does the logic of *funü* personification of nations compare with the logic of the global branding machine? Nadia Kaneva defines nation branding as "a compendium of discourses and practices aimed at reconstituting nationhood through marketing and branding paradigms" (2011:118). Nation branding is usually done through government-sponsored initiatives, often in conjunction with corporate sponsors, and is intended to increase a country's soft power through promoting positive images of the country abroad, in order to attract overseas investment and increase tourism and trade. It is also intended for domestic audiences as well, to promote a sense of national cohesion and well-being among citizens. Nation brands are designed and managed by a small elite. Their success at the goal of creating positive sentiment abroad is dubious, but to the extent that they are successful, they are even more imbricated in the global capitalist identity machine.

Nation branding actually very rarely uses personification as a strategy, being primarily focused on city planning, showcase events, and more abstract logos and slogans. However, Japan is a notable exception. Various Japanese government initiatives have named Hello Kitty and Doraemon as "cultural ambassadors," and in 2009 the Ministry of Foreign Affairs sent three women around the world cosplaying iconic types—the Schoolgirl, the Lolita, and the Harajuku Teen—as "Ambassadors of Cute," part of a wide-ranging campaign to promote the image of "Cool Japan" (Miller 2011a). As Michal Daliot-Bul (2009) and Laura Miller (2011a) argue, the government was largely appropriating subcultural images that were already global, while ignoring the creative labor of youth subculture participants, especially young women, both at home and in Europe and the United States.

In Taiwan, politicians and parties have also appropriated the aesthetics of Japanese manga/anime to brand themselves. During the 1998 election for the mayor of Taipei, the DPP produced an "A-Bian doll," a cute representation of its candidate, Chen Shui-bian ("A-Bian" was his folksy nickname). The dolls sold out, and when Chen ran for president in 2000, a whole series of A-Bian products was sold, including stuffed toys, plastic figurines, and piggy banks. The A-Bian figures were designed with the same kind of roundness, blankness, and neotenic proportions that characterizes logo characters such as Hello Kitty. In fact, they did not include any of the features that political cartoonists emphasized when drawing Chen, such as his rectangular wire-frame glasses.[6] The cartoonified A-Bian products were extremely popular with young DPP supporters, and Yin Chuang (2011) links the use of the *kawaii* (cuteness) aesthetic in these dolls to the process of democratization through the growth of consumer culture. Although many of Chen's young supporters became disillusioned with Chen after his election (he was reelected by a much smaller margin in 2004, his party lost the presidency in 2008, and Chen is currently in jail for embezzlement), cartoon images and *ang-a* of politicians continue to be widely used in Taiwanese election campaigns, by both parties. The current president of Taiwan, Tsai Ing-wen (DPP), has appropriated cute cartoons of herself, originally produced by fan-supporters, into official publicity materials for various government initiatives.

Although they may occasionally look alike, personifications within the manga/anime and *ang-a* modes of animation work very differently from nation brands constructed by government agencies and professional designers. One difference lies in the fact that nation brands tend to be made through a process of stripping down, while manga/anime characters tend to come to life through a process of fleshing out (see chapter 1). In East Asia the logic of corporate branding and the logic of cute intersect along the axis of abstraction. For branding managers, the larger the corporation and the more diffuse its range of products, the more abstract the logo should be. Small OEM (original equipment manufacturer) businesses tend to think of brands as traditional trademarks, as signs that secure the goodwill of customers accrued through consistent quality over time. In contrast, for multinational corporations that market a wide range of products manufactured through outsourcing to factories around the world, the logo reflects an "attitude," a condensation of the corporation and its products into an abstract "happy object," to use Sara Ahmed's (2004) term—not a simple assurance of what customers already know about the company, but a "love mark" that elicits affection and loyalty regardless of the types of material products it may be attached to.

In the context of personified logos, then, more textured and detailed character designs are for specific products aimed at niche markets. Creating a character to represent a wider range of products is, for designers, a process of stripping down, of taking away details and textures. For example, I interviewed a group of designers who were tasked with creating a logo character for a new social media site that a large gaming company was about to launch, where fans of all their various games would be encouraged to chat with each other. Designers of the company's game characters spent a lot of time filling out the characters—giving them backstories and distinctive characteristics, making their movements variable and realistic. But for designing the social network character, they needed something that would be "acceptable to everyone" and have a "healing" effect. They therefore needed an "uncomplicated" character design to "transmit the image of the company to the customers." In the end, they created a very simple geometric character in two colors, whose only expressive features were a single eye in the center (a small black dot inside a lighter-colored larger circle) and short, stick-like arms and legs. The theory behind this paring down of detail is that the fewer features a character has (the more blank it is), the more open it is to the projection of different emotions.

In branding, the larger and more diffuse the entity (product lines, corporations), the more static and abstract the brand tends to be. Nations, even those like Japan that claim racial and cultural homogeneity, are extremely diverse and diffuse communities. Thus, nation-branding projects tend to focus on static objects—architecture, monuments—or logos that are very abstract or consist of only a few highly conventional symbols. Manga/anime personifications, in contrast, maintain vitality through superscription, through the constant addition of new, often contradictory narrative and visual details. In the discourse of nation branders, history, diversity, and even vitality itself may be qualities that the brand attempts to capture, but they cannot be qualities of the brand itself. If they do become qualities of the brand itself, then the brand becomes incoherent and escapes the control of its makers/owners.

Another, related difference between the fan-animated personification and the brand lies in how information networks function. In corporate branding, brand makers and owners usually hope that the meaning of the brand will circulate in one of two ways. The meaning may circulate in broadcast fashion, with allowances for variations in interpretation. That is, different consumers may interact with the brand in different ways, but they do not interact with each other. A good example here is Hello Kitty. As Christine Yano's (2013) extended research shows, different groups of consumers are attracted to Hello Kitty for different reasons—for her cuteness, for nostalgia, even for a certain campy-retro "coolness"—and the Sanrio Company is not only happy with this but encourages diverse interpretations (within limits). But these different consumer groups do not seem to talk to each other or to borrow directly from each other. In a way, Hello Kitty's famous blankness, including her missing mouth, makes her the perfect broadcast medium, allowing the "masses" to project their emotions onto her one by one, as individuals. On the other hand, in the more recent trend of "viral branding," marketers rely on consumers' own social networks to spread the brand. But this kind of branding tends to arouse anxiety among managers about brand dissolution (Moore 2003).

One use of the personification of communities to combat the ravages of postindustrial capitalism, rather than to merely compete within it, is the creation of mascot characters for towns and cities in Japan (Birkett 2012; Occhi 2012). Mascot characters for towns are usually commissioned by local government agencies and designed by professionals, although they may also be created by local amateurs. They are often part of initiatives to attract tourists, although for the amateur group from a small deindustrializing city that Mary Birkett (2012) studied, creating a mascot character was directed more toward the younger generations of local residents, giving them something to revive their pride and engender emotional investment in their hometown.

I think this is a great practical tactic for reanimating communities that are losing their imaginability. But local mascots may run into the usual problems that come with trying to take down the master's house with the master's tools. Local mascots, in other words, still in some ways follow the logic of corporate branding. Most blend iconic elements representing the features of the real town with the aesthetics of *kawaii*. They also seem to follow the broadcast model of branding, speaking to audiences primarily as individual consumers. This may, however, be changing as events in which local mascots from all over Japan compete and interact with audiences are becoming popular (Occhi 2012) and as these mascots are circulating on Internet platforms far beyond their local contexts—for instance, when many fans used Kumamon, the already highly commercialized mascot of Kumamoto Prefecture, to express their sympathy for victims of the earthquake there in April 2016.

*Funü* personification insists on heterogeneity of interpretation and on social circulation, so that semiotic supplement continually builds and dissipates, giving the characters, their world, and fandom itself vitality. The "semiotic vulnerability" that Moore (2003) argues is inherent in the brand as a combination of semiotic and material qualities is, for APH fans, a source of attraction and pleasure rather than anxiety.

At this point, it should go without saying that one final difference between the brand and the personifications in APH is that personifications, unlike the brand, cannot be owned. Like fans of other media franchises, APH fans often put disclaimers—such as "I do not own these characters" or "*Axis Powers Hetalia* is the property of Hidekaz Himaruya"—above the amateur fiction and art they post online. These disclaimers are meant for the broader public, a hedge against legal action by the corporations who hold licenses for the characters. But when APH fans are writing to each other—for instance, when they are arguing over whether a characterization in a *tongrenzhi* has strayed too far from the canon personality—they tend to make statements such as "The characters don't belong to any one of us" or "The characters belong to all of us."

While many fans told me it is "natural" for the home nation character to be most popular, it is significant that none of them claimed that people from a given country had more right (or responsibility) to represent it than fans from elsewhere. Fans often take up new elements for their representations of their home nation from images and narratives created by fans in other nations. For instance, Taiwanese cosplayers acknowledge that the practice of making Wan Niang's hair wavy rather than straight (as it is in the canon) originated with a mainland Chinese cosplayer. When they are researching a character, fans do sometimes look for *tongrenzhi* produced by fans from that country, but they generally do not give these representations more weight than others. As one mainland Chinese fan put it, "China has five thousand years of history, the costumes are different in each era, and the regions are all different. The Han are the majority, but China is multicultural; there are lots of minority peoples. Wang Yao represents what foreigners know best about China. It's easier to condense the image of a country like that from the outside." Most fans implicitly understand that in a taxonomic system of nationality, (non-in)consistency is easier to maintain from a perspective that transcends self-identity.

While there is much in APH *funü* fandom that is flatly identitarian and conservative, there are a few aspects of the process of personifying nations here that present alternatives to the neoliberal identity machine. In particular, APH fans have three valuable insights into national identity. First, national identities are constructed through relationships (both literal relationships, in the *fujōshi* formula, and the semiotic relationship of contrasting qualities). Second, their affective power comes from a lack of fixity rather than from coherence (they are always in the process of "doing," never "done," to use Holloway's terms). And third, they cannot be owned.

The main lesson I would draw from APH's longevity and vitality, and from what fans see as the origins of that longevity and vitality, is that if we want our imagined communities to stay alive, we need to open them up to what we might call object relations with the imagined communities of others. What I mean here is that we might need to be less protective of our self-identities. The practice of identity politics has largely been based on the idea that legitimate identity must be defined from the inside, that it is only members of a community that have the right to speak for that community. But one thing that APH and its fandom teaches us is that (non-in)consistency—presence and vitality—cannot come only from the inside, since characters/identities can have those qualities only within larger worlds. If only Taiwanese fans re-created the character of Wan Niang, the fandom would not last very long.

Let me conclude by asking this: Might we see imagined communities such as the nation, not as identity categories that certain people belong to, but as objects in the process of animation, objects that belong to everyone and no one? What the practice of anthropomorphizing nations as cartoon characters acknowledges is that communities are also things, objects that can become actors only if they are acted upon.

# Animation and Futurity

Performance is a process of becoming. Animation is a process of making. The two are, in practice, always intertwined; every act of becoming makes something, and in every act of making, the maker becomes someone new.

Becoming seems to lead naturally toward the future. Performers take external social roles into their selves and re-create them, inevitably transformed, through embodiment. In this conclusion, I want to ask what it might mean to think of the future in terms of animation—that is, how we remake the world by projecting and materializing parts of our selves. I want to start a conversation about how we might conceptualize politics, in the broadest sense, through the lens of animation, to try to figure out some ways that the concept of animation might inspire strategies for activism in our current globalized, digital media environment, just as the concept of performance inspired strategies for activism when broadcast media were dominant.

In the twentieth century, performance proved to be good to think with for activists seeking to develop strategies to challenge the status quo and ontology of hierarchized identity categories such as gender, race, and class. Two major modes of performance activism developed that are still frequently used today, with differing effects. The first strategy is Brechtian alienation effect—that is, developing a type of reflexive performance that reveals, through a variety of techniques, the ways that identities are constructed and naturalized. The way that drag performance was used within queer activism in the 1990s is exemplary here. While the mainstream of the gay and lesbian movement focused on proving that gay people are "normal," in underground theaters and marches organized by groups such as ACT UP, Queer Nation, and the Lesbian Avengers, drag kings and queens took center stage, using exaggerated and self-reflexive gender performance and camp humor to make the gap between biological sex and social gender identity visible, to expand the range of imaginable gender identities, and to draw connections between sexual, racial, gender, and class oppression.

The second way that performance has been used in radical politics is to create spaces for what Augusto Boal (1979) called "rehearsal for revolution"—allowing marginalized people to think through and practice different ways of approaching specific political problems. Boal's Theater of the Oppressed, developed in the brief years of Allende's socialist government in Chile in the 1970s, included exercises to help peasants and workers both defamiliarize themselves from the habitus acquired through their everyday work and refamiliarize themselves with their bodies' potential for new modes of expressivity. It also included exercises to explore how class position affects people's habitual reactions to the same sorts of situations, and "invisible theater," in which actors/workers would bring some of the scenarios they had rehearsed in workshops into public spaces, drawing interested passersby into the sort of dialogue that might lead to organizing.

What might be an animation equivalent of political drag? What would an Animation of the Oppressed look like? Certainly, examples of animation-based activism abound, from the Bread and Puppet Theater, to Miyazaki Hayao's environmentalist animated cinema inspiring more direct political action among fans, to the indigenous activism that resulted in Bolivia's Legislative Assembly investing Mother Earth with legal personhood and rights in 2010. My purpose here is not to describe or evaluate existing or potential activist strategies; I am not qualified to do that. I do think, though, that anthropology has something to offer to the project of imagining a politics of animation. One of the main purposes of ethnography is to make generally available specialized knowledge, particularly of marginalized groups. In 1972, Esther Newton published *Mother Camp*, an ethnographic study of drag queens in Chicago and St. Louis, based on her PhD dissertation. Most of her research was conducted before Stonewall, and her informants were not activists. In fact, most of them were ambivalent about, or entirely uninterested in, the small, middle-class gay and lesbian movement at the time. Nonetheless, Newton's ethnography was influential in how gender studies scholars in the 1990s reconceptualized gender and sexuality and in how activists thought of theater as a tool (e.g., Judith Butler 1990; Case 1989). Newton outlined the practical knowledge that professional drag queens had developed over the years about the relationship between embodiment and identity and made it available for political activism.

What I want to do now is something like what Newton did, to make available for activism some of the knowledge that Taiwanese puppeteers, fans, designers, and followers of Chinese folk religion have acquired about how one goes about giving things lives of their own. So let me try to sum up some of the things I have learned in Taiwan about animation.

First, if we want to think seriously about the politics of animation, we need to rethink our concepts of fetishism and psychic projection. As I noted in chapter 6, "fetishism" is used in the Marxist tradition as a term for, as Holloway (2002) puts it, "the separation of done from doing," the original sin of capitalism. But historians and anthropologists have been reexamining the origins of the fetish in the interactions of Portuguese traders and Africans in the seventeenth century (Pietz 1985, 1987), and as David Graeber puts it, "fetishes are gods in the process of construction"—fetishism is "social creativity," a process in which the makers' "awareness of the illusion makes no difference" (2007:113, 146). African fetishes are, if I may rephrase Graeber's argument, consciously produced animations, much as Taiwanese gods are. Certainly, the work of most professional animators today is just as alienated as any other labor under capitalism. But fans see their (nonprofessional, unpaid) work of re-creating and adding to the density of animated characters as a labor of love, and they express a strong desire to expand and protect their community and to make fandom a welcoming virtual environment. While I don't want to romanticize fandom as a pure realm outside of capitalism (it is not), I also think it's worth considering that animation fans can point us toward how noncoercive collective world-making can work.

"Psychic projection" is also usually used as a negative term. In North America, if a family member, lover, or friend tells you that you're projecting, you are probably being accused of a kind of self-deception, possibly one that leads to the coercion of others. Most object relations psychology focuses on the process of individuation—of escaping the projections of others, especially parents—rather than on how individuals contribute to and nurture each other's selves. While there is certainly much discussion of the negative effects of bad parenting, there is not much discussion (beyond Winnicott's discussion of the role of the "good-enough mother") of what positive projection might look like, on the part of either parent or child or within adult relationships (psychoanalyst Christopher Bollas' [1992] meditations on the intersubjectivity of analyst and analysand are something of an exception).

Anthropologists have long sought to de-universalize the idea of the self as a coherent, independent source of agency. One of the insights that looking at animation anthropologically provides, as I tried to show in chapter 6, is that identity can be thought of as a collective project of animation, that we may not own our own identities, and that that not-owning may not always be experienced as misrecognition or deprivation. My point here is that when we think of futurity in terms of investing human qualities, whether in humans or in nonhuman objects, we cannot determine the value of that future, its oppressiveness or freedom, in advance. Animation is, as McKenzie (2001:18) says of performance, "a stratum of power/knowledge," neither more nor less than potential.

One of my main goals in writing this book has been to show how the concept of animation provides an alternative for thinking of worlds and identities as either possessions or Others, a way of thinking of both as me/not me. I think that the Taiwanese *ang-a* mode of animation gives us one model for how to think about the relationship between humans and their environment outside of humans creating the environment (animation as "playing God") and outside of the environment as completely independent of human creativity (the animist view of everything in the world having its own preexisting spirit).

One of the most common ways of imagining futurity is through biological reproduction. Children, as politicians, educators, and earnest charity fund-raisers tell us every day, are the future. Biological reproduction is also often used as a metaphor for labor that is not alienated. We "give birth" to ideas, to music, to art. We call the beloved object on which we labor and into which we pour parts of our selves (the PhD dissertation, the customized motorcycle) "my baby." Perhaps the most hopeful way of thinking about animation futurity is to rethink this metaphor along the lines of Khalil Gibran's *On Children*:

> Your children are not your children.
> They are the sons and daughters of Life's longing for itself.
> They come through you but not from you,
> And though they are with you yet they belong not to you.

We can choose how to animate our worlds, but others must live in them, and vice versa. Your fictional characters, your gods, your identities—they are not yours. They come from and belong to no one and everyone. They have their own lives.

# Notes

## Introduction

1.  *Po-te-hi* (*budaixi* in Mandarin) literally means "cloth bag theater." It is also sometimes called *chiang-tiong-hi* (in Mandarin: *zhangzhongxi*), or "theater in the palm of the hand." *Po-te-hi* and *koa-a-hi* (in Mandarin: *gezaixi* or *gezixi*, often translated as "Taiwanese Opera"), a genre of musical theater that dates to around the turn of the twentieth century, are often paired as representative national folk arts. Both *po-te-hi* and *koa-a-hi* are performed in the Holo (Minnan) dialect.

2.  Animator Kyle Balda, who has worked as a character designer and an animation supervisor for Pixar, Industrial Light and Magic, and other large studios, described himself this way at a lecture he gave at the Museum of Fine Arts in Taipei on October 30, 2009. I later found out from talking to other American professional animators that this self-description is very common.

3.  Clifford Geertz, in "Religion as a Cultural System," distinguished models *of*, which make reality comprehensible, and models *for*, which serve as blueprints for the manipulation of reality. He argued that "culture patterns" such as religion "have an intrinsic double aspect": "they give meaning, that is, objective conceptual form, to social and psychological reality both by shaping themselves to it and by shaping it to themselves" (Geertz 1973:93).

4.  The island of Taiwan was settled by people from the Chinese mainland starting in the seventeenth century. The majority of these settlers came from Fujian Province, directly across the Taiwan Strait, especially the areas of Zhangzhou and Quanzhou, and spoke the Holo (Hokkien, or Minnan) language. A smaller group were of the Hakka ethnic minority. Both groups are considered ethnically Chinese, and both Holo and Hakka are in the

Chinese language family. Another group of Chinese people migrated to Taiwan after the Chinese Communist Party won control of the mainland in 1949, mostly soldiers who came with Chiang Kai-shek and his Chinese Nationalist Party (KMT) army. These migrants came from all over China and spoke a wide variety of Chinese languages, although most spoke Mandarin, which was made the "national language" (Guoyu) of Taiwan in 1945, as either a first or second language. Today people whose mother tongue is Holo make up approximately 70 percent of the population, Hakka people are approximately 15 percent, and the (patrilineal) descendants of post-1945 Chinese migrants constitute around 12 percent. Before the island was settled by the Chinese, there were numerous Austronesian indigenous peoples living on the island, who had been there for thousands of years. Today indigenous people are less than 3 percent of the population. There are also over 40,000 migrant workers from Southeast Asia now working in Taiwan, and around 140,000 marriage migrants from Southeast Asia. Marriage migrants may apply for Taiwanese citizenship if they give up citizenship in their country of origin; migrant workers are allowed to work legally in Taiwan for only twelve years and are not eligible for citizenship.

This book is focused on the animation practices of the Holo-speaking majority, which have roots in Chinese history. Some aspects of indigenous Taiwanese and Southeast Asian culture have been appropriated into Chinese-Taiwanese animation (for instance in the use of cute cartoons of indigenous peoples as logo characters, or the use of indigenous or Southeast Asian music within puppetry), and indigenous Taiwanese in their teens to 30s, and the children of Taiwanese-Southeast Asian marriages, participate in the fandoms of Japanese, American, and locally produced animation. The indigenous and Southeast Asian people in Taiwan have their own, very different traditions of animation practice, which are outside of the scope of this book.

5.   Wan-chia Wang (2010) cites the organizer of the 2010 Taiwan Golden Comic Awards http://gca.moc.gov.tw/gca/2018/default_en.aspclaiming that 95 percent of the comics available in the Taiwanese market in 2009 were Japanese manga. I heard similar estimates from artists, publishers, and vendors I interviewed in 2015.

6.   The Chinese title translates to English as *The Animalized Postmodern: How Otaku Are Influencing Japanese Society.*

7.   I should also mention what are perhaps the best-known Taiwanese animations outside Taiwan, the animated news/news parody videos produced by Next Media Animation, which is based in Taipei. Although NMA's

growing fame is a source of national pride, and many of its videos focus on Taiwanese politics and use local imagery, the company was founded by Hong Kong entrepreneur Jimmy Lai, and NMA's style and use of digital technology are seen in Taiwan as global, or American, rather than local.

8. "Pili" is an onomatopoeia for the sound of thunder and means "astounding."

9. For examples of the "traditional culture creative industries" discourse that celebrate the Pili Company, see Caituanfaren Zhonghua Minsu Yishu Jijinhui (2005); Zhang Qionghui (2003); and Lü (2006).

10. A digital version of the exhibit is online at http://gofigures.ioe.sinica .edu.tw.

## Chapter 1: Animation versus Performance

1. According to Hutchby (2001:27), "affordances . . . are properties of things; yet those properties are not determinate or even finite, since they only emerge in the context of material encounters between actors and objects" (see also Gibson 1979). For example, for a human being, one affordance of a fist-size stone would be its potential to be used to open walnuts or mash grain, while for a mouse, the rock's affordances would include providing shade and a hiding space.

2. Both Artaud and Brecht were, significantly, inspired by Asian theater genres. We should keep in mind that the development of the performance model has a long history of troubling the East-West dichotomy, which the emergence of the animation model is, so far, continuing.

3. Television technology, like radio, was originally designed and adapted for a variety of uses, including military, education, and communication purposes. But when it was taken over by commercial interests after World War II, it was developed exclusively as a technology for the home. Commercial television began in 1946 with local stations in the New York area, owned and promoted by radio companies, including RCA, NBC, and CBS. These companies went on to form national networks. Because television grew out of radio, it used the same marketing model of making profits primarily through the sale of advertisement time. Between 1946 and 1955, the percentage of American households owning a television set rose form 0.02 percent to 64 percent, and the number of stations rose from 6 to 458. By 1960, people in the United States were watching television an average of 3.5 hours a day (Edgerton 2010:90–93).

4. For most media scholars, the golden age of American television lasted from 1948 to the early 1960s.

5. *Wikipedia*, s.v. "History of Computer Animation," accessed July 1, 2018, https://en.wikipedia.org/wiki/History_of_computer_animation.

6.  There has been some work on sound in animation but, as in cinema studies generally, surprisingly little.

7.  There are also fields within scientific and information technology research that might be seen as kinds of animation—artificial life, robotics, and human-computer interface design, for example. These fields have been prominent in the emerging field of the sociology/anthropology of science.

8.  That many people contribute to the creation of characters in live-action cinema (including the scriptwriter, director, cinematographer, lighting director, etc.) is an aspect of cinema that, under the performance paradigm, has received very little attention.

9.  We can, of course, add or subtract to this list of sign systems for different technes of animation. Cinema animation, for example, also involves codes of background music, composition and framing, number of cels projected per second, etc.).

10. Christopher Bolton (2002) does something very like this in his article on Oshii's remediation of bunraku in *Ghost in the Shell*.

11. James Cameron's 2009 film *Avatar* broke box office records in Taiwan and is still rerun regularly on cable television. The film's title was translated as *A-fan-da* in Mandarin, the Chinese transliteration of the Sanskrit, although the more common term is *huashen*, which is used in nonreligious as well as religious contexts (as in "She is the *huashen* of Guanyin," meaning that someone is compassionate).

12. Many keyboard face cartoons that are now popular throughout East Asia were invented by Japanese girls specifically for cell-phone texting (see Miller 2011b). To see Wan Wan's emoticon characters, you can go to her blog: Wan Wan, *Wan Wan de Tuya Rizhi* (Wan Wan's graffiti diary).

## Chapter 2: The *Ang-a*

1.  For a rich ethnography of both the practices and ideologies of artificial-life scientists in the United States and Europe, see Helmreich (1998).

2.  For more in-depth analyses of the utopian potential and uncanniness of AL and AI in speculative fiction, see Nelson (2001). Several feminist scholars have noted that fantasies of disembodied intelligence are associated with masculinity in North America and Europe and may be perceived as utopian or dystopian along gender lines (Hayles 1999; Helmreich 1998).

3.  There is a Chinese myth of the origin of humankind. The goddess Nüwa is said to have molded the first people out of clay. These were the aristocrats. She then dragged a rope through wet mud, and the clumps that were dislodged became the common people. There are several reasons why I think

that this myth is not particularly relevant to the Taiwanese *ang-a* mode of animation. Wu Hung (2006) has argued that the myth may have been modeled after new animation practices (changes in how tomb figurines were made) rather than the other way around. More importantly, Nüwa is a relatively obscure goddess in Taiwan. There are only a few temples in Taiwan dedicated to Nüwa, in contrast with the thousands dedicated to Mazu. Although many people are familiar with the myth of Nüwa repairing the sky, which I have seen referenced in fine art and popular culture, I have never once, in over two decades of fieldwork, heard a Taiwanese person make an unelicited reference to the myth of Nüwa creating mankind from mud. This situation contrasts sharply with the ubiquity of citations of Genesis in a wide variety of contexts among not only Jews and Christians but also others in North America and Europe.

4. Pronounced "bye-bye." The term is Holo; in Mandarin the verb "to worship" is simply *bai*, but it requires an object.

5. It is difficult to find a perfect English word to translate *shenxiang*. The word is composed of the characters for "god" and "image" and refers to sacralized statues of deities for worship. I find the direct translation "deity image," used by some scholars, to be too ambiguous, since not all images of gods are sacred, as *shenxiang* are. While I sympathize with Alfred Gell's insistence on revaluing the word "idol," in Taiwan and Japan the word "idol" (*ouxiang*) is primarily used to refer to young attractive stars of the cinema, music, and television industries. I decided to use "icon" (even though, like "deity image," it generally refers to both two- and three-dimensional objects), mainly because aspects of the ancient Greek and Eastern Orthodox tradition of the *ikon* or *eikon*—visual mimesis and divine presence—are associations I want to emphasize and because the term seems to have the fewest negative or irrelevant associations.

6. The Holo term *sian* (*xian* in Mandarin) refers to a wide range of beings with supernatural powers who are not gods, ghosts, or demonic. It can include human Daoists who have mastered some physical or medical discipline to the point of never aging. Other common translations of *xian* are "fairy" and "celestial."

7. There are two other meanings of the character *ou*, which are also continuous from the Zhou dynasty to the present. One meaning is "companion," which also emerges from the idea of the double, as in the modern bureaucratic term for a spouse, *pei ou*. A third, apparently unrelated meaning of *ou* is "by chance, randomly, or occasionally," as in the adverb *ouran*. The meaning of "companion" clearly resonates in the ways that contemporary

Taiwanese interact with various types of human-form figures. As I discuss in the next chapter, the idea of chance is also linked to certain types of contemporary *ou* through marketing and ritual practices.

8. *Ang-a* of living celebrities are also produced in Taiwan. But these *ang-a* represent the intangible "star personae" (Dyer 1986) of these celebrities rather than their private selves or biological beings.

9. There are some exceptions—deities or spirits that are not human. There are a few old trees and rocks in rural Taiwan that have names and are worshipped. There are also some animal gods that are worshipped through animal-form statues, but these statues are never placed on altars and are rarely thought of as having individual personalities or stories. The most common animal deity in Taiwan is Lord Tiger (Hu Ye), the servant of the Earth God (Tudi Gong). Statues of a crouching tiger are placed on the ground beneath the Earth God's altar. Wei-Ping Lin tells the story of a village where a god was worshipped in the shape of a frog. Originally, a statue of the frog was located in a shrine outside the temple. When the villagers decided they wanted to worship the god inside the temple, they had a new *shenxiang* carved and placed on the altar, which had a human body and face but retained a few froglike features such as green skin (Wei-Ping Lin, pers. comm.).

10. These descriptions are summarized from Liu Wensan (1981) and Wei-Ping Lin (2008).

11. Following anthropological ethics, I use pseudonyms when describing and quoting individual fans I interviewed.

12. These dolls are called "Xiao Yu *wawa*" because they were first made using mass-produced plastic dolls of a Japanese manga character whose name is pronounced as "Xiao Yu" in Mandarin. Later, Taiwanese boutique owners had similar dolls made specially for the purpose of being fashioned into versions of the Pili characters, which were manufactured in Taiwan.

13. Among Pili fans, the term *fenshen* is used far less often than the term *ben-zun* and usually refers to full-sized puppets rather than plastic toys.

14. The Pili Company makes several puppets for each main character. The literary puppet is the one that is used for filming most scenes; the military puppet is used to film fighting scenes, in which the puppet will be thrown around and could be damaged. The military puppets are considered secondary (*fuzun*) because they are in some ways replacements for the literary puppets, and they are also called (stunt) double actors (*tishen yanyuan*). But since both the literary and military puppets perform in the original videos, both may be considered *benzun*.

15. In an analysis of the Pili franchise using Baudrillard, one Taiwanese scholar-fan argued:

> Under the situation where reality cannot be reflected, then the more real than the real, the "hyper-real," appears. At this time, the symbol/image appears to be "alive." The Pure White Lotus, Su Huanzhen [the main protagonist of the Pili series], is an obvious example. . . . Aside from the television screen, his image can be found in photo albums, posters, cell-phone accessories, notebooks and many other products. . . . [S]*imulation can be used to achieve the process of deification,* to usurp legitimacy for itself. In sum, *simulation does not completely deny the existence of reality, because after all, the puppet "Su Huanzhen" actually does exist.* Nevertheless, the reality produced by simulation [*nixiang*] already surpasses reality. (Hong 2005:103; italics mine)

> Even in an analysis that closely resembles analyses of the Japanese media mix as a postmodern phenomenon, this Taiwanese writer feels compelled to use the metaphor of deification and to assert the persistence of the reality of the *benzun* puppet of Su Huanzhen.

16. The portrayal of the face in a different style from the body (or more accurately, clothed body), sometimes by different artists, is characteristic of several historical genres of Chinese painting, including ancestor portraits and some schools of literati portraiture (Wu Hung 2005).

17. The relative importance of *zaoxing* and face for character recognition and (non-in)consistency tends to be different for icons and Pili puppets (although this is changing, as I discuss in chapter 3). The face of a deity may vary greatly from icon to icon, since carvers often work from images that come to them, or to someone else, in dreams. But Mazu is always recognizable from her beaded headpiece, and Guan Yin from her flowing robes and the vase she usually carries. *Zaoxing* is even more important for the recognition of more obscure gods. With the main Pili protagonists, however, the *zaoxing* may change quite often, but the face stays the same. Thus, although Su Huanzhen has been incarnated in many different puppets over the past twenty years of the Pili serials and changes costumes and hairstyles, his "butterfly eyebrows" and wide mouth stay the same. These features are present not only in the puppets used in the canon videos but also in the more cartoony "cute" (*Q-ban*) graphic style and in more abstract versions, such as cute dough figurines made by fans. (Images of different incarnations of Su Huanzhen over the years are available in the

section titled "The Pili International Multimedia Company's Hand-Puppet Video Serials" of the online museum exhibit "Go, Figures! The Culture and Charisma of Statues, Puppets, and Dolls," available at http://gofigures.ioe .sinica.edu.tw.)

This is not to say that the face is not also important in icons, or the *zaoxing* for Pili characters. Guan Yin's mole or decorative mark in the center of her forehead and Guan Gong's red face and long beard are as traditional as their accessories. In a common game played at Pili fan gatherings, close-up photos of parts of a character's *zaoxing* are projected on a screen and fans must guess which character it is. But in general, an icon will fail (that is, be unrecognizable to worshippers and perhaps to the god being invited inside) if it does not have enough of the core features of that god's *zaoxing*, while a representation of a Pili character will "fail" (that is, appear too far "out of character") if too many core features of the face are changed.

18.   Different genres of local puppetry and local opera may have slightly different role taxonomies. These are the role categories for traditional *po-te-hi*.

19.   Analogism is not the only worldview that one could induce from a review of the historical record of premodern China or even within Han-dynasty Daoist metaphysics. My aim here is merely to show that there are continuities between this particular strain of metaphysical thought in imperial China and animation practices in contemporary Taiwan.

20.   The *Feng shen bang* is a collection of stories usually translated as *Investiture of the Gods*. The title of the Pili book might be translated as something like *Pili's Divine Registry, Zodiac Version*.

21.   Of course, this type of analogism abounds in cinema animation—Walt Disney's *Robin Hood* (1973), in which Robin Hood is a (cunning) fox and Little John a (big, strong, not very smart) bear, is one obvious example, as are the Japanese wartime cartoons analyzed by Lamarre (2008), in which different animal species represent different human "races." My point here is not to say that analogism is a feature unique to the Chinese *ang-a* mode of animation, but to distinguish this mode of animation from Azuma's theory of database consumption.

## Chapter 3: The Cutification of the Gods

1.   The term *gongzai* comes from Hong Kong; it is a Cantonese word meaning "doll" or "toy figurine," very similar to the Holo *ang-a*, with connotations of childish cuteness.

2.   The English letter "Q" is often used by young Taiwanese as a transliteration of the English "cute." It also means "chewy" or "al dente."

3. Immortals (*xian*) are technically lesser than gods (*shenming*), but the line is fuzzy and the Eight Immortals, for instance, are worshipped exactly as if they were gods, with their own temples and spirit mediums.

4. The *shenming gongzai* also resemble *yuru kyara* in that they can be embodied by live actors wearing giant masks that cover the entire head (see Occhi 2012), as they were in a series of television ads for FamilyMart's fourth series of toys.

5. Color photographs of FamilyMart's Good Gods Figurines and of several examples of cute deity figurines commissioned by temples in Taiwan can be viewed in the online version of the museum exhibit I curated (Institute of Ethnology, Academia Sinica, 2018).

6. In chapter 2, I outlined a Taiwanese mode of animation in which the *ang-a* is invested with specific human qualities (personality, affect, and charisma) through specific types of actions (ritual, iconographic, and communicational practices). The process by which religious icons are invested with a god's soul and power provides a model of and for how people interact with *po-te-hi* puppets and, in some ways, with commercial character toys as well. Taiwanese fans may read even imported character toys through the lens of the *ang-a* mode of animation—for instance, when they view copyright in terms of genealogies of substance and mimesis rather than in terms of intellectual property.

7. Many people use Daoism as a synonym for folk religion, and many who identify as Buddhist also worship Daoist gods at folk religious temples. The American Institute in Taiwan (2014) asserts: "Researchers and academics estimate that as much as 80 percent of the population believes in some form of traditional folk religion."

8. The only way in which the *shenming gongzai* designers and collectors I interviewed differed significantly from the collectors of Japanese manga/anime and Pili puppet collectors I interviewed was that fewer than 10 percent of the former self-identified as Buddhist, a much smaller portion than in the general population. This may have to do with the growth of large Buddhist organizations, such as the Buddhist Compassion Tzu Chi Association and Fo Guang Shan, such that young people may feel that identifying as Buddhist means claiming membership in such an organization, and they may be more comfortable identifying as followers of folk religion even if their religious practice includes worship of buddhas and bodhisattvas and individual practices such as sutra reading and meditation.

9. For more on the atmosphere of "hot and noisy," which characterizes bustling markets, restaurants, and parties, as well as temple festivals, and

the way it invites movement between commitment and detachment, see Hatfield (2010, chap. 1).

10. I have given all interviewees pseudonyms. However, where the names of designers are publicly known, as in the case of Penny Lin, I use their legal name or pen name when discussing their artworks and maintain their anonymity when discussing their personal lives.

11. For Christians to complain about Chinese folk religious shrines in places of business owned by non-Christians is quite unusual—even more so for a shop owner to acquiesce—and this is the only time I have heard of it. The kind of evangelical Christians who publicly claim that buddhas, bodhisattvas, and Daoist deities are "demonic" are a small minority within the Taiwanese Christian community, but some churches in Taiwan, funded by American evangelical organizations, have become more vocal in the past decade, promoting "family values" legislation and organizing protests against the annual LGBT Pride Parade in Taipei (the largest in Asia).

12. *Kyarakutā* is a Japanese phoneticization of the English "character" and usually refers to cute logo and mascot characters rather than to other types of fictional characters. It is often shortened to *kyara*.

13. This is an unusual story. There are two gods of medicine, Bao Sheng Da Di and Shen Nong, who are often appealed to for their healing powers. Families also often pray to Mazu and Guan Yin for healing. I have never heard of anyone else praying to the City God for this purpose. Xiao Long and his father may have prayed to the City God to heal his mother because of the family connection to the City God's cult.

14. I want to thank Wei-Ping Lin and the students in her Taiwanese Religion class who pointed out the differences between Hindu and Chinese religious images in this respect when I presented this research to them in May 2010.

15. Aside from deity toys, many other toys produced in Taiwan in the mid-2000s expressed a *taike* sensibility. These include a series of plastic toys based on the "betel nut beauties" (young women, usually wearing skimpy outfits, who sell betel nuts and cigarettes to drivers from glass booths by the roadside), designed and manufactured by the Tommy Bear Company, which were very popular with young collectors in 2005–2006.

16. Chiang makes the connection between the pragmatism of folk religion and commercialization by claiming that efficacy is a market value. This argument is problematic, given that neither classical economists nor Marxists would conflate the market value of a product with its use value.

17. She said this in a conversation after I had turned off my tape recorder, so this quote is an approximation based on my handwritten notes after the interview ended.

## Chapter 4: *Ang-a* Globalization

1. Huang Qianghua is a pen name; he sometimes also uses his legal name, Huang Wenzhang.

2. Only three television stations were operating in Taiwan in 1970, and programming in Holo was restricted. Ratings were assessed through random telephone calls. Thus, the 97 percent rating was not as shocking as it would be now. However, the cultural impact of the Shi Yanwen series should not be underestimated. The series' popularity incited panic about its influence on children, and it has become a collective generational memory of the "fifth graders" (those born in the 1960s). The characters were revived in 1994 by Huang Junxiong and another of his sons, Huang Ligang, in the Jin Guang digital video *wuxia po-te-hi* series. This series has continued to 2019 under Huang Ligang's direction and is the Pili series' main competitor.

3. Updated information is available on the Pili International Multimedia Company website.

4. No relation to Chris and Vincent Huang (Huang Qianghua and Huang Wenze).

5. I am using the spellings of the names from the English subtitles in the official DVD set. Oddly, these names are romanizations of the pronunciations in Mandarin. Romanizations of the characters' Japanese names also appear in the opening titles: Shang Bu Huan = Sho Fu Kan; Lin Xue Ya = Rin Setsu A.

6. Su Huanzhen is the main protagonist of the Pili series. His name in Holo is So Hoanchin. I will use "Su Huanzhen" hereafter. In everyday conversation the Mandarin pronunciation is more commonly used by fans, most of whom are more fluent in Mandarin than Holo.

7. However, the name "Lop" comes from the historical name of the desert in which the kingdom of Lou Lan was located.

8. Historically, the Han army actually demanded tribute from Lou Lan and eventually invaded and occupied it. But no mention of this is made in *The Arti*. In *The Arti*, visitors from Chang An are apparently so common in Lou Lan that the teahouse there has a whole menu of Han Chinese dishes for the tourists.

9. For more on the novel, see *Wikipedia*, s.v. "Thunderbolt Fantasy," accessed July 1, 2018, https://en.wikipedia.org/wiki/Thunderbolt_Fantasy. A

novelization of *The Arti* was also written, but it does not vary much from the film.

10. For an example of a Taiwanese animated film that did blend representations of folk Daoist magic with an environmental theme successfully, see *Grandma and Her Ghosts* (*Mofa a-ma*, 1988, directed by Shaudi Wang). Here, Daoist magic is framed, not within the *wuxia* genre, but within a nostalgic family drama about a boy from the city visiting his grandmother in the countryside.

11. Interestingly, in the English Wikipedia plot summary, the stone giant is called a "golem," drawing attention to the fact that the use of writing on paper placed inside a figure is not a means of animation limited to the Chinese tradition.

**Chapter 5: Cosplay**

1. A few *po-te-hi* films were made, but they were not commercial successes.

2. In *po-te-hi*, as in Peking Opera, the four traditional role types are *sheng*, *dan*, *jing*, and *chou*. The *jing* is a general, often with a painted face, and the *chou* is a clown. In *koa-a-hi*, the actors are first trained in general male and female role types and may then study various male and female clown role types. The term *jing* is not used in *koa-a-hi*, although there are older military male roles that are similar.

3. While most Taiwanese scholars and puppeteers maintain that the puppet's movements imitate those of opera actors, I did meet one performer who had experience in both opera and puppetry and claimed the opposite. She gave me a beautiful, if historically unprovable, demonstration of how the way Chinese opera actors lift their feet and arms is modeled on the movements of marionettes.

4. In a comparison of two randomly selected fight scenes (one minute each)—one from a 1994 series, *Xin Yunzhou da ruxia*, produced by Huang Junxiong, and one from a 1999 Pili series, *Pili lei ting*—I found that the average length of shots had been reduced from approximately 2.5 seconds to 1.06 seconds, with the longest shot in the sequence reduced from 9 seconds to 3. In the 1994 clip, the camera moves along only two axes, left to right and backward and forward, maintaining the sense of the set as a proscenium stage. In the 1999 clip, the camera most often moves on the left-right axis, but in an arc rather than along a straight line, giving the impression of a more three-dimensional stage space. It zooms in and out and also tilts left and right, up and down. The camera also moves back and forth between a proscenium view of the action, as in the earlier clip, and a point of view that is in the middle of the action, either from the point

of view of one of the characters or in a central position around which the characters move.

5. See, for example, the article on "Wood-Be Idols" in Tsai (2004).

6. The word "pose" was said in English, a common practice.

7. The movement style of Taiwanese television ancient costume dramas (*guzhuangxi*) is based on softened, naturalized versions of the stylized movements of *koa-a-hi*. At the height of *koa-a-hi*'s popularity on television, from the 1970s to 1990s, many actresses performed in both.

8. For discussion of the relationship between photography and self-identity in Taiwan before the introduction of smartphones and social media, see Adrian (2003) on how wedding salon photo albums simultaneously create and memorialize the self-as-bride.

9. One group of Pili cosplayers came closer to the performance approach to cosplay than others. These were the members of the Limitless Cosplay Theater (Wuxian Renxing Jutuan). The founders of this troupe started cosplaying when they were officers of a regional fan club for one of the characters. They were among the fans I interviewed regularly over a long period of time. In 2005 they founded the Limitless Theater, registering it as a legal business enterprise. They have a contract with the Pili Company, and all jobs they accept must be approved by the company. They perform at fan club events, at promotional events for the Pili Company, and at promotional events for other businesses that the company has agreed to work with. They also take some jobs cosplaying manga and anime characters at events organized by game companies and manga publishers.

    In order to professionalize, they took several classes in Chinese martial arts, *koa-a-hi*, and spoken drama. None of these classes, however, included any kind of Method acting training; most were focused on physical technique and skills such as blocking. One of the main ways the Limitless troupe's performances differ from the ones they used to perform as fan club officers is that they now voice the characters themselves, sometimes speaking the lines onstage and sometimes recording the dialogue in a professional sound studio. The leader of the troupe told me that the reason they did this was that "we're actors now, people, not puppets." At the same time that they were becoming actors rather than puppets, they started planning to expand their repertoire beyond cosplay, to start playing characters created especially for them, rather than characters from puppetry and manga/anime series.

10. Pili cosplayers say they tend to cosplay until an older age than most cosplayers of Japanese manga/anime, which they attribute to the fact that most of the Pili characters are adults rather than adolescents.

11.  I found a similar range of professions among the women I interviewed who were writing fan fiction; that group also included professional women such as a lawyer and a pharmacist.

12.  The three men I conducted short interviews with at cosplay/*tongrenzhi* conventions were a high school student, a factory worker, and a construction worker. The latter two were cosplaying as part of a character group organized by their girlfriends, who were in low-paying service industry jobs.

13.  David Graeber makes a similar point, arguing that the concept of immaterial labor is "transparently absurd" because it "goes back to dilemmas in Italian workerism in the '70s and '80s." He writes:

> On the one hand, there was a stubborn Leninist assumption . . .
> that it must always be the most 'advanced' sector of the proletariat
> that makes up the revolutionary class. Computer and other infor-
> mation workers were the obvious candidates here. But the same
> period saw the rise of feminism and the Wages for Housework
> movement, which put the whole problem of unwaged, domestic
> labor on the political table in a way that could no longer simply be
> ignored. The solution was to argue that computer work and house-
> work were really the same thing. Or, more precisely, were becoming
> so. (Graeber 2008:6)

14.  Panics over working women since the 1970s have been mostly over their "failure" to marry and have children rather than over their appearance or demeanor becoming more masculine.

15.  See Grosz (1994) for a thorough critique.

16.  Haraway's 1985 essay, "A Manifesto for Cyborgs," is the classic articulation of this position. Also see Stone (1995). These fantasies are just as prominent, if not more so, in the Japanese popular culture that heavily influences Taiwan, although here they seem both more ambivalent and less gendered. See Bolton (2002) and Orbaugh (2002).

### Chapter 6: *Ang-a* Identity Politics

1.  This section is based on analyses of online and self-published APH fan fiction, manga, and artwork, online fan discussions (on Chinese- and English-language sites), and participant-observation at fan events in Taiwan between 2012 and 2014, as well as secondary sources. I also conducted semi-structured interviews with eighteen APH fan fiction writers in Taiwan, as well as with a group of four fans in the PRC, one in Hong Kong, and two in Thailand, and shorter, informal interviews with fans

from Indonesia and the Philippines whom I met selling APH fan art in Singapore.

2. I take the dialogue here from the English dubbed version.

3. When I asked why the other official pairing, Germany and Italy, was not popular in Taiwan, I was told that Taiwanese people don't find brainless characters like Italy appealing, so Germany is more frequently paired with the snobbish and artistic Prussia.

4. I heard Zizek speak about this at a lecture in Chicago in the late 1990s, but he makes similar points in a talk available on YouTube (Zizek 2018).

5. It is common practice, at least in Taiwanese fan works, to have minor characters from the canon stand in for the author or for the point of view of a typical *funü* (Silvio 2011).

6. Images of some A-Bian toys are available in the "Political Figures" section of the online museum exhibit "Go, Figures! The Culture and Charisma of Statues, Puppets, and Dolls" (see Institute of Ethnology 2018).

# Glossary of Key Terms in Mandarin, Holo, and Japanese

| Mandarin<br>(國語/中文)<br>Romanized using<br>the pinyin system | Holo<br>(閩南語/台語)<br>Romanized using<br>the Péh-oē-jī<br>system | Japanese<br>(日本語)<br>Romanized using<br>the Hepburn<br>system | English meaning |
|---|---|---|---|
| | ang-á<br>尪仔 | | Puppet, doll, figurine |
| | ang-á-sian<br>尪仔仙 | | A puppet |
| bàibài<br>拜拜 | pài-pài | | To worship |
| bàn<br>扮 | | | To dress as, to act the part of |
| bàn xiān<br>扮仙 | pān-sian | | A ritual performed before an opera or stage performance at a temple festival |
| bànyǎn jiǎosè<br>扮演角色 | | | To play a role; cosplay |
| bǎoyòu<br>保佑 | pó-pì | | Blessings, protection |
| běnzūn<br>本尊 | pún-chun | | The original icon, the icon from which a *fenshen* icon is made |
| bùdàixì<br>布袋戲 | pò·-tē-hì | | Southern Chinese glove puppet theater |
| bùxiétiáo<br>不協調 | | | Incoherent; lacking harmony |

225

| Mandarin (國語/中文) Romanized using the pinyin system | Holo (閩南語/台語) Romanized using the Péh-oē-jī system | Japanese (日本語) Romanized using the Hepburn system | English meaning |
|---|---|---|---|
| cái 才 | | | Talent, genius |
| cáituánfǎrén 財團法人 | | | Foundation, nonprofit corporation |
| cāo 操 | | | To manipulate (the verb used for puppeteering) |
| | | chibi ちび チビ | A style of cartoon character with an extra-large head and childish features |
| chóngbài ǒuxiàng 崇拜偶像 | | | To worship idols |
| chǒu 丑 | | | The clown character type in Chinese opera and puppetry |
| chūchǎngshī 出場詩 | | | A poem recited by a character when making an entrance |
| chuántǒng wénhuà, chuàngyì chǎnyè 傳統文化創意產業 | | | The traditional cultural creative industries |
| cì yuán 次元 | | jigen 次元 | Dimension |
| dāidāi 呆呆 | | | Blank, stupid |
| dàn 旦 | tòa$^n$ | | The female role in opera or puppetry |
| dàobǎn 盜版 | | | To pirate; pirated (goods) |
| dǎobō 導播 | | | Director (for television) |
| diànyīn Sān Tàizǐ 電音三太子 | | | Electronic San Taizi |
| diànyǐnghuà 電影化 | | | Cinematization |

| Mandarin (國語/中文) Romanized using the pinyin system | Holo (閩南語/台語) Romanized using the Péh-oē-jī system | Japanese (日本語) Romanized using the Hepburn system | English meaning |
| --- | --- | --- | --- |
| diāoxiàng<br>雕像 | | | A carved statue. |
| dǒngshìzhǎng<br>董事長 | | | CEO |
| fēn xiāng<br>分香 | hūn hiu$^n$ | | Literally, to divide the incense; the process in which incense from the burner of an icon is placed inside its branch icon |
| fēnshēn<br>分身 | hūn-sin | | A branch icon made with ash from the incense burner of another icon of the same deity |
| fú<br>符 | | | A Daoist charm (for healing or protection) |
| Fú Lù Shòu<br>福祿壽 | | | Happiness, success, and longevity (three blessings; also the Three Immortals) |
| fǔnǚ<br>腐女 | | fujōshi<br>腐女子 | A woman who reads and/or writes fiction or manga featuring male-male romantic and/or sexual relationships; a campy self-designation that is a homophone for a generic term for "woman," which literally means "rotten woman" |
| gēzǎixì,<br>gēzǐxì<br>歌仔戲 | koa-á-hì | | Taiwanese Opera |

| Mandarin (國語/中文) Romanized using the pinyin system | Holo (閩南語/台語) Romanized using the Péh-oē-jī system | Japanese (日本語) Romanized using the Hepburn system | English meaning |
|---|---|---|---|
| gōng 攻 | | seme 攻め | The penetrator, or top, role in BL (boys' love) fiction |
| gōng miào 宮廟 | | | An unregistered temple |
| gōngzǎi 公仔 | | | (From the Cantonese) A doll or figurine |
| guān 官 | | | Official; an official; high office |
| guān pèi 官配 | | | An "official pairing," a pair of characters who have a close relationship in an original work |
| hārizu 哈日族 | | | The Japanophile tribe; young Taiwanese people who are fans of Japanese popular culture and fashion |
| huāliǎn 花臉 | | | The painted-face role in opera or puppetry |
| huàshēn 化身 | | | An avatar or embodiment |
| huí niáng jiā 回娘家 | | | To return to one's mother's home (from one's husband's home) |
| jìsìquān 祭祀圈 | | | Worship circle (a term used in Taiwanese folk religious scholarship, referring to the population that worships a particular deity) |
| jíxiángwù 吉祥物 | | | A lucky charm, mascot, or logo character |

| Mandarin (國語/中文) Romanized using the pinyin system | Holo (閩南語/台語) Romanized using the Péh-oē-jī system | Japanese (日本語) Romanized using the Hepburn system | English meaning |
|---|---|---|---|
| jiāo 教 | | | To teach; a teaching |
| jiǎosè 角色 | | | Role, character |
| jiǎosè bànyǎn 角色扮演 | | | Cosplay, role-playing |
| jiēshòudù 接受度 | | | Acceptability |
| jìng 淨 | | | The older military male role in opera or puppetry |
| kāi guāng diǎn yǎn 開光點眼 | khai-kong 開光 | | The ritual to open the eyes (of a new icon) |
| guīlěixì 傀儡戲 | ka-lé-hì | | Southern Chinese marionette puppetry |
| | | kami 神 | God; a spirit (in Shinto) |
| kàn xiàng 看相 | | | Fortune-telling by reading facial features |
| kě ài 可愛 | | kawaii かわいい | Cute, adorable |
| kèbǎn yìnxiàng 刻板印象 | | | Stereotype |
| | kim-kong-hì 金光戲 | | A style of puppetry featuring special effects |
| | | kosu-pure コスプレ | Cosplay |
| kuàijì 會計 | | | A bookkeeper or accountant |
| | | kyarakuta キャラクター | Character |
| liǎn xíng 臉型 | | | The form of a face |
| liàngxiàng 亮相 | | | A held pose in Chinese opera |

| Mandarin (國語/中文) Romanized using the pinyin system | Holo (閩南語/台語) Romanized using the Péh-oē-jī system | Japanese (日本語) Romanized using the Hepburn system | English meaning |
| --- | --- | --- | --- |
| liáoyùxì 療癒系 | | iyashi 癒し | Healing, comfort (here describing a category of cute character goods) |
| líng 靈 | | | Supernatural power, efficacy |
| línghún 靈魂 | | | Soul |
| língyàn 靈驗 | | | Manifestation of supernatural power |
| lúzhǔ 爐主 | | | The keeper of the incense burner, a temple organization leader |
| méng 萌 | | moe 萌え | A feeling of excitement or attachment aroused by manga/anime characters; to experience that feeling |
| méngdiǎn 萌點 | | | *Moe* points |
| méngqǐlái 萌起來 | | | To "*moe* up," to start to feel *moe*; to have a story idea sprout in one's mind |
| mínjiān xìnyǎng 民間信仰 | | | (Chinese) Folk religion |
| mínjiān zōngjiào 民間宗教 | | | (Chinese) Folk religion |
| mínzú xìng 民族性 | | | Ethnicity, ethnic-ness |
| mínzú yìshí 民族意識 | | | Ethnic consciousness |
| mò 末 | | | The old male role in Chinese opera or puppetry |

| Mandarin<br>(國語/中文)<br>Romanized using<br>the pinyin system | Holo<br>(閩南語/台語)<br>Romanized using<br>the Péh-oē-jī<br>system | Japanese<br>(日本語)<br>Romanized using<br>the Hepburn<br>system | English meaning |
|---|---|---|---|
| mù ǒu<br>木偶 | | | A wooden puppet |
| nǐxiàng<br>擬像 | | | A simulacrum |
| | | ningyō jōruri<br>人形浄瑠璃 | A genre of Japanese puppetry |
| ǒu<br>偶 | | | An anthropomorphic figure |
| ǒu dòngmàn<br>偶動漫 | | | Puppetry-animation |
| ǒu rén<br>偶人 | | | An anthropomorphic figure |
| pèi shén<br>配神 | | | The accompanying gods (as opposed to the primary god worshipped in a specific temple) |
| | pòah-poe<br>跋杯 | | Divination using two moon-shaped blocks |
| Q-bǎn<br>Q版 | | | A cute version (of a character) |
| qīfù<br>欺負 | | | To bully |
| qīnqiēgǎn<br>親切感 | | | Intimacy |
| ràng tā kànqǐlái huó shēng shēng de<br>讓它看起來活生生的 | | | Make it appear to be alive |
| rènào<br>熱鬧 | lāu-jiát<br>鬧熱 | | "Hot and noisy," a term describing an exciting atmosphere when a crowd is gathered |
| rénqíng<br>人情 | | | Feeling between people, favors |

| Mandarin (國語/中文) Romanized using the pinyin system | Holo (閩南語/台語) Romanized using the Péh-oē-jī system | Japanese (日本語) Romanized using the Hepburn system | English meaning |
|---|---|---|---|
| rénwén sùyǎng 人文素養 | | | Civilized quality |
| rìběn xuètǒng de shāngpǐn 日本血統的商品 | | | Products with a Japanese bloodline |
| rù shén 入神 | jíp-sîn | | To bring in the god, to invite the god to enter (part of the ritual to sacralize an icon) |
| | | seiyū 声優 | A voice actor |
| | | sekai 世界 | World; from kabuki, a narrative chronotope, in opposition to "variation," a particular narrative. Otsuka Eiji uses the term for what fans would call the "universe" of a media franchise. |
| shàngbānzú 上班族 | | | Office worker tribe |
| shén guài 神怪 | | | Gods and monsters |
| shēn ké 身殼 | | | Body-shell, the body as a vessel |
| shén lì 神力 | | | Divine force |
| shēng 生 | seng | | The male role in Chinese opera or puppetry |
| shēngmìnglì 生命力 | | | Vitality, life force |
| shénlíng 神靈 | | | Divine soul/power |

| Mandarin (國語/中文) Romanized using the pinyin system | Holo (閩南語/台語) Romanized using the Péh-oē-jī system | Japanese (日本語) Romanized using the Hepburn system | English meaning |
|---|---|---|---|
| shénmíng gōngzǎi 神明公仔 | | | Deity toys |
| shénxiàng 神像 | | | An icon, a statue of a god for worship |
| | | shukō 趣向 | Variation (as opposed to "world," in kabuki); a particular narrative within a world chronotope |
| shǔxìng 屬性 | | | Attribute, property of a person or thing |
| shùwèi wǔxiá bùdàixì 數位武俠布袋戲 | | | Digital knights-errant puppetry |
| shuài qì 帥氣 | | | A dashing manner, the quality of being attractive in a masculine way |
| shòu 受 | | uke 受け | The receptor, or bottom, role in BL (boys' love) fiction |
| shōu jīng | siu-kia$^n$ 收驚 | | An exorcism ritual |
| táikè 台客 | | | A derogatory term for a Taiwanese (as opposed to Chinese) person; the name for a campy style that exaggerates stereotypical markers of Taiwanese working-class culture |
| tìshēn yǎnyuán 替身演員 | | | A body-substitute actor, a stunt double |
| | tōa sian ang-á 大仙尪仔 | | Large masks worn to represent some gods in temple processions |

| Mandarin (國語/中文) Romanized using the pinyin system | Holo (閩南語/台語) Romanized using the Péh-oē-jī system | Japanese (日本語) Romanized using the Hepburn system | English meaning |
|---|---|---|---|
| tóngrén 同人 | | | People who write *tongrenzhi* |
| tóngrénnǚ 同人女 | | | Women who write and read *tongrenzhi* |
| tóngrénzhì 同人誌 | | dōjinshi 同人誌 | Amateur comics that feature characters from media franchises (usually manga/anime characters) |
| | | tsundere ツンデレ | A character who appears cold but is passionate underneath |
| tú 徒 | | | A disciple or student |
| wán 玩 | | | To play |
| wán ǒu 玩偶 | | | A doll |
| wénhuà fùxìng yùndòng 文化復興運動 | | | The Cultural Renaissance movement |
| wén xì ǒu 文戲偶 | | | A literary puppet (one used for nonfighting scenes) |
| wúliáo 無聊 | | | Boring, meaningless |
| wúshénlùn 無神論 | | | Atheism |
| wǔlín 武林 | | | The martial forest, the world/chronotope of the Pili series and of the *wuxia* genre in general |
| wǔ xì ǒu 武戲偶 | | | A martial puppet (one used for fight scenes) |

| Mandarin (國語/中文) Romanized using the pinyin system | Holo (閩南語/台語) Romanized using the Péh-oē-jī system | Japanese (日本語) Romanized using the Hepburn system | English meaning |
|---|---|---|---|
| wǔxiá 武俠 | | | A genre of Chinese fiction featuring wandering swordsmen; sometimes translated as "knights-errant" fiction |
| xì ǒu 戲偶 | | | A puppet |
| xì qǔ 戲曲 | | | Musical theater (the generic term for traditional Chinese opera) |
| xiān 仙 | | | An immortal; a measure word for a puppet |
| xiǎngxiàng 想像 | | | Imagination |
| xiàngxué 相學 | | | Fortune-telling by reading facial features |
| xiǎo húnhún 小混混 | | | A petty criminal, a loafer |
| xiétiào 協調 | | | To negotiate or harmonize; coherent, harmonious |
| xíngtī 形體 | | | Physical form |
| xìntú 信徒 | | | A believer, a worshipper (of a particular god) |
| yǎn 演 | | | To perform |
| | | yandere ヤンデレ | A person who appears to be nice but is secretly psychotic |
| yǎnshén 眼神 | | | Gaze |

| Mandarin<br>(國語/中文)<br>Romanized using<br>the pinyin system | Holo<br>(閩南語/台語)<br>Romanized using<br>the Péh-oē-jī<br>system | Japanese<br>(日本語)<br>Romanized using<br>the Hepburn<br>system | English meaning |
|---|---|---|---|
| yángwáwá<br>洋娃娃 | | | A baby doll |
| yīn<br>陰 | | | Dark, negative |
| yīnyuán<br>姻緣 | | | Marriage destiny |
| yuánfèn<br>緣分 | iân (iân-hūn)<br>緣 (緣分) | | Relational destiny |
| | | yuru kyara<br>ゆるキャラ | Wobbly characters,<br>often used as part of<br>marketing campaigns |
| zá<br>雜 | | | Miscellaneous |
| zào<br>造 | | | To make |
| zàoxíng<br>造型 | | | Outward appearance<br>(dress and makeup) |
| zàoxíng zǔ<br>造型組 | | | The appearance<br>bureau (in the Pili<br>Company) |
| zháinán (individual/s)<br>宅男<br>yùzháizú (group<br>designation)<br>御宅族 | | otaku<br>おたく<br>オタク | Geek, nerd; someone<br>obsessed with one<br>thing; serious male<br>fan(s) of manga/<br>anime |
| zhǎngzhōngxì<br>掌中戲 | chiáng-tiong-hì | | Theater in the palm of<br>the hand; an alternate<br>term for *po-te-hi* |
| zhèntóu<br>陣頭 | tīn-thâu | | A temple procession;<br>the troupes that<br>perform temple<br>processions |
| zhèngbǎn<br>正版 | | | The official edition,<br>the copyrighted<br>edition |

| Mandarin<br>(國語/中文)<br>Romanized using<br>the pinyin system | Holo<br>(閩南語/台語)<br>Romanized using<br>the Péh-oē-jī<br>system | Japanese<br>(日本語)<br>Romanized using<br>the Hepburn<br>system | English meaning |
|---|---|---|---|
| zhǔ shén<br>主神 | | | The main god (in a temple) |
| zhuǎn xìng<br>轉性 | | | To change sex; gender-switch (a type of character in *tongrenzhi*) |
| zǒngjīnglǐ<br>總經理 | | | Managing director, general manager |
| zōngjiāo<br>宗教 | | | Religion |
| zōngjiāoxìng<br>zhōubiān shāngpǐn<br>宗教性週邊商品 | | | Tie-in products of a religious nature |
| zǒu xiù<br>走秀 | | | A fashion show; to walk a runway |
| zūn<br>尊 | chun | | The measure word for an icon or a puppet |

# Glossary of Names

**Artworks and Character Names**

A Xi (Arti-C) 阿西

*Dongli jian youji* (Thunderbolt Fantasy—Sword Seekers) 東離劍遊紀

*Feng shen bang* (Investiture of the Gods) 封神榜

*Mofa a-ma* (Grandma and Her Ghosts) 魔法阿媽

*Qi ren mima: Guluobu zhi mi* (The Arti: The Adventure Begins) 奇人密碼：古羅布之謎

*Sheng shi chuan shuo* (Legend of the Sacred Stone) 聖石傳說

Su Huanzhen (Holo: Sò˙Hoân Chin) 素還真

Wan Lang 灣郎

Wan Niang 灣娘

*Xi hu die meng* (Butterfly Lovers) 西蝴蝶夢

*Xi meng ren sheng* (The Puppetmaster) 戲夢人生

*Yaxiya rihe* (A Good Day for Asia) 亞細亞日和

Ye Xiao Chai (Holo: Iáp Sió The) 葉小釵

*Yidaili* 義呆利 *Axis Powers* (Chinese); ヘタリア *Axis Powers* (Japanese); *Axis Powers Hetalia*

*Yunzhou da ru xia—Shi Yanwen* (Holo: *Hunchiu tai lu kiap—Su Iambun*) (Shi Yanwen, the Confucian Swordsman of Yunzhou) 雲州大儒俠史艷文

*Zheng wang ji* (*Battle for the Throne*) 爭王記

**People and Organizations**

Azuma Hiroki 東浩紀

Chang Hsun 張珣

Chang Li-yun 張芷雲

Chen Hsinchih 陳杏枝

Chen Longting 陳龍廷
Chen Pingyuan 陈平原
Chen Qiufan 陳秋帆
Chiu Hai-Yuan 瞿海源
Chu Ruey-Ling 朱瑞玲
Chuang Yin 莊佳穎
Guojia Tongxun Weiyuanhui (National Communications Commission) 國家通訊委員會
He Zi 禾子
Hong Mengkai 洪盟凱
Huang Haidai 黃海岱
Huang Huei-fung 黃滙峰
Huang Junxiong 黃俊雄
Huang Liang-hsun 黃亮勛
Huang Neng-yang 黃能揚
Huang Qianghua 黃強華 (a.k.a. Huang Wenzhang 黃文章, a.k.a. Chris Huang)
Huang Shu-ling 黃淑鈴
Huang Wenze (a.k.a. Vincent Huang) 黃文擇
Huang Yuming 黃毓銘
Jiang Wuchang 江武昌
Lai Honglin 賴宏林
Leng Bin 冷彬
Li Xinyi 李信宜
Lin Mei-jung 林美容
Lin Pen-Hsuan 林本炫
Lin Shangzuo 林上祚
Lin Shihong (Penny Lin) 林士弘
Lin Wei-Ping 林瑋嬪
Liu Wensan 劉文三
Otsuka Eiji 大塚 英志
Pili Guoji Duomeiti Gufen Youxian Gongsi (Pili International Multimedia Company, Ltd.) 霹靂國際多媒體股份有限公司
Su Shuobin 蘇碩斌
Tsai Ventine (Cai Wenting) 蔡文婷
Urobuchi Gen 虛淵 玄

Wan Wan 灣灣
Wang Jia-Shiang 王嘉祥
Wang Pei-ti 王佩廸
Wu Mingde 吳明德
Wuxian Renxing Jutuan (Limitless Cosplay Theater) 無限人形劇團
Xie Yuqi 謝豫琦
Xie Zhongyi 謝忠義
Yamaguchi Yuko 山口裕子、森綾
Yomota Inuhiko 四方田犬彥

# Bibliography

A Jie. 2016. "*Dongli jian youji* wu lei tuijian: Qian tan Lao Xu #2" [Thunderstruck recommendation for *Thunderbolt Fantasy—Sword Seekers*: Brief discussion of Old Urobuchi #2]. YouTube video, 5:22, posted October 8, 2016. Accessed July 1, 2018. https://www.youtube.com/watch?v=tkxUhVBXxt0.

Adrian, Bonnie. 2003. *Framing the Bride: Globalizing Beauty and Romance in Taiwan's Bridal Industry*. Berkeley: University of California Press.

Ahmed, Sara. 2004. *The Cultural Politics of Emotion*. Edinburgh: Edinburgh University Press.

Allison, Anne. 1994. *Nightwork: Sexuality, Pleasure, and Corporate Masculinity in a Tokyo Hostess Club*. Chicago: University of Chicago Press.

——. 2006. *Millennial Monsters: Japanese Toys and the Global Imagination*. Berkeley: University of California Press.

American Institute in Taiwan. 2014. *International Religious Freedom Report for 2014: Taiwan Part*. Taipei: American Institute in Taiwan. https://www.ait.org.tw/international-religious-freedom-report-2014-taiwan-part/.

Anderson, Benedict. 1991. *Imagined Communities: Reflections on the Origin and Spread of Nationalism*. New York: Verso.

Annett, Sandra. 2011. "Animating Transcultural Communities: Animation Fandom in North America and East Asia from 1906–2010." PhD diss., University of Manitoba.

Arvidsson, Adam. 2006. *Brands: Meaning and Value in Media Culture*. New York: Routledge.

Au, Wagner James. 2008. *The Making of Second Life: Notes from the New World*. New York: Collins.

Austin, John. 1962. *How to Do Things with Words*. Oxford: Clarendon Press.

Azuma Hiroki. 2009. *Otaku: Japan's Database Animals*. Translated by Jonathan E. Abel and Shion Kono. Minneapolis: University of Minnesota Press.

Barthes, Roland. 1982. *Empire of Signs*. Translated by Richard Howard. New York: Hill and Wang.

Baudrillard, Jean. 1994. *Simulacra and Simulation*. Translated by Sheila Faria Glaser. Ann Arbor: University of Michigan Press.

Bechdel, Alison. 2012. *Are You My Mother? A Comic Drama*. Boston: Houghton Mifflin Harcourt.

Belting, Hans. 1994. *Likeness and Presence: A History of the Image before the Era of Art*. Translated by Edmund Jephcott. Chicago: University of Chicago Press

Berardi, Franco "Bifo." 2009. *The Soul at Work: From Alienation to Autonomy*. Translated by Francesca Cadel and Giuseppina Mecchia. Los Angeles: Semiotext(e).

Berger, Patricia. 1998. "Body Doubles: Sculpture for the Afterlife." *Orientations* 29 (2): 46–53.

Bird-David, Nurit. 1999. " 'Animism' Revisited: Personhood, Environment, and Relational Epistemology." *Current Anthropology* 40 (1): 67–91.

Birkett, Mary. 2012. " 'Amateur' Mascots on the Loose: The Pragmatics of Kawaii (Cute)." BA honors thesis, University of Michigan.

Blair, M. M. 2010. " 'She Should Just Die in a Ditch': Fan Reactions to Female Characters in Boys' Love Manga." In *Boys' Love Manga: Essays on the Sexual Ambiguity and Cross-Cultural Fandom of the Genre*, edited by Antonia Levi, Mark McHarry, and Dru Pagliassotti, 110–125. Jefferson, NC: McFarland and Co.

Boal, Augusto. 1979. *Theatre of the Oppressed*. London: Pluto Press.

Boellstorff, Tom. 2008. *Coming of Age in Second Life: An Anthropologist Explores the Virtually Human*. Princeton, NJ: Princeton University Press.

Bogatyrëv, Peter. [1937–1938] 1982. "A Contribution to the Study of Theatrical Signs: The Perception of the Signs in Puppet Theater, Theater with Live Actors, and Art in General." In *The Prague School: Selected Writings, 1929–1946*, edited by Peter Steiner, 55–64. Austin: University of Texas Press.

Bogost, Ian. 2012. *Alien Phenomenology, or What It's Like to Be a Thing*. Minneapolis: University of Minnesota Press.

Bollas, Christopher. 1992. *Being a Character*. New York: Routledge.

Bolter, Jay David, and Richard Grusin. 1999. *Remediation: Understanding New Media*. Cambridge, MA: MIT Press.

Bolton, Christopher. 2002. "From Wooden Cyborgs to Celluloid Souls: Mechanical Bodies in Anime and Japanese Puppet Theater." *Positions* 10 (3): 729–771.

Bornstein, Kate. 1998. *My Gender Workbook: How to Become a Real Man, a Real Woman, the Real You, or Something Else Entirely*. New York: Routledge.

Boyer, Pascal. 1996. "What Makes Anthropomorphism Natural: Intuitive Ontology and Cultural Representations." *Journal of the Royal Anthropological Institute* 2 (1): 83–97.

Brown, Bill. 2001. "Thing Theory." *Critical Inquiry* 28 (Autumn): 1–22.

Brown, Robert L. 1998. "The Miraculous Buddha Image: Portrait, God, or Object?" In *Images, Miracles, and Authority in Asian Religious Traditions*, edited by Richard H. Davis, 37–54. Boulder, CO: Westview Press.

Brown, Steven T. 2008. "Machinic Desires: Hans Bellmer's Dolls and the Technological Uncanny in *Ghost in the Shell 2: Innocence*." *Mechademia* 3:222–253.

Butler, Jeremy G. 1991. "'I'm Not a Doctor, but I Play One on TV': Characters, Actors and Acting in Television Soap Opera." *Cinema Journal* 30 (4): 75–91.

Butler, Judith. 1988. "Performative Acts and Gender Constitution: An Essay in Phenomenology and Feminist Theory." *Theatre Journal* 40 (4): 519–531.

———. 1990. *Gender Trouble: Feminism and the Subversion of Identity*. New York: Routledge.

———. 1993. *Bodies That Matter: On the Discursive Limits of "Sex."* New York: Routledge.

Caituanfaren Zhonghua Minsu Yishu Jijinhui (Chinese Folk Arts Foundation), ed. 2005. *Taiwan Budaixi yu Chuantong Wenhua Chuangyi Chanye Yantaohui Wenji* [Collected essays from the Taiwan Po-te-hi and Traditional Culture Creative Industries Symposium]. Yilan County: Guoli Chuantong Yishu Zhongxin.

Case, Sue-Ellen. 1989. "Toward a Butch-Femme Aesthetic." In *Making a Spectacle: Feminist Essays on Contemporary Women's Theater*, edited by Lynda Hart, 282–299. Ann Arbor: University of Michigan Press.

Chang Hsun. 2003. *Wenhua Mazu: Taiwan Mazu xinyang yanjiu lunwenji* [Cultural Mazu: Collection of essays on Taiwan Mazu belief]. Taipei: Academia Sinica Institute of Ethnology.

Chen Hsinchih. 2012. "Zuxian xinyang bianqian de chu tan" [The change of ancestor worship in Taiwan]. In *Taiwan de shehui bianqian, 1985–2005: Xinli, jiazhi yu zongjiao* [Social change in Taiwan, 1985–2005: Psychology, values, and religion], edited by Chu Ruey-Ling, Chiu Hai-Yuan, and Chang Li-yun, 107–149. Taipei: Academia Sinica Institute of Sociology.

Chen Longting. 1999. "Budaixi renwu de zhengzhi quanshi: Cong Shi Yanwen dao Su Huanzhen" [A political interpretation of *po-te-hi* characters: From Shi Yanwen to Su Huanzhen]. *Taiwan feng wu* [Taiwan folkways] 49 (4): 171–188.

———. 2007. *Taiwan budaixi fazhan shi* [The history of the development of Taiwanese *po-te-hi*]. Taipei: Qianwei Chubanshe.

Chen, Mel. 2012. *Animacies: Biopolitics, Racial Mattering, and Queer Affect*. Durham, NC: Duke University Press.

Chen Pingyuan. 1995. Qiangu wenren xiake meng: Wuxia xiaoshuo leixing yanjiu [The ancient swordsman dream of the literati: Genre research on the *wuxia* novel]. Taipei: Maitian Renwen.

Chen Qiufan. 1993. Ren xiang xue [Study of the human face]. Taipei: Long Nian Wenhua.

Chen, Yu-fu, and Jake Chung. 2017. "Number of Married Couples in Decline; Singles Hit 4.4m." *Taipei Times*, October 25. http://www.taipeitimes.com /News/taiwan/archives/2017/10/25/2003681012.

Chiu Hai-Yuan. 2012. "Zongjiao yu shushu taidu he xingwei de bianqian (1985– 2005): Jianshi shisuhua de yingxiang" [Changes in religious and occult behaviors (1985–2005): Examining the effects of secularization]. In *Taiwan de shehui bianqian, 1985–2005: Xinli, jiazhi yu zongjiao* [Social change in Taiwan, 1985–2005: Psychology, values, and religion], edited by Chu Ruey-Ling, Chiu Hai-Yuan, and Chang Li-yun, 241–291. Taipei: Academia Sinica Institute of Sociology.

Cholodenko, Alan. 1991. Introduction to *The Illusion of Life*, edited by Alan Cholodenko, 9–36. Sydney: Power Publications.

———. 2007. Introduction to *The Illusion of Life II: More Essays on Animation*, edited by Alan Cholodenko, 13–98. Sydney: Power Publications.

Chu Ruey-Ling, Chiu Hai-Yuan, and Chang Li-yun, eds. 2012. *Taiwan de shehui bianqian, 1985–2005: Xinli, jiazhi yu zongjiao* [Social change in Taiwan, 1985–2005: Psychology, values, and religion]. Taipei: Academia Sinica Institute of Sociology.

Chuang, Yin. 2011. "Kawaii in Taiwan Politics." *International Journal of Asia-Pacific Studies* 7 (3): 1–17.

Clammer, John, Sylvie Poirier, and Eric Schwimmer, eds. 2004. *Figured Worlds: Ontological Obstacles in Intercultural Relations*. Toronto: University of Toronto Press.

Clart, Philip, and Charles B. Jones, eds. 2003. *Religion in Modern Taiwan*. Honolulu: University of Hawai'i Press.

Comaroff, John L., and Jean Comaroff. 2009. *Ethnicity, Inc.* Chicago: University of Chicago Press.

Condry, Ian. 2013. *The Soul of Anime: Collaborative Creativity and Japan's Media Success Story*. Durham, NC: Duke University Press.

crasnowy. 2018a. "Bao wu" [Precious thing]. *Tongrenzhi* posted online in five parts. Accessed July 1, 2018. Part 1: https://www.ptt.cc/bbs/APH/M.1242313170 .A.DBA.html. Part 2: https://www.ptt.cc/bbs/APH/M.1242405762.A.912 .html. Part 3: https://www.ptt.cc/bbs/APH/M.1243181666.A.4B3.html. Part 4: https://www.ptt.cc/bbs/APH/M.1243345225.A.551.html. Part 5: https://www .ptt.cc/bbs/APH/M.1243786980.A.C59.html.

———. 2018b. "Ruguo tamen shi zhishi" [If they were butlers]. *Tongrenzhi* posted online. Accessed July 1, 2018. https://www.ptt.cc/bbs/APH/M .1243865032.A.3D8.html.

Daliot-Bul, Michal. 2009. "Japan Brand Strategy: The Taming of 'Cool Japan' and the Challenges of Cultural Planning in a Postmodern Age." *Social Science Japan Journal* 12 (2): 247–266.

Deleuze, Gilles. 1986. *Cinema 1: The Movement-Image*. Translated by Hugh Tomlinson and Barbara Habberjam. Minneapolis: University of Minnesota Press.

Descola, Philippe. 2013. *Beyond Nature and Culture*. Translated by Janet Lloyd. Chicago: University of Chicago Press.

Diamond, Elin. 1988. "Brechtian Theory/Feminist Theory." *TDR* 32 (1): 82–94.

Dibbell, Julian. 1998. *My Tiny Life: Crime and Passion in a Virtual World*. New York: Henry Holt and Co.

Duara, Prasenjit. 1988. "Superscribing Symbols: The Myth of Guandi, Chinese God of War." *Journal of Asian Studies* 47 (4): 778–795.

Dyer, Richard. 1986. *Heavenly Bodies: Film Stars and Society*. New York: St. Martin's Press.

———. 1992. *Only Entertainment*. New York: Routledge.

Ebrey, Patricia. 1997. "Portrait Sculptures in Imperial Ancestral Rites in Song China." *T'oung Pao: International Journal of Chinese Studies* 83:42–92.

Eck, Diana L. 1985. *Darsan: Seeing the Divine Image in India*. Chambersburg, PA: Anima Books.

Edgerton, Gary R. 2010. *The Columbia History of American Television*. New York: Columbia University Press.

Eisenstein, Sergei. 1986. *Eisenstein on Disney*. [Essays from 1940–1941] Edited by Jay Leyda. Translated by Alan Upchurch. Calcutta: Seagull Books.

Faure, Bernard. 1998. "The Buddhist Icon and the Modern Gaze." *Critical Inquiry* 24 (3): 768–813.

Feuchtwang, Stephan. 1992. *The Imperial Metaphor: Popular Religion in China*. New York: Routledge.

Frazer, James. [1911] 1925. *The Golden Bough: A Study in Magic and Religion*. Vol. 1. New York: Macmillan.

Freedman, Alisa. 2009. "*Train Man* and the Gender Politics of Japanese 'Otaku' Culture: The Rise of New Media, Nerd Heroes and Consumer Communities." *Intersections: Gender and Sexuality in Asia and the Pacific* 20. http://intersections.anu.edu.au/issue20/freedman.htm.

Fullerton, Howard N., Jr. 1999. "Labor Force Participation: 75 Years of Change, 1950–98 and 1998–2025." *Monthly Labor Review* 122 (December): 3–12. http://www.bls.gov/mlr/1999/12/art1full.pdf.

Galbraith, Patrick. 2009. "*Moe*: Exploring Virtual Potential in Post-Millennial Japan." *Electronic Journal of Contemporary Japanese Studies*. http://www.japanesestudies.org.uk/articles/2009/Galbraith.html.

Geertz, Clifford. 1973. *The Interpretation of Cultures*. New York: HarperCollins.

Gell, Alfred. 1998. *Art and Agency: An Anthropological Theory*. Oxford: Clarendon Press.

Gershon, Ilana. 2010a. *The Breakup 2.0: Disconnecting over New Media*. Ithaca, NY: Cornell University Press.

———. 2010b. "Media Ideologies." *Journal of Linguistic Anthropology* 20 (2): 283–293.

———. 2011. "Neoliberal Agency." *Current Anthropology* 52 (4): 537–555.

———. 2014. "Selling Your Self in the United States." *PoLAR: Political and Legal Anthropology Review* 37 (2): 281–295.

———. 2016. "'I'm Not a Businessman, I'm a Business, Man': Typing the Neoliberal Self into a Branded Existence." *HAU: Journal of Ethnographic Theory* 6 (3): 223–246.

Gibran, Khalil. 2018. "On Children." Accessed July 1, 2018. http://www.katsandogz .com/onchildren.html.

Gibson, James. 1979. *The Ecological Approach to Perception*. London: Houghton Mifflin.

Gilligan, Carol. 1982. *In a Different Voice: Psychological Theory and Women's Development*. Cambridge, MA: Harvard University Press.

Goffman, Erving. 1959. *The Presentation of Self in Everyday Life*. New York: Anchor.

———. 1963. *Stigma: Notes on the Management of Spoiled Identity*. Englewood Cliffs, NJ: Prentice-Hall.

———. 1974. *Frame Analysis: An Essay on the Organization of Experience*. New York: Harper and Row.

———. 1979. *Gender Advertisements*. New York: Harper and Row.

Gombrich, E. H. 1963. *Meditations on a Hobby Horse and Other Essays on the Theory of Art*. Chicago: University of Chicago Press.

Gordon, Beverly. 2006. *The Saturated World: Aesthetic Meaning, Intimate Objects, Women's Lives, 1890–1940*. Knoxville: University of Tennessee Press.

Gouldner, Alvin. 1970. *The Coming Crisis of Western Sociology*. New York: Basic Books.

Government Information Office. 2003. *The Story of Taiwan*. Accessed September 30, 2003. http://www.gio.gov.tw/info/taiwan-story/economy/eframe/frame3 .htm.

Graeber, David. 2007. *Possibilities: Essays on Hierarchy, Rebellion, and Desire*. Oakland, CA: AK Press.

———. 2008. "The Sadness of Post-Workerism, or 'Art and Immaterial Labour' Conference: A Sort of Review." *The Commoner*. https://libcom.org/library /sadness-post-workerism.

Grosz, Elizabeth A. 1994. *Volatile Bodies: Toward a Corporeal Feminism*. Bloomington, IN: Indiana University Press.

Hamm, John Christopher. 2005. *Paper Swordsmen: Jin Yong and the Modern Chinese Martial Arts Novel*. Honolulu: University of Hawai'i Press.

Hansen, Valerie. 1990. *Changing Gods in Medieval China, 1127–1276*. Princeton, NJ: Princeton University Press.

Haraway, Donna J. 1985. "A Manifesto for Cyborgs: Science, Technology, and Socialist Feminism in the 1980s." *Socialist Review*, no. 80: 65–108.

Hardt, Michael. 1999. "Affective Labor." *Boundary 2* 26 (2): 89–100.

Hardt, Michael, and Antonio Negri. 2000. *Empire*. Cambridge, MA: Harvard University Press.

Harrell, Stevan. 1977. "Modes of Belief in Chinese Folk Religion." *Journal for the Scientific Study of Religion* 16 (1): 55–65.

Hastings, Adi, and Paul Manning. 2004. "Introduction: Acts of Alterity." *Language and Communication* 24:291–311.

Hatfield, DJ W. 2010. *Taiwanese Pilgrimage to China: Ritual, Complicity, Community*. New York: Palgrave.

Hayles, N. Katherine. 1999. *How We Became Posthuman: Virtual Bodies in Cybernetics, Literature, and Informatics*. Chicago: University of Chicago Press.

He Zi. 1997. "Su Huanzhen: Wenhe haoren" [Su Huanzhen: Tender superman]. In *Pili yingxiong da butie: Zui xiai de budaixi renwu* [Pili heroes roster: Favorite puppet characters], edited by Chen Feiwen, 33–35. Taipei: Shibao Wenhua.

Helmreich, Stefan. 1998. *Silicon Second Nature: Culturing Artificial Life in a Digital World*. Berkeley: University of California Press.

Heng, H. Jiuan. 2003. "The Emergence of Pure Consciousness: The Theater of Virtual Selves in the Age of the Internet." In *Technology and Cultural Values on the Edge of the Third Millennium*, edited by Peter D. Hershock, Marietta Stepaniants, and Roger T. Ames. Honolulu: University of Hawai'i Press.

Hochschild, Arlie. 2003. *The Managed Heart: Commercialization of Human Feeling*. 20th anniversary ed. Berkeley: University of California Press.

Holloway, John. 2002. *Change the World without Taking Power: The Meaning of Revolution Today*. Ann Arbor, MI: Pluto Press.

Hong Mengkai. 2005. "Da bu yuxiang houxiandai—Pili jie zhi *Du cheng xie yin*" [Taking a big step toward postmodern culture: Pili's *Castle Sealed in Blood*]. In *Taiwan budaixi yu chuantong wenhua chuangyi chanye yantaohui wenji* [Collected essays from the Taiwan Po-te-hi and Traditional Culture Creative Industries Symposium], edited by Caituanfaren Zhonghua Minsu Yishu Jijinhui (Chinese Folk Arts Foundation), 96–111. Yilan County: Guoli Chuantong Yishu Zhongxin.

Howard, Angela Falco. 2006. "From the Han to the Southern Song." In *Chinese Sculpture*, edited by Angela Falco Howard, Wu Hung, Li Song, and Yang Hong, 201–356. New Haven, CT: Yale University Press.

Howard, Angela Falco, Wu Hung, Li Song, and Yang Hong, eds. 2006. *Chinese Sculpture*. New Haven, CT: Yale University Press.

Hsiao, Chi-fang. 2014. "The Cultural Translation of U.S. Television Programs and Movies: Subtitle Groups as Cultural Brokers in China." PhD diss., University of California, Los Angeles.

Huang Liang-hsun. 2018. "Fangtan *Qi ren mima: Guluobu zhi mi* bianju ji yishu zongjian Huang Liangxun" [Interview with the scriptwriter and art director of *The Arti: The Adventure Begins*, Huang Liang-hsun]. Interview with Taipei Film Commission. YouTube video, 7:10. Accessed July 1, 2018. https://www.youtube.com/watch?v=5ft1M-3Cmq8&feature=youtu.be.

Huang Minming. 2001. "Taiwan diqu de laodong zhuanxing" [Labor transformation in the Taiwan region]. *Zixun shehui yanjiu* [Journal of Information Society] 1 (July): 257–278.

Huang Neng-yang. 2001. "Quanqiuhua shidai li de bentu wenhua gongye—Yi dianshi budaixi wei li" [The local cultural industry in the globalization era: A case study of TV puppetry]. MA thesis, National Chung Cheng University.

Huang Qianghua [Chris Huang]. 1999. *Pili xingzuo Feng shen bang* [Pili Zodiac: Intervention of the Gods]. Taipei: Shangye Zhoukan Chubanshe.

Huang, Shu-ling. 2011. "Nation-Branding and Transnational Consumption: Japan-Mania and the Korean Wave in Taiwan." *Media, Culture and Society* 33 (1): 3–18.

Hutchby, Ian. 2001. *Conversation and Technology: From the Telephone to the Internet*. Cambridge, UK: Polity.

Institute of Ethnology, Academia Sinica. 2018. "Go, Figures! The Culture and Charisma of Statues, Puppets, and Dolls." Online museum exhibit. Accessed July 1, 2018. http://gofigures.ioe.sinica.edu.tw/en/index.html.

Iwabuchi, Koichi. 2002. *Recentering Globalization: Popular Culture and Japanese Transnationalism*. Durham, NC: Duke University Press.

———. 2010. "Undoing Inter-national Fandom in the Age of Brand Nationalism." *Mechademia* 5:87–96.

Jenkins, Henry. 1992. *Textual Poachers: Television Fans and Participatory Culture*. New York: Routledge.

———. 2006. *Convergence Culture: Where Old and New Media Collide*. New York: New York University Press.

Jensen, Casper Bruun, and Anders Blok. 2013. "Techno-animism in Japan: Shinto Cosmograms, Actor-Network Theory, and the Enabling Powers of Non-human Agencies." *Theory, Culture and Society* 30 (2): 84–115.

Jentsch, Ernst. [1906] 1997. "On the Psychology of the Uncanny." *Angelaki* 2 (1):7–16.

Jiang Wuchang. 1990. "Budaixi jian shi" [A brief history of *po-te-hi*]. *Min su qu yi* [Journal of Chinese ritual, theater and folklore] 67/68:66–126.

Jones, Charles B. 2003. "Religion in Taiwan at the End of the Japanese Colonial Period." In *Religion in Modern Taiwan*, edited by Philip Clart and Charles B. Jones, 10–35. Honolulu: University of Hawai'i Press.

Jordan, David. 1972. *Gods, Ghosts, and Ancestors: Folk Religion in a Taiwanese Village*. Berkeley: University of California Press.

Jullien, François. 1999. *The Propensity of Things: Toward a History of Efficacy in China*. Translated by Janet Lloyd. New York: Zone Books.

Kaneva, Nadia. 2011. "Nation Branding: Toward an Agenda for Critical Research." *International Journal of Communication* 5:117–141.

Kaplin, Stephen. 2001. "A Puppet Tree: A Model for the Field of Puppet Theatre." In *Puppets, Masks, and Performing Objects*, edited by John Bell, 18–25. Cambridge, MA: MIT Press.

Keane, Webb. 2007. *Christian Moderns: Freedom and Fetish in the Mission Encounter*. Berkeley: University of California Press.

Keeler, Ward. 1987. *Javanese Shadow Plays, Javanese Selves*. Princeton, NJ: Princeton University Press.

Kelts, Roland. 2006. *Japanamerica: How Japanese Pop Culture Has Invaded the U.S.* New York: Palgrave Macmillan.

Kesner, Ladislav. 1991. "Portrait Aspects and Social Functions of Chinese Ceramic Tomb Sculpture." *Orientations* 22 (8): 33–42.

———. 1995. "Likeness of No One: (Re)presenting the First Emperor's Army." *Art Bulletin* 77 (1): 115–132.

———. 2007. "Face as Artifact in Early Chinese Art." *RES* 51 (Spring): 33–56.

Kinsella, Sharon. 1995. "Cuties in Japan." In *Women, Media, and Consumption in Japan*, edited by Brian Moeran and Lise Scov. New York: Curzon Press.

———. 1998. "Japanese Subculture in the 1990s: Otaku and the Amateur Manga Movement." *Journal of Japanese Studies* 24 (2): 289–316.

Kirsch, Stuart. 2014. "Imagining Corporate Personhood." *PoLAR: Political and Legal Anthropology Review* 3 (2): 207–217.

Koma, Kyoko. 2013. "Kawaii as Represented in Scientific Research: The Possibilities of Kawaii Cultural Studies." *Hemispheres* 28:5–19.

Kong, Lily, Chris Gibson, Louisa-May Khoo, and Anne-Louise Semple. 2006. "Knowledges of the Creative Economy: Towards a Relational Geography of Diffusion and Adaptation in Asia." *Asia Pacific Viewpoint* 47 (2): 173–194.

Kotani, Mari. 2018. "Interview: Mari Kotani, Pioneer of Japanese Cosplay—Origins." Interview with Ohwada, Keio University. Online video with transcript, 11:00. Accessed February 10, 2018. https://www.futurelearn.com /courses/intro-to-japanese-subculture/0/steps/23609.

Lai Honglin. 2001. "Pili budaixi zhi huanxiang zhuti piping" [A fantasy theme criticism of Pili puppet show]. MA thesis, Fu Jen University.

Lamarre, Thomas. 2008. "Speciesism, Part I: Translating Races into Animals in Wartime Animation." *Mechademia* 3:75–96.

———. 2009. *The Anime Machine: A Media Theory of Animation*. Minneapolis: University of Minnesota Press.

Latour, Bruno. 1993. *We Have Never Been Modern*. Cambridge, MA: Harvard University Press.

———. 2005. *Reassembling the Social: An Introduction to Actor-Network-Theory*. New York: Oxford University Press.

Lazzarato, Maurizio. 1996. "Immaterial Labor." In *Radical Thought in Italy: A Potential Politics*, edited by Paolo Virno and Michael Hardt, 133–147. Minneapolis: University of Minnesota Press.

Leavitt, Alex, and Andrea Horbinski. 2012. "Even a Monkey Can Understand Fan Activism: Political Speech, Artistic Expression, and a Public for the Japanese Dōjin Community." *Transformative Works and Cultures* 10. http://journal .transformativeworks.org/index.php/twc/article/view/321/311.

Lee, Ming-Tsung. 2004. "Absorbing 'Japan': Transnational Media, Cross-cultural Consumption, and Identity Practice in Contemporary Taiwan." PhD diss., King's College, University of Cambridge.

Leng Bin. 2002. *Ai shang Shinupi: Snoopy in Our Memories* [In love with Snoopy: Snoopy in our memories]. Taipei: Guo Bao.

———. 2003. *Ai shang Shinupi: Women de Shinupi shoucang 2* [In love with Snoopy: Our Snoopy collection 2 (Snoopy in Our Memories 2)]. Taipei: Guo Bao.

Leve, Lauren. 2011. "Identity." *Current Anthropology* 52 (4): 513–535.

Li Song. 2006. Introduction to *Chinese Sculpture*, edited by Angela Falco Howard, Wu Hung, Li Song, and Yang Hong, 1–6. New Haven, CT: Yale University Press.

Li Xinyi, ed. 2008. *Zhong shen fa wei zhuan da qian* [The gods show their power, earn big money]. Taipei: Xin Fu Ti An Wenhua.

Lin Pen-Hsuan. 2012. "Dili liudong yu zongjiao xinyang bianqian" [Geographical mobility and religious change in Taiwan]. In *Taiwan de shehui bianqian, 1985–2005: Xinli, jiazhi yu zongjiao* [Social change in Taiwan, 1985–2005: Psychology, values, and religion], edited by Chu Ruey-Ling, Chiu Hai-Yuan, and Chang Li-yun, 151–189. Taipei: Academia Sinica Institute of Sociology.

Lin Shangzuo. 2008. "Jiang Canteng: Zongjiao shangpinhua tai fanlin" [Chiang Tsanteng: The commercialization of religion is going overboard]. *China Times*, February 3.

Lin Wei-Ping. 2002. "Taiwan Han ren de shenxiang: Tan shen ruhe juxiang" [Icons of the Taiwanese Han people: A discussion of how gods are objectified.] *Taiwan Journal of Anthropology* 1 (2): 115–147.

———. 2008. "Conceptualizing Gods through Statues: A Study of Personification and Localization in Taiwan." *Comparative Studies in Society and History* 50 (2): 454–477.

———. 2015. *Materializing Magic Power: Chinese Popular Religion in Villages and Cities*. Cambridge, MA: Harvard University Asia Center.

Liu Wensan. 1981. *Taiwan shenxiang yishu* [The art of Taiwanese icons]. Yishu Jia Xian Kan 18. Taipei: Yishu Jia Chubanshe.

Lü Aihui. 2006. "Huang jia san xiongdi: Chuangzao wenhua qiji" [The three brothers Huang: Creating a cultural miracle]. *Feifan xinwen E zhoukan* [UBN weekly] 27 (October 22–28): 58–61.

MacAloon, John. 1984. *Rite, Drama, Festival, Spectacle: Rehearsals toward a Theory of Cultural Performance*. Philadelphia: ISHI.

Macpherson, C. B. 1962. *The Political Theory of Possessive Individualism: From Hobbes to Locke*. Oxford: Oxford University Press.

Malaby, Thomas. 2009. *Making Virtual Worlds: Linden Lab and Second Life*. Ithaca, NY: Cornell University Press.

Manning, Paul. 2009. "Can the Avatar Speak?" *Journal of Linguistic Anthropology* 9 (2): 310–325.

———. 2010. "The Semiotics of Brand." *Annual Review of Anthropology* 39:33–49.

Manning, Paul, and Ilana Gershon. 2013. "Animating Interaction." *HAU: Journal of Ethnographic Theory* 3 (3): 107–137.

Manovich, Lev. 2001. *The Language of New Media*. Cambridge, MA: MIT Press.

Martin, Fran. 2008. "Comics as Everyday Theory: The Counterpublic World of Taiwanese Women Fans of Japanese Homoerotic Manga." In *Cultural Theory in Everyday Practice*, edited by Nicole Anderson and Katrina Schlunke, 164–176. Oxford: Oxford University Press.

Masuzawa, Tomoko. 2005. *The Invention of World Religions, or, How European Universalism Was Preserved in the Language of Pluralism*. Chicago: University of Chicago Press.

———. 2007. "Troubles with Materiality: The Ghost of Fetishism in the Nineteenth Century." In *Religion: Beyond a Concept*, edited by Hent de Vries, 647–667. New York: Fordham University Press.

McCloud, Scott. 1993. *Understanding Comics: The Invisible Art*. New York: William Morrow.

McKenzie, Jon. 2001. *Perform or Else: From Discipline to Performance*. New York: Routledge.

Meadows, Mark Stephen. 2005. *I, Avatar: The Culture and Consequences of Having a Second Life*. Berkeley, CA: New Riders.

Miller, Laura. 2010. "Japan's Zoomorphic Urge." *ASIANetwork Exchange* 17 (2): 69–82.

———.2011a. "Cute Masquerade and the Pimping of Japan." *International Journal of Japanese Sociology* 20:18–29.

———. 2011b. "Subversive Script and Novel Graphs in Japanese Girls' Culture." *Language and Communication* 31:16–26.

Miyake, Toshio. 2013. "Doing Occidentalism in Contemporary Japan: Nation Anthropomorphism and Sexualized Parody in *Axis Powers Hetalia*." *Transformative Works and Cultures*, no. 12 (March). http://journal.transformativeworks.org/index.php/twc/article/view/436/392.

Moore, Robert. 2003. "From Genericide to Viral Marketing: On 'Brand.'" *Language and Communication* 23:331–357.

Mori Masahiro. [1970] 2012. "The Uncanny Valley: The Original Essay by Masahiro Mori." Translated by Karl F. MacDorman and Norri Kageki. *IEEE Spectrum*. http://spectrum.ieee.org/automaton/robotics/humanoids/the-uncanny-valley.

Morse, Margaret. 1998. *Virtualities: Television, Media Art, and Cyberculture*. Bloomington: Indiana University Press.

Nadeau, Randall, and Chang Hsun. 2003. "Gods, Ghosts, and Ancestors: Religious Studies and the Question of 'Taiwanese Identity.'" In *Religion in Modern Taiwan*, edited by Philip Clart and Charles B. Jones, 280–299. Honolulu: University of Hawai'i Press.

Napier, Susan J. 2005. "The Problem of Existence in Japanese Animation." *Proceedings of the American Philosophical Society* 149 (1): 72–79.

———. 2006. "The World of Anime Fandom in America." *Mechademia* 1:47–64.

———. 2007. *From Impressionism to Anime: Japan as Fantasy and Fan Cult in the Mind of the West*. New York: Palgrave MacMillan.

Nardi, Bonnie. 2010. *My Life as a Night Elf Priest: An Anthropological Account of "World of Warcraft."* Ann Arbor: University of Michigan Press.

Naremore, James. 1988. *Acting in the Cinema*. Berkeley: University of California Press.

National Communications Commission. 2011. Weihou ershao tongchuan quanyi NCC gongbu "Ershao tongshun chuanbo zhengci wangling ji xingdong celüe" [Protecting children's access rights: NCC publication "Children's information broadcasting policy online and action strategy"]. http://www.ncc.gov.tw/chinese/content.aspx?site_content_sn=2747.

Nelson, Victoria. 2001. *The Secret Life of Puppets*. Cambridge, MA: Harvard University Press.

Newton, Esther. 1979. *Mother Camp: Female Impersonators in America*. Chicago: University of Chicago Press.

Ngai, Sianne. 2005. "The Cuteness of the Avant-Garde." *Critical Inquiry* 31 (4): 811–847.

———. 2012. *Our Aesthetic Categories: Zany, Cute, Interesting*. Cambridge, MA: Harvard University Press.

Nozawa, Shunsuke. 2012. "The Gross Face and Virtual Fame: Semiotic Mediation in Japanese Virtual Communication." *First Monday* 17 (3). https://doi.org /10.5210/FM.V17I3.3535.

———. 2013. "Characterization." *Semiotic Review*, no. 3. https://www.semioticreview .com/ojs/index.php/sr/article/view/16.

Nye, Joseph. 1990. "Soft Power." *Foreign Policy* 80:153–171.

Occhi, Debra. 2012. "Wobbly Aesthetics, Performance and Message: Comparing Japanese *Kyara* with Their Anthropomorphic Forebears." *Asian Ethnology* 71 (1): 109–132.

Ocha, Machiko. 2006. *Train Man: A Shojo Manga*. Based on the story by Hitoro Nakano. Translated and adapted by Makoto Yukon. New York: Ballantine Books.

Omi, Michael, and Howard Winant. 1986. *Racial Formation in the United States: From the 1960s to the 1980s*. New York: Routledge and Kegan Paul.

Orbaugh, Sharalyn. 2002. "Sex and the Single Cyborg: Japanese Popular Culture Experiments in Subjectivity." *Science Fiction Studies* 29 (3): 436–452.

———. 2008. "Emotional Infectivity: Cyborg Affect and the Limits of the Human." In *Mechademia 3*: 150–172. Minneapolis: University of Minnesota Press.

Osnos, Evan. 2014. *The Age of Ambition: Chasing Fortune, Truth, and Faith in the New China*. New York: Farrar, Straus and Giroux.

Otsuka, Eiji. 2010. "World and Variation: The Reproduction and Consumption of Narrative." Translated and with introduction by Marc Steinberg. *Mechademia* 5: 99–116. Minneapolis: University of Minnesota Press. Originally published in 1989 in *Monogatari shōhiron* [A theory of narrative consumption], by Otsuka Eiji.

Overseas Compatriot Affairs Council. 2012. "Longitudinal Survey of Migrants to the U.S. from Taiwan, 2012: Filling Statement—Questionnaire A (for First-Time Respondents)." http://www.ocac.gov.tw/ocac/file/attach/1152 /file_1853.doc.

Patten, Fred. 2004. *Watching Anime, Reading Manga: 25 Years of Essays and Reviews*. Berkeley, CA: Stone Bridge Press.

Peachey, Anna, and Mark Childs, eds. 2011. *Reinventing Ourselves: Contemporary Concepts of Identity in Virtual Worlds*. London: Springer.

Piaget, Jean. 1975. "The Concept of Life." In *The Child's Conception of the World*, translated by Joan Tomlinson and Andrew Tomlinson, 194–206. Totowa, NJ: Littlefield, Adams.

Pietz, William. 1985. "The Problem of the Fetish, I: The Origin of the Fetish." *RES: Anthropology and Aesthetics* 9:5–17.

———. 1987. "The Problem of the Fetish, II: The Origin of the Fetish." *RES: Anthropology and Aesthetics* 13:23–45.

Pili International Multimedia Company. 2000. *Pili Guoji Duo Meiti Qiye jie* [Introduction to Pili International Multimedia Enterprise]. Publicity pamphlet.

———. 2002. Untitled publicity pamphlet.

———. 2015. "Gongkai shuoming shu: Faxing 104 niandu yuangong ren gu quan pinzheng" [Public Document: 2015 Employee Warrant]. Accessed July 1, 2018. http://home.pili.com.tw/company/prospectus/201509_8450 _B1c_20170925_110526.pdf.

———. 2018. "Pili Wang" [Pili Net]. Accessed July 1, 2018. http://www.pili.com.tw/.

Rée, Jonathan. 1992. "Internationality." *Radical Philosophy* 60:3–11.

Rehak, Bob. 2003. 'Playing at Being: Psychoanalysis and the Avatar.' In *The Video Game Theory Reader*, edited by Mark J.P. Wolf and Bernard Perron, 103–128. New York: Routledge.

Ruizendaal, Robin. 2006. *Marionette Theatre in Quanzhou*. Leiden: Brill.

Sangren, P. Steven. 1987. *History and Magical Power in a Chinese Community*. Stanford, CA: Stanford University Press.

———. 2000. *Chinese Sociologics: An Anthropological Account of the Role of Alienation in Social Reproduction*. London: Athlone Press.

Schechner, Richard. 1985. *Between Theater and Anthropology*. Philadelphia: University of Pennsylvania Press.

———. 2006. *Performance Studies: An Introduction*. 2nd ed. New York: Routledge.

Schwartz, Hillel. 1992. "Torque: The New Kinaesthetic of the Twentieth Century." In *Incorporations*, edited by Jonathan Crary and Sanford Kwinter. New York: Zone Books.

Sconce, Jeffrey. 2000. *Haunted Media: Electronic Presence from Telegraphy to Television*. Durham, NC: Duke University Press.

Sedgwick, Eve Kosofsky. 1990. *Epistemology of the Closet*. Berkeley: University of California Press.

Seraph. 2009. *Yaxiya rihe* [Good day for Asia]. Taipei: Self-published *tongrenzhi*.

Shahar, Meir. 1996. "Vernacular Fiction and the Transmission of God's Cults in Late Imperial China." In *Unruly Gods: Divinity and Society in China*, edited by

Meir Shahar and Robert P. Weller, 184–211. Honolulu: University of Hawai'i Press.

———. 1998. *Crazy Ji: Chinese Religion and Popular Literature*. Cambridge, MA: Harvard University Press.

Shahar, Meir, and Robert P. Weller, eds. 1996. *Unruly Gods: Divinity and Society in China*. Honolulu: University of Hawai'i Press.

Shershow, Scott Cutler. 1995. *Puppets and "Popular" Culture*. Ithaca, NY: Cornell University Press.

Siggstedt, Mette. 1991. "Forms of Fate: An Investigation of the Relationship between Formal Portraiture, Especially Ancestral Portraits, and Physiognomy (*Xiangshu*) in China." In *International Colloquium on Chinese Art History, 1991: Proceedings*, part 2. Taipei: National Palace Museum.

Silvio, Teri. 1999. "Reflexivity, Bodily Praxis, and Identity in Taiwanese Opera." *GLQ: A Journal of Gay and Lesbian Studies* 5 (4): 585–604.

———. 2006. "Informationalized Affect: The Body in Taiwanese Digital-Video Puppetry and COSplay." In *Embodied Modernities: Corporeality, Representation, and Chinese Cultures*, edited by Fran Martin and Larissa Heinrich, 195–217. Honolulu: University of Hawai'i Press.

———. 2007. "Remediation and Local Globalizations: How Taiwan's 'Digital Video Knights-Errant Puppetry' Writes the History of the New Media in Chinese." *Cultural Anthropology* 22 (2): 285–313.

———. 2008. "Pop Culture Icons: Religious Inflections of the Character Toy in Taiwan." In *Mechademia 3*: 200–221. Minneapolis: University of Minnesota Press.

———. 2009. "Tai/Kuso/Camp: 'New Opeila' and the Structure of Sensibility." *Inter-Asia Cultural Studies* 10 (3): 341–360.

———. 2010. "Animation: The New Performance?" *Journal of Linguistic Anthropology* 20 (2): 422–438.

———. 2011. "BL/Q: The Aesthetics of Pili Puppetry Fan Fiction." In *Popular Culture in Taiwan: Charismatic Modernity*, edited by Marc L. Moskowitz, 149–166. New York: Routledge.

———. 2017. "Crying Songs and Their Fans: The Material and Affective Economy of Taiwanese Opera, 1945–1975." *Positions* 25 (3): 469–505.

Singer, Milton, ed. 1959. *Traditional India: Structure and Change*. Philadelphia: American Folklore Society.

Smith-Rosenberg, Carroll. 1975. "The Female World of Love and Ritual: Relations between Women in Nineteenth Century America." *Signs* 1 (1): 1–29.

Sodano, Dustin. 2016. "Mobile Taiwan: A Look at a Highly Mobile Market." *eMarketer*, December 16. https://www.emarketer.com/Article/Mobile-Taiwan-Look-Highly-Mobile-Market/1014877.

Spigel, Lynn. 1992. "Installing the Television Set: Popular Discourses on Television and Domestic Space, 1948–1955." In *Private Screenings: Television and the Female Consumer*, ed. Lynn Spigel and Denise Mann, 3–39. Minneapolis: University of Minnesota Press.

Stalberg, Roberta. 1984. *China's Puppets*. San Francisco: China Books.

Steinberg, Marc. 2012. *Anime's Media Mix: Franchising Toys and Characters in Japan*. Minneapolis: University of Minnesota Press.

Stern, Daniel. 1985. *The Interpersonal World of the Infant: A View from Psychoanalysis and Developmental Psychology*. New York: Basic Books.

Stone, Allucquère Rosanne. 1995. *The War of Desire and Technology at the Close of the Mechanical Age*. Cambridge, MA: MIT Press.

Stuart, Jan, and Evelyn Rawski. 2001. *Worshipping the Ancestors: Chinese Commemorative Portraits*. Stanford: Stanford University Press.

Su Shuobin. 2012. "Chuan shen shi xieshi: Ri zhi Taiwan de sheying renzhi yu minjian xiaoxiang" [Expressive realism: Photographic perception and folk portraiture in Japanese-occupied Taiwan]. In *Jindai xiaoxiang yiyi de lunban* [Contesting the meanings of modern portraiture], edited by Liu Ruiqi, 380–410. Taipei: Yuanliu.

*Taipei Times*. 2006. "Local Internet Penetration Increasing." February 7. http://www.taipeitimes.com/News/biz/print/2006/02/27/2003294917.

Taussig, Michael. 1993. *Mimesis and Alterity: A Particular History of the Senses*. New York: Routledge.

Thomas, Jolyon Baraka. 2012. *Drawing on Tradition: Manga, Anime, and Religion in Contemporary Japan*. Honolulu: University of Hawai'i Press.

Tillis, Steve. 1992. *Toward an Aesthetics of the Puppet: Puppetry as a Theatrical Art*. New York: Greenwood Press.

———. 2001. "The Art of Puppetry in the Age of Media Production." In *Puppets, Masks and Performing Objects*, edited by John Bell, 172–185. Cambridge, MA: MIT Press.

Truong, Alexis Hieu. 2013. "Framing Cosplay: How 'Layers' Negotiate Body and Subjective Experience through Play." *Intersections: Gender and Sexuality in Asia and the Pacific*. http://intersections.aru.edu.au/issue32/truong/htm.

Tsai Ventine [Cai Wenting]. 2004. *Xian ge bu chuo: Taiwan xiqu gushi* [Hold that note! Stories from Taiwan's stage.] Taipei: Guanghua Zazhi [Sinorama].

Tseng, Shu-fen, Yu-Ching You, and Chin-Chang Ho. 2002. "New Economy, Underemployment, and Inadequate Employment." *Zixun Shehui Yanjiu* [Journal of Information Society] 3 (July): 215–237.

Turkle, Sherry. 1984. *The Second Self: Computers and the Human Spirit*. New York: Simon and Schuster.

———. 1995. *Life on Screen: Identity in the Age of the Internet*. New York: Touchstone.

Turner, Victor. 1967. *The Forest of Symbols: Aspects of Ndembu Ritual*. Ithaca, NY: Cornell University Press.

Urobuchi Gen. 2017. Interview with Taiwanese blogger A Jie. YouTube video. Accessed and transcribed February 10, 2017. https://www.youtube.com/watch?v=o1hVSayjgSo.

Veltrusky, Jiri. 1983. "Puppetry and Acting." *Semiotica* 47 (1/4): 69–122.

Viveiros de Castro, Eduardo. 2012. *Cosmological Perspectivism in Amazonia and Elsewhere: Four Lectures Delivered at the Department of Social Anthropology, University of Cambridge, February–March 1998*. Hau Masterclass Series. http://www.haujournal.org/index.php/masterclass/issue/view/Masterclass%20Volume%201.

Wan Wan. 2018. *Wan Wan de tuya rizhi* [Wan Wan's graffiti diary]. Personal blog. Accessed July 20, 2018. http://cwwany.pixnet.net/blog.

Wang, Georgette. 1984. "Televised Puppetry in Taiwan: An Example of the Marriage between a Modern Medium and a Folk Medium." In *Continuity and Change in Communication Systems: An Asian Perspective*, edited by Georgette Wang and Wimal Dissanayake, 169–180. Norwood, NJ: Ablex.

Wang Pei-ti. 2015. "COSER, Weiniang yu kuaxingbie de xiawucha shijian" [Afternoon tea with cosplayers, fake girls, and transgenders]. In *Dongman shehuixue: Bie shuo de haoxiang hai you jiu* [Manga/anime sociology: Don't say there's still hope for us], interview transcript edited by Wang Pei-ti, 141–164. Taipei: Qiyi Guo Wenchuang.

Wang, Wan-chia. 2010. "Taiwan's Comic Renaissance." Translated by Chuang Kung-ru. *Taiwan Panorama*, December 7. http://www.taiwan-panorama.com/en/show_issue.php?id=2010129912070E.TXT&table=3&cur_page=1&distype=text#.

Williams, Raymond. 1986. *Marxism and Literature*. Oxford: Oxford University Press.

———. 1990. *Television: Technology and Cultural Form*. London: Routledge.

Winge, Theresa. 2006. "Costuming the Imagination: Origins of Anime and Manga Cosplay." *Mechademia* 1:65–76.

Winnicott, D. W. 1971. *Playing and Reality*. New York: Routledge.

Wolf, Arthur. 1974. "Gods, Ghosts, and Ancestors." In *Religion and Ritual in Chinese Society*, edited by Arthur Wolf, 131–182. Stanford: University of California Press.

Wolf, Margery. 1972. *Women and the Family in Rural Taiwan*. Stanford, CA: Stanford University Press.

Wu Hung. 2005. "On Tomb Figurines: The Beginning of a Visual Tradition." In *Body and Face in Chinese Visual Culture*, edited by Wu Hung and Katherine Tsiang, 13–48. Cambridge, MA: Harvard University Press.

———. 2006. "From the Neolithic to the Han." In *Chinese Sculpture*, edited by Angela Falco Howard, Wu Hung, Li Song, and Yang Hong, 17–104. New Haven, CT: Yale University Press.

Wu Hung and Katherine Tsiang. 2005. Introduction to *Body and Face in Chinese Visual Culture*, edited by Wu Hung and Katherine Tsiang, 1–10. Cambridge, MA: Harvard University Press.

Wu Mingde. 2005. *Taiwan budaixi biaoyan yishu zhi mei* [The beauty of Taiwanese *po-te-hi* performance art]. Taipei: Taiwan Xuezhe.

Xie Yuqi. 2002. *Duo-la-A-meng shoucang da ji he* [The Doraemon collector's set]. Taipei: Guo Bao.

Xie Zhongyi. 2009. "Gu miao you Haimian Baobao xiao pengyou zui ai!" [An ancient temple has SpongeBob SquarePants, the children's favorite!]. China Television Service online news, November 11. http://news.cts.com.tw/cts /society/200911/200911240349637.html.

Yamaguchi Yuko. 2011. *KITTY de yanlei* [Tears of Kitty]. Translated from Japanese into Chinese by Huang Yanting. Taipei: Buke Wenhua.

Yang, Mayfair Mei-hui. 2004. "Goddess across the Taiwan Strait: Matrifocal Ritual Space, Nation-State, and Satellite Television Footprints." *Public Culture* 16 (2): 209–238.

Yano, Christine. 2013. *Pink Globalization: Hello Kitty's Trek across the Pacific*. Durham, NC: Duke University Press.

Yomota Inuhiko. 2007. *Ke ai de liliang da* [Cute is strong]. Translated from Japanese into Chinese by Chen Guangfen. Taipei: Tianxia Yuan Jian. Originally published in 2006 as *"Kawaii" Ron*.

Yu, Wei-hsin. 2015. "Women and Employment in Taiwan." Brookings, September 14. https://www.brookings.edu/opinions/women-and-employment-in-taiwan/.

Zhang Qionghui, ed. 2003. *Huang Qianghua, Huang Wenze yu Pili budaixi* [Huang Qianghua, Huang Wenze, and Pili *po-te-hi*]. Taipei: Shenghuo Meixue Guan.

Zhang Zhen. 2001. "Bodies in the Air: The Magic of Science and the Fate of Early 'Martial Arts' Film in China." *Postscript* 20 (2–3): 43–60.

Zizek, Slavoj. 2018. "Slavoj Zizek Racist Jokes! Must Watch." Interview. YouTube video, 9:50. Accessed July 1, 2018. https://www.youtube.com/watch?v =xQsZMzcfYa0.

# Index

2-D (*er ciyuan*), 34, 83, 179, 196–199
2.5-D, 83–84
3-D (*san ciyuan*), 34, 46, 83, 130, 179, 196–199
7-Eleven, 126, 133

Aardman Animation, 2
acceptability (*jieshoudu*), 92, 98–101
activism: environmental, 206; fan, 179; identity-based, 32, 33, 40; queer, 32, 205–206
Actors Studio, 22, 167
Actor network theory, 36
ACT UP, 32, 205
affective labor, 51, 120, 170–172, 173–174. *See also* emotional work
affordances, 20, 21, 146, 211n1
agency, external theory of, 64–65, 67–70; internal theory of, 64–67
Ahmed, Sara, 201
Allison, Anne, 38, 51, 57–58, 127, 151
analogism, 83, 139; in *ang-a* mode of animation, 80, 84–86, 190; Chinese, 84–85, 216n19; in cinema animation, 216n21; concept of fate in, 115; definition of, 84; in *wuxia*, 136
ancestor portraits, 77, 78–79, 215n16
*ang-a* (*ou*), 15, 55–56; animating process, 117; anthropomorphic nature, 63–64; as artifact, 63; charisma of, 75–76; coherence concepts, 81, 82; definition, 55–56; genealogy of 58–59; external agency of, 67–70; as having lineages, 70–74; internal agency of, 64–67;

linguistic associations, 59; of living celebrities, 214n8; as material representation of a character, 60; medium for communication between virtual personalities and living people, 68–70; medium within a network of media, 62–63, 76–77; relationship with narrative, 60–61
*ang-a* mode of animation, 16, 55–58, 63, 70; alternative way of thinking about relationship between humanity and environment, 58, 208; applied to imported character toys, 74, 217n6; difference from Japanese manga/anime mode of animation, 79–82, 84–85; overlap with database consumption, 90, 108, 197; overlap with other modes of animation, 86–87
*ang-a-sian*, 57
*anima*, 54
animal deities, 214n9
animism, 19, 37; definition of, 83–84, in Japanese manga/anime, 41, 58, 138
anthropomorphism, 178, in branding, 40; in cartoons, 185; of gods, 64, 66. *See also* personification
Artaud, Antonin, 22, 211n2
artificial intelligence (AI), 54–55, 56, 212n2
artificial life (AL), 54, 55, 56, 212n2
*The Arti: The Adventure Begins* (*Qi ren mima: Guluobu zhi mi*), 130–132, 139, 219n8; digital technology use in, 144; Disney marketing model, 141; failure to capture American audience,

# About the Author

Teri Silvio is an associate research fellow at the Institute of Ethnology, Academia Sinica, Taipei. She has conducted ethnographic research on puppetry, animation, design, fandoms, theater, and gender and sexuality in Taiwan, Hong Kong, China, and Southeast Asia. Silvio has published in *Cultural Anthropology*, *Journal of Linguistic Anthropology*, *Positions*, and *Mechademia*.